THE PUERTO RICAN CUATRO CHORD BIBLE

(BEADG Standard Tuning)

by

Tobe A. Richards

A Fretted Friends Publication for Cabot Books

Published by:
Cabot Books
Copyright © 2007 & 2016 by Cabot Books
All rights reserved.

First Edition September 2007
Second Edition February 2016

ISBN-13: 978-1-906207-36-6

No part of this publication may be reproduced in any form
or by any means without the prior consent of the publisher.

Cabot Books
3 Kenton Mews
Henleaze
Bristol
BS9 4LT
United Kingdom

Visit our online site at www.frettedfriendsmusic.com
e-mail: cabotbooks@blueyonder.co.uk

TABLE OF CONTENTS

Introduction..4-5

Fingering..5

Chord Theory & FAQs..6-7

Understanding Chord Boxes..8

Puerto Rican Cuatro Fingerboard & Tuning Layout..........9

Chords Covered in this Book..10

Slash Chords...11

Using a Capo or *Capo D'astra*......................................11

C Chords...12-16

C♯/D♭ Chords..17-21

D Chords...22-26

D♯/E♭ Chords..27-31

E Chords...32-36

F Chords...37-41

F♯/G♭ Chords..42-46

G Chords...47-51

G♯/A♭ Chords..52-56

A Chords...57-61

A♯/B♭ Chords..62-66

B Chords...67-71

Major Slash Chords...72-75

A Selection of Moveable Chord Shapes......................76-79

The Puerto Rican Cuatro Family Factfile....................80-81

Alternative Chord Name Chart...82

Notes..83-85

Chord Window Blanks...86-110

INTRODUCTION

The Puerto Rican Cuatro Chord Bible provides the musician with 1,728 chords in all keys, featuring 68 different chord types, with 3 variations of each standard chord. 144 major slash chords are also included, together with 48 moveable chord shape diagrams (providing access to a further 576 barré and standard moveable chords) making this the most comprehensive reference guide for the Puerto Rican cuatro currently available. For many years now, guitarists have been able to pick up a songbook and instantly play the songs in front of them, either with the help of one of the many published guides, or through the chord boxes supplied with most popular music. With the help of this *Chord Bible*, beginners and experienced Puerto Rican cuatro players alike will be able to take advantage of the many songbooks, fake books and musical compendiums by any artist you would care to name, from *The Beatles* to *Joan Baez*, from *Planxty* to *The Pogues* or *Springsteen* to *Simon & Garfunkel*. With 68 different chordal variations in all keys, virtually any song should be playable!

Having a good chordal knowledge should arguably be the bedrock in any fretted or keyboard musicians armoury. Whether you're playing rock, pop, folk, jazz, blues, country or other types of music, it's impossible to supply a suitable accompaniment to any vocal or solo instrumental music without providing a chordal or harmonic backing. The subtle nuance of an added ninth chord over a major chord is something that can't be captured simply by playing a melody line. In theory it is possible to approximate the harmonic intervals of any music using a limited palette of chords - probably around ten to twelve. But wherever possible it's best to use correct harmonies if they're available to you.

Having five courses of strings, the Puerto Rican cuatro is obviously limited to five note chords, but by making acceptable compromises and omitting the least important parts of that chord, even the most complex musical structures are possible. For instance, in the case of an eleventh, the third is generally omitted without the character of the chord being adversely affected. Equally, the root or key note isn't always necessary to achieve an effective approximation of the full chord. The third is rarely missing from the majority of chords (other than elevenths) as it determines whether the key is major or minor - although this isn't a hard and fast rule, particularly in folk music where the root and fifth form the basis of most traditional music. These two intervals are generally the starting point for a number of open tunings of instruments as diverse as the guitar, the Irish bouzouki and the mountain dulcimer. The same interval is also used in a lot of heavy rock where a fifth chord is described as a *power chord*. Even though a power chord is technically neither major nor minor, it's more often used as an alternative for a major chord in most popular music.

One question which often pops up is *how many chords do I need to learn?* The smart answer is '*how long is a piece of string?*', which is true, but it doesn't actually answer the question if you don't know where to start. My advice would be to begin with simple chord clusters like the popular G, C, D and Em progression and gradually work in new ones as you advance. If you intend playing within a rock format, it's probably sensible to learn the E, A, B sequence which is the staple of most guitarists and bassists. As a generalisation, jazz probably requires the greatest chordal knowledge of any form of music, so the learning curve will be longer if you're planning to pick up any songbook and instantly produce a recognisable version of your favourite *Duke Ellington* or *Steely Dan* number. The only truth as far as harmonic knowledge goes is you can never learn *too* much!

In this series of chord theory books, I've included a comprehensive selection of configurations of chords in all keys. As I mentioned previously, this will enable you to pick up virtually any songbook or fake book (topline melody and chord symbols) and look up the chord shape that's needed. Obviously, you'll come across the occasional song which doesn't conform to the normal harmonic intervals which you find in this, or any other chord theory publication, but with a little experimentation and experience, you'll be able to make a reasonable stab at it. For instance, most players would be more than a little bemused if they suddenly came across an instruction to play a *Gbmaj7add6/D*. Fortunately, this is fairly unusual, but from the knowledge you'll have learned, you'll be able to use a similar chord or work it out note by note. Put simply, if *every* theoretically possible chord shape were to be included in this or any other book, the result would resemble something akin to several volumes of the *Yellow Pages*!

FINGERING

Always a tricky subject and one which seems to generate a lot of discussion and differing opinions as to which method is correct. Personally, I take the view that it's a largely fruitless exercise, as the number of variables involved make a definitive answer unlikely. So what I've decided to do in this book is to choose fingering positions which feel comfortable to me. Some chord shapes will dictate the fingering used, but others will be down to personal preference. If you can practise your two and three finger chords using different fingers, it will make your playing a lot more fluid when you change to another chord shape. But if you develop habits which limit you to one playing position, it isn't the end of the world either, if you can make the transitions seamless.

The only rules, if you could loosely call them that, are:-

a) Don't abandon using your pinky or little finger if you're just beginning to play, as you'll eventually need it for some of the four finger chords which frequently crop up.

b) Try to avoid fretting with the thumb unless you're learning an instrument like the mountain dulcimer which requires a longer stretch. I know a number of players employ it on slimmer necked instruments, but I personally feel it leads to bad habits.

c) Keep your left hand fingernails short or fretting becomes a major problem. Obviously do the reverse if you're a lefty.

d) If you're a beginner and you're naturally left handed, don't get persuaded into buying a right handed instrument - it won't work! The learning curve will be steeper and you'll never get the fluidity you'd achieve with your natural hand. Most acoustic instruments can be adapted for a left hander apart from cutaway guitars and f-style mandolins etc., by reversing the nut and strings. For the non-reversible instruments, always go for a left handed model.

e) Learn to barré with other fingers apart from your index finger. This will prove invaluable with more complex chords and increase finger strength as well.

f) Don't be afraid to use fingerings further up the neck in combination with open strings as these will give you interesting new voicings and are generally quite popular in folk music. A number of these are provided in this book.

g) The Puerto Rican cuatro can be played with a pick or fingerpicks. Alternatively, fingernails can be used if you're accustomed to this method of playing. Using a pick or fingerpicks generally produces a brighter sound with more attack.

CHORD THEORY & FAQs

Q What is a chord?
A It's a collection of three or more notes played simultaneously. The exceptions in this book are the fourths and fifths (power chords) which aren't in the strictest sense, true chords. For convenience sake, they are classed as such.

Q What is a triad?
A A chord containing three notes. For example, G Major, Bm, D+ or Asus4.

Q What are intervals?
A Intervals are the musical distance between notes in a musical scale. For instance in the scale of C Major, C is the 1st note, D is the 2nd note, E the 3rd and so on. So if you're playing the chord of C Major, your intervals will be 1–3–5 or C as the *first* note, E as the *third* note and G as the *perfect fifth*.

Q What is a chromatic scale and which intervals does it contain?
A: A chromatic scale encompasses all twelve notes in a musical scale, including the sharps and flats. It's also the basis for the naming of *every* chord in existence. See the staff diagram below to see the intervals:

Q What is a seventh chord?
A: In its most basic form, an additional note beyond the triad. Sevenths can be either major or flattened. For instance, returning to our old friend, the key of C, a *Cmaj7* has an added *B* on top of the *C–E–G* triad. The resultant chord has a mellow quality often found in jazz. Now if you take the B and flatten it by dropping the fourth note in your chord down to a B flat, you get a C7.

Q: Then why isn't it called a C minor seventh?
A: Technically this *is* a minor seventh note, but this would create a lot of confusion when naming chords, as you already have a minor interval option in your triad (in the key of C major, E flat), so it's always referred to as a 7th to differentiate between it and a major seventh.

Q: What is an extension?
A: A chord which goes beyond the scope of triads and sevenths. Basically, extensions are additional notes placed above the triad or seventh in a musical stave, fingerboard or keyboard. It's important to understand these are, for theoretical purposes, always placed above the seventh. Or in layman's terms, higher up the scale. The confusion comes when you start to realise a 9th is identical to a 2nd - in the scale of C – a D note.

Q: So why is the ninth note the same as the second note?
A: This takes a little grasping, but if you remember that if your note goes higher than the seventh it's a 9th, but if it's lower, it'll be a 2nd. An example of this would be Csus2, which contains the root

note of C, a 2nd or suspended D note and a G, the perfect 5th. You'll see this even more clearly if you look at the piano keyboard diagram below. Count from the C up to the following D beyond the 7th (B note). From the C to the second D is exactly nine whole notes.

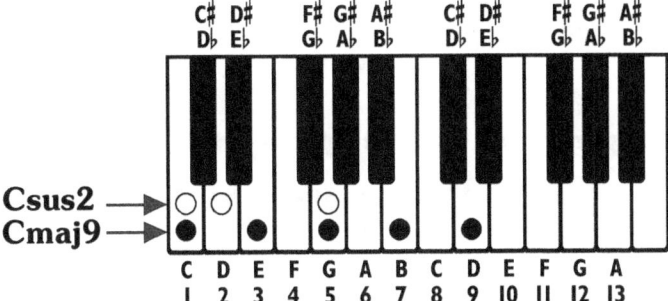

Q: *Do any other extensions share a common note?*
A: Yes, other examples include the *11th*, which is also a *4th* and the *13th* which shares a note with the *6th*.

Q: *What are inversions?*
A: In the root version of a chord, the notes run in their correct order from lowest to highest. In the case of G major, it would be G–B–D. With an inversion of the same chord the notes would run in a different order. For example, the first inversion of G major would be B–D–G and the second, D–G–B. In general, triads sound more or less the same when they're inverted, but that's certainly not the case with sevenths and extensions which can sound quite different and occasionally discordant when the notes are jumbled up in certain configurations. Inversions can also produce different chords using the same basic notes. A good example of this would be *C6 (C-E-G-A)* which produces an *Am7 (A-C-E-G)* when it's inverted (both contain the notes of C–E–G–A, but in a different order). The major variations are in the tonal properties of the chords, making them sound quite different from one another.

Q: *Do elevenths and thirteenths have any particular properties?*
A: Yes. In most cases the 3rd is omitted from eleventh chords and the 11th from the majority of thirteenths as they're deemed unnecessary and arguably, create unwanted dissonance.

Q: *Some chords are called by different names in different music books. What should I do?*
A: The alternative chord name reference chart at the back of the book should help sort out the confusion.

Q: *What is a suspended chord?*
A: It's simpler to think of suspended chords as a stepping stone to a major or resolving chord. In effect the third has been left in a state of suspension by either raising it to a fourth (sus4) or lowering it to a second (sus2). Sevenths also provide versions of the suspended chord in the form of C7sus4 or C7sus2 (using the key of C as an example).

Q: *What is a diminished chord?*
A: A diminished chord has a dissonent quality to it where the third and fifth notes in a triad are flattened by a semi-tone. Again, using C as an example, C major (C-E-G) is altered to Cdim (C-E♭-G♭). A second version of a dimished chord is also used in many forms of music, the diminished seventh. This retains the elements of a standard diminished chord, adding a double flat in the seventh (C-E♭-G♭-B♭♭). A B♭♭ in this case is, to all intents and purposes, really an A note.

Q: *What is an augmented chord?*
A: An augmented chord basically performs the opposite task to a diminished one. Instead of lowering the fifth by a semitone, it raises it by the same interval. A C+ (augmented) chord contains the triad of C-E-G♯. The major root and third are retained and the fifth is sharpened.

UNDERSTANDING THE CHORD BOXES

The three diagrams below show the chord conventions illustrated in this guide. Most experienced fretted instrument players should be familiar with them. The suggested fingering positions are only meant as a general guide and will depend, in many instances, on hand size, finger length and flexibility, so feel free to experiment. The location of the black circles is unalterable, though, if you want to produce the correct voicing.

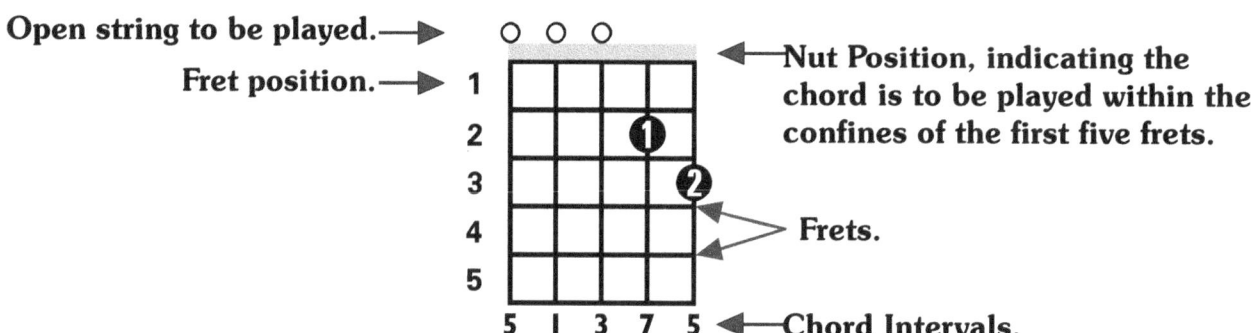

Open string to be played. →

Fret position. →

← Nut Position, indicating the chord is to be played within the confines of the first five frets.

→ Frets.

← Chord Intervals.

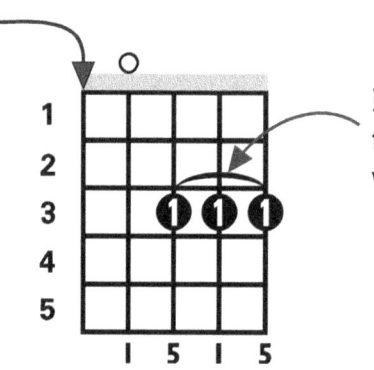

If there are no markers above or below the string, the string should not be played.

Barré chord (in this example, a three string barré to be fretted with the index finger).

Suggested fingering. In this case the 1st or index finger marker is displayed.

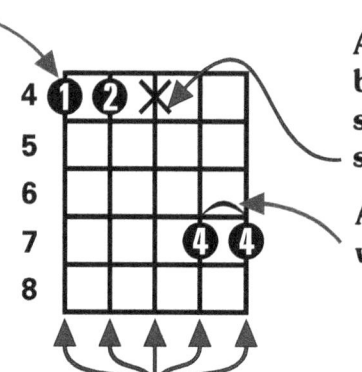

A damped string is represented by an 'X' on or above the string. This indicates the string shouldn't be played.

A two string barré to be played with the fourth finger.

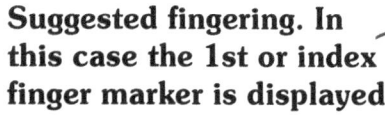

Left to right: 5th, 4th, 3rd, 2nd and 1st courses of strings.

Whether a fretted instrument has single strings or pairs of strings, the chord boxes in this book, other chord dictionaries and songbooks treat it as a four stringed instrument. This convention is common to all double or triple course instruments such as the mandolin or tiple, making the diagrams a lot less confusing and free from unnecessary clutter.

PUERTO RICAN CUATRO FINGERBOARD & TUNING LAYOUT

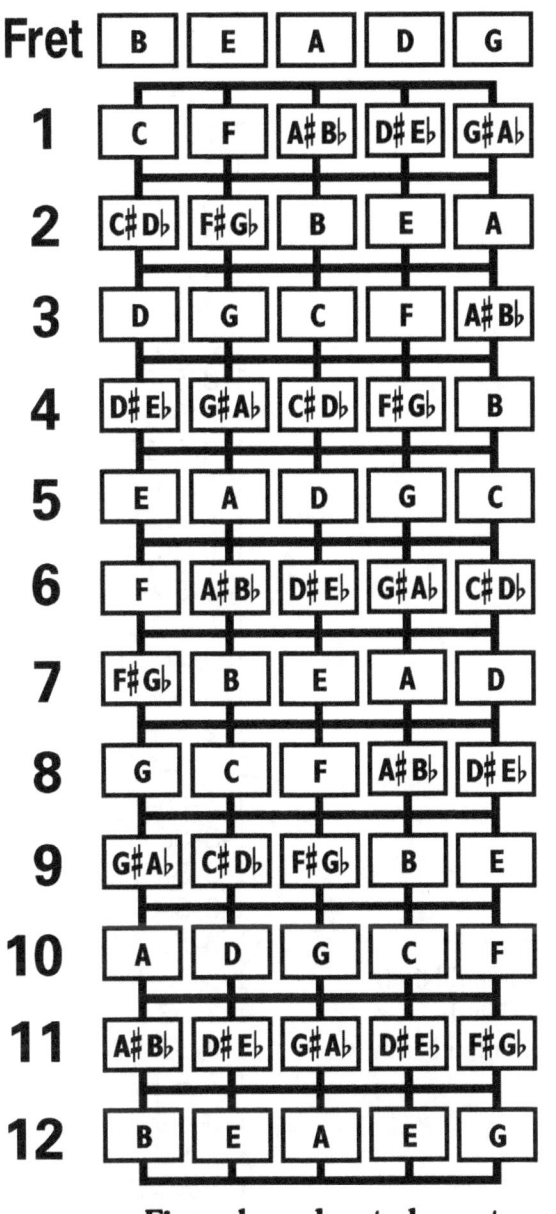

Fingerboard note layout

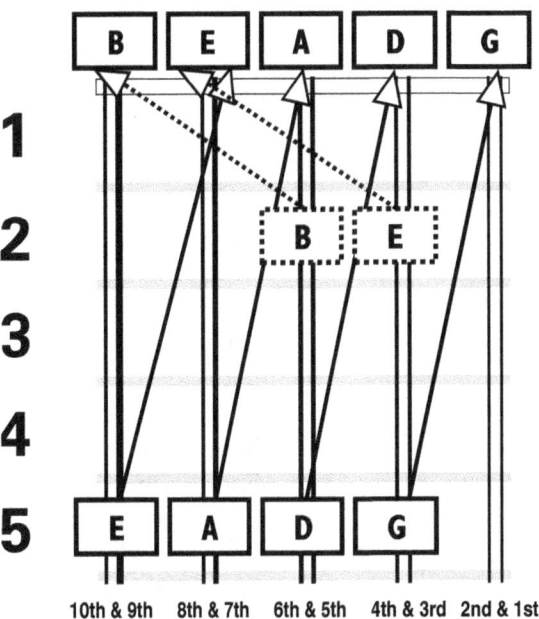

Tuning the Puerto Rican Cuatro by fretting at given intervals on the fingerboard. The broken boxes and lines indicate the correct positions to tune the outer 10th and 8th octave strings.

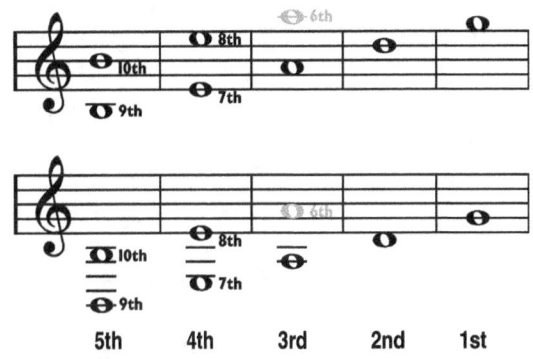

Puerto Rican Cuatro tuning in standard notation. written (top) and true pitch (bottom).

To tune your Puerto Rican Cuatro accurately, it's best to use an electronic chromatic tuner, but if there isn't one available, you can tune it to a guitar or piano/electronic keyboard. The following tuning grid gives the correct fingering positions on the guitar fingerboard and piano keyboard.

Puerto Rican Cuatro	Guitar	Piano
1st & 2nd string (G)	1st string (E) fretted at the 3rd fret	1st G above middle C
3rd & 4th string (D)	2nd string (B) fretted at the 3rd fret	1st D above middle C
5th & 6th string (A)	3rd string (G) fretted at the 2nd fret	1st A below middle C
6th octave string (A)	1st string (E) fretted at the 5th fret (G)	1st A above middle C
7th string (E)	4rh string (D) fretted at the 2nd fret	1st E below middle C
8th octave string (E)	1st open string (E)	1st E above middle C
9th string (B)	5th string (A) fretted at the 2nd fret	2nd B below middle C
10th octave string (B)	2nd open string (B)	1st B below middle C

THE CHORDS COVERED IN THIS BOOK

Chord	Chord Name in Full	Harmonic Interval
C	Major	1–3–5
Cm	Minor	1–F3–5
C-5	Major Diminished Fifth	1–3–F5
C°	Diminished	1–F3–F5
C4	Fourth	1–4
C5	Fifth or Power Chord	1–5
Csus2	Suspended Second	1–2–5
Csus4	Suspended Fourth	1–4–5
Csus4add9	Suspended Fourth Added Ninth	1–4–5–9
C+	Augmented	1–3–S5
C6	Major Sixth	1–3–5–6
Cadd9	Major Added Ninth	1–3–5–9
Cadd11	Major Added Eleventh	1–3–5–11
Cm6	Minor Sixth	1–F3–5–6
Cm-6	Minor Diminished Sixth	1–F3–5–F6
Cmadd9	Minor Added Ninth	1–F3–5–9
C6add9	Major Sixth Added Ninth	1–3–5–6–9
Cm6add9	Minor Sixth Added Ninth	1–F3–5–6–9
C°7	Diminished Seventh	1–F3–F5–DF7
C7	Seventh	1–3–5–F7
C7sus2	Seventh Suspended Second	1–2–5–F7
C7sus4	Seventh Suspended Fourth	1–4–5–F7
C7-5	Seventh Diminished Fifth	1–3–F5–F7
C7+5	Seventh Augmented Fifth	1–3–S5–F7
C7-9	Seventh Minor Ninth	1–3–5–F7–F9
C7+9	Seventh Augmented Ninth	1–3–5–F7–S9
C7-5-9	Seventh Diminished Fifth Minor Ninth	1–3–F5–F7–F9
C7-5+9	Seventh Diminished Fifth Augmented Ninth	1–3–F5–F7–S9
C7+5-9	Seventh Augmented Fifth Minor Ninth	1–3–S5–F7–F9
C7+5+9	Seventh Augmented Fifth Augmented Ninth	1–3–S5–F7–S9
C7add11	Seventh Added Eleventh	1–3–5–F7–11
C7+11	Seventh Augmented Eleventh	1–3–5–F7–S11
C7add13	Seventh Added Thirteenth	1–3–5–F7–13
Cm7	Minor Seventh	1–F3–5–F7
Cm7-5	Minor Seventh Diminished Fifth	1–F3–F5–F7
Cm7-5-9	Minor Seventh Diminished Fifth Minor Ninth	1–F3–F5–F7–F9
Cm7-9	Minor Seventh Minor Ninth	1–F3–5–F7–F9
Cm7add11	Minor Seventh Added Eleventh	1–F3–5–F7–11
Cm(maj7)	Minor Major Seventh	1–F3–5–7
Cmaj7	Major Seventh	1–3–5–7
Cmaj7-5	Major Seventh Diminished Fifth	1–3–F5–7
Cmaj7+5	Major Seventh Augmented Fifth	1–3–S5–7
Cmaj7+11	Major Seventh Augmented Eleventh	1–3–5–7–S11
C9	Ninth	1–3–5–F7–9
C9sus4	Ninth Suspended Fourth	1–4–5–F7–9
C9-5	Ninth Diminished Fifth	1–3–F5–F7–9
C9+5	Ninth Augmented Fifth	1–3–S5–F7–9
C9+11	Ninth Augmented Eleventh	1–3–5–F7–9–S11
Cm9	Minor Ninth	1–F3–5–F7–9

Chord	Chord Name in Full	Harmonic Interval
Cm9-5	Minor Ninth Diminished Fifth	1–F3–F5–F7–9
Cm(maj9)	Minor Major Ninth	1–F3–5–7–9
Cmaj9	Major Ninth	1–3–5–7–9
Cmaj9-5	Major Ninth Diminished Fifth	1–3–F5–7–9
Cmaj9+5	Major Ninth Augmented Fifth	1–3–S5–7–9
Cmaj9add6	Major Ninth Added Sixth	1–3–5–6–7–9
Cmaj9+11	Major Ninth Augmented Eleventh	1–3–5–7–9–S11
C11	Eleventh	1–3–5–F7–9–11
C11-9	Eleventh Diminished Ninth	1–3–5–F7–F9–11
Cm11	Minor Eleventh	1–F3–5–F7–9–11
Cmaj11	Major Eleventh	1–3–5–7–9–11
C13	Thirteenth	1–3–5–F7–9–11–13
C13sus4	Thirteenth Suspended Fourth	1–4–5–F7–9–11–13
C13-5-9	Thirteenth Diminished Fifth Minor Ninth	1–3–F5–F7–F9–11–13
C13-9	Thirteenth Minor Ninth	1–3–5–F7–F9–11–13
C13+9	Thirteenth Augmented Ninth	1–3–5–F7–S9–11–13
C13+11	Thirteenth Augmented Eleventh	1–3–5–F7–9–S11–13
Cm13	Minor Thirteenth	1–F3–5–F7–9–11–13
Cmaj13	Major Thirteenth	1–3–5–7–9–11–13

Key: F = Flat   S = Sharp   DF = Double Flat

SLASH CHORDS

What is a slash chord? Put simply, they're standard chords with an added note in the bass. *So what differentiates a C chord from a C/G when the G is already part of that chord, in this case, the fifth?* Theoretically, nothing, but the difference is very apparent when you actually sound the chord. The G bass is emphasised to provide a different feel to the harmonics. Slashes are also commonly found when the music calls for a descending bassline. For example; C, C/B, C/A and C/G.

The note after the slash indicates the bass note being played. For instance C/D would be an instruction to play a C chord with a D bass.

Slash Note. Generally found on the 5th & 4th courses.

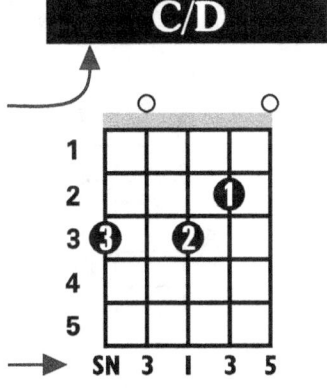

How do I play a slash chord that isn't listed in this book? Well, firstly, it would be an almost impossible task to cover every possible slash chord in existence, because the variations are potentially even greater than with standard chords. What you can do, within the confines of this guide, is to find the part of the chord before the slash in the main body of the book and then look for the nearest bass note on the fourth or fifth courses of strings. To find the right bass note, consult the fingerboard layout on *page 9*.

USING A CAPO (OR *CAPO D'ASTRA*)

Using a capo is a quick and easy way of changing key to suit a different vocal range or to join in with with other musicians playing in a different key. For the uniniated, a capo is a moveable bar that clamps onto the fingerboard of fretted instruments. It works in much the same way as using a finger barré to hold down the strings. They come in a variety of designs and prices, the simplest using a metal rod covered in rubber and sprung with elastic. For the Puerto Rican cuatro, look for a guitar capo.

C Chords

C
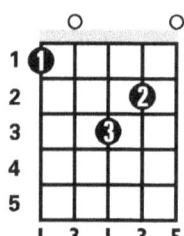

Cm
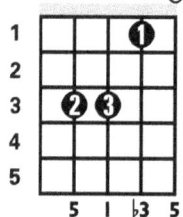

C7
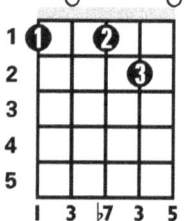

Cm7
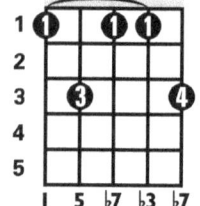

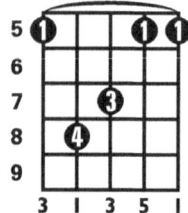
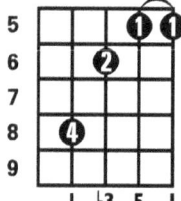
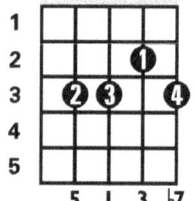
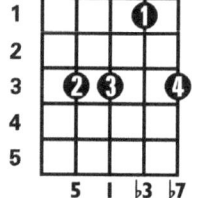

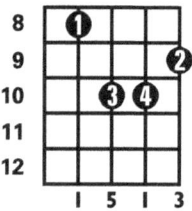
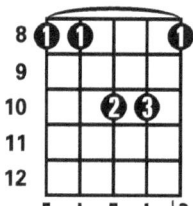
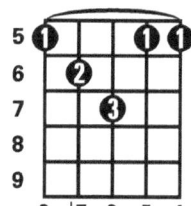
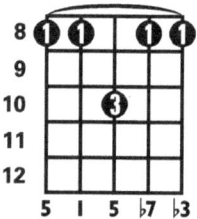

C5
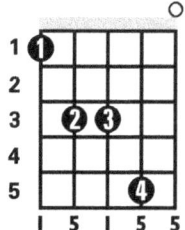

C6
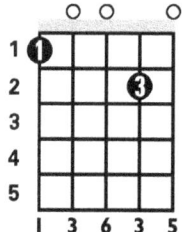

Cm6
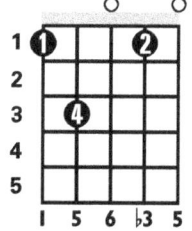

Cmaj7
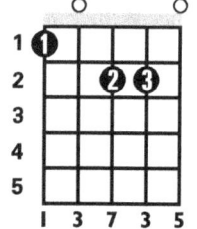

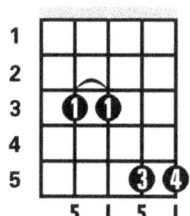
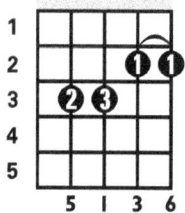
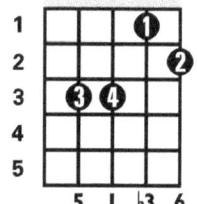
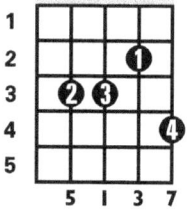

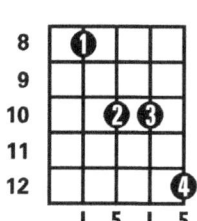
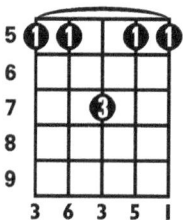
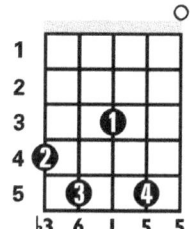
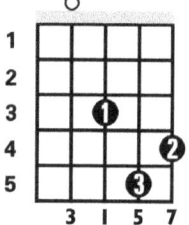

C Chords

C°
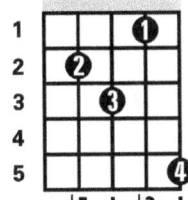
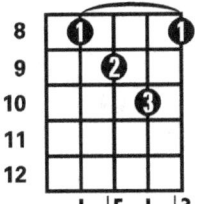
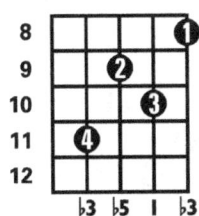

C°7
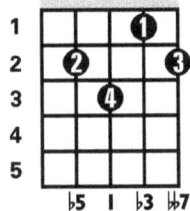
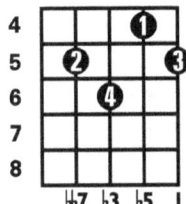
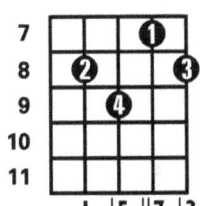

C-5
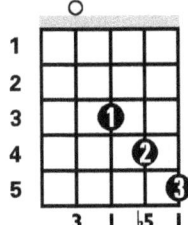
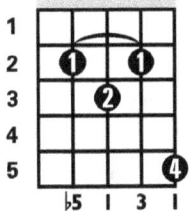

C+
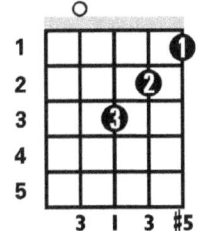
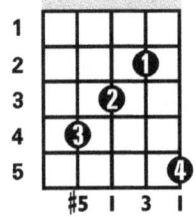
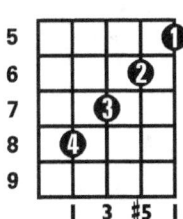

Csus2
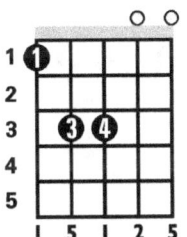
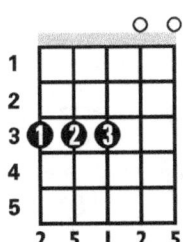
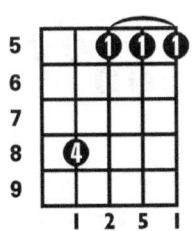

Csus4
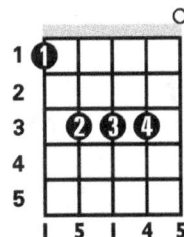
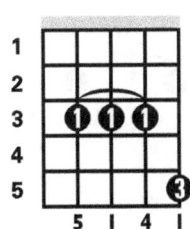
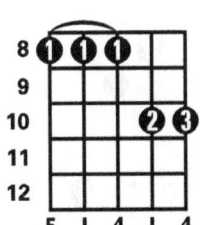

C7sus4
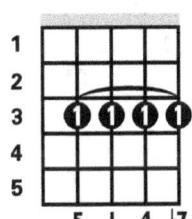
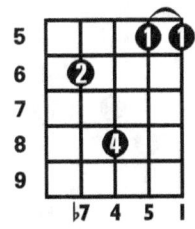
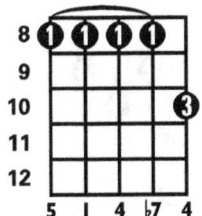

Cm7-5
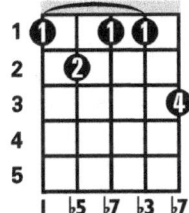
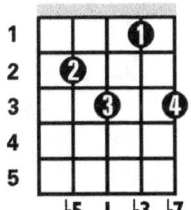
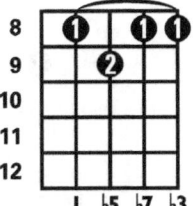

C Chords

Cadd9	Cmadd9	C6add9	Cm6add9
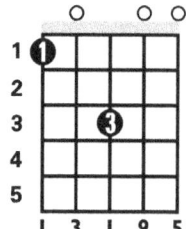	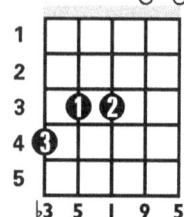	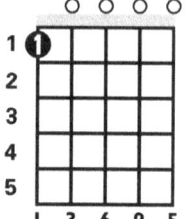	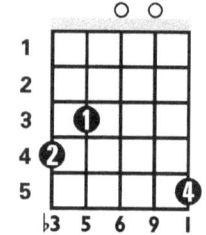
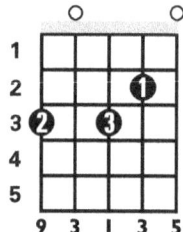	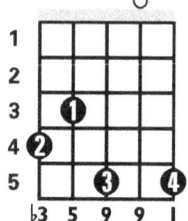	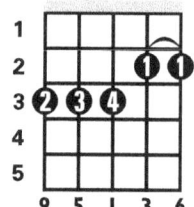	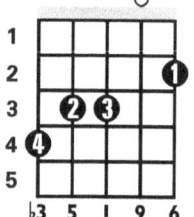
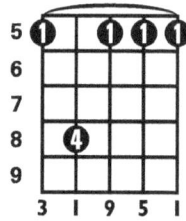	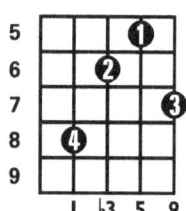	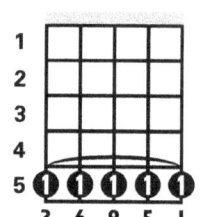	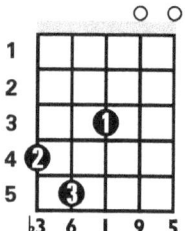

C7-5	C7+5	C7-9	C7+9
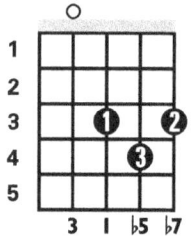	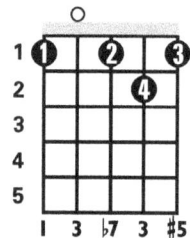	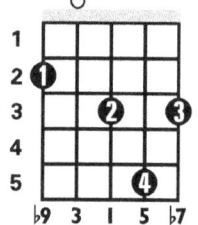	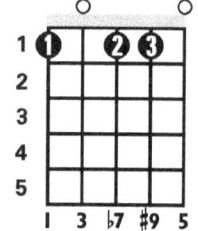
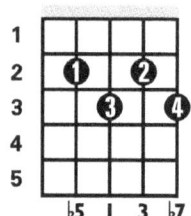	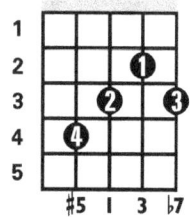	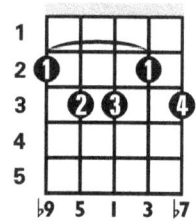	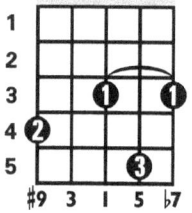
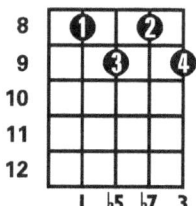	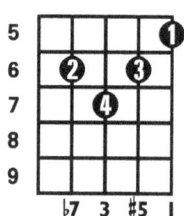	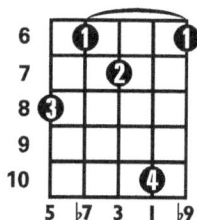	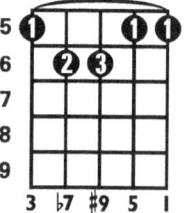

C Chords

Cm(maj7)
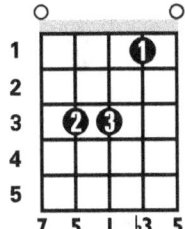
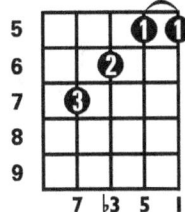
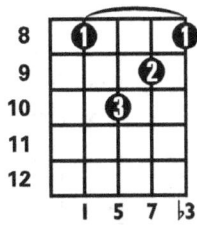

Cmaj7-5
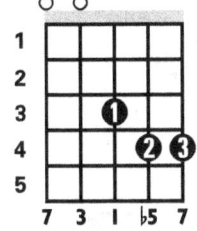
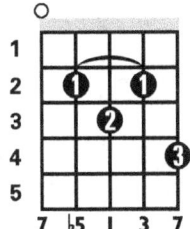
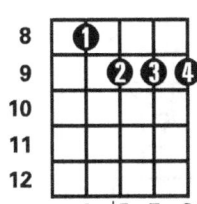

Cmaj7+5
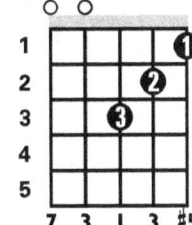
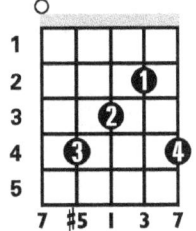
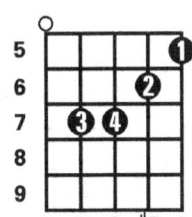

C9
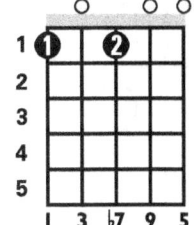
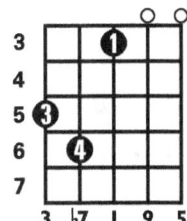
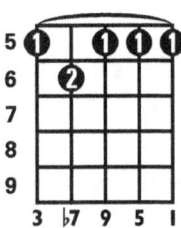

Cm9
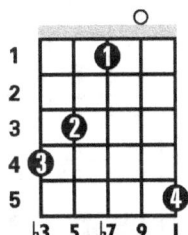
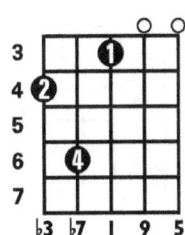
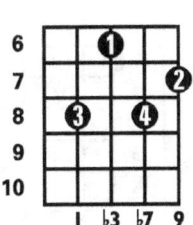

Cmaj9
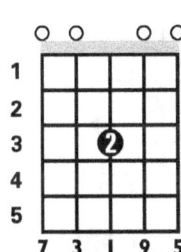
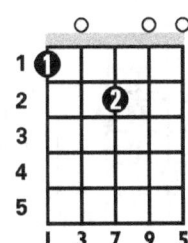
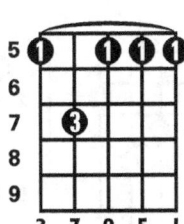

C11
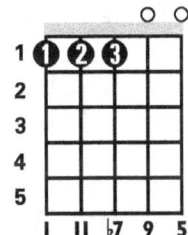
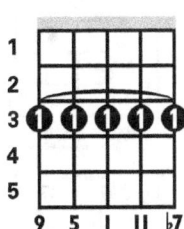
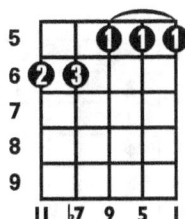

C13
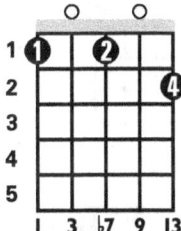
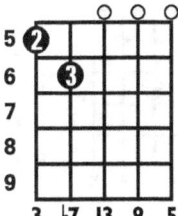
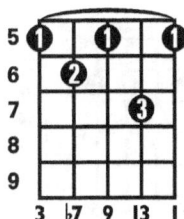

C Chords (Advanced)

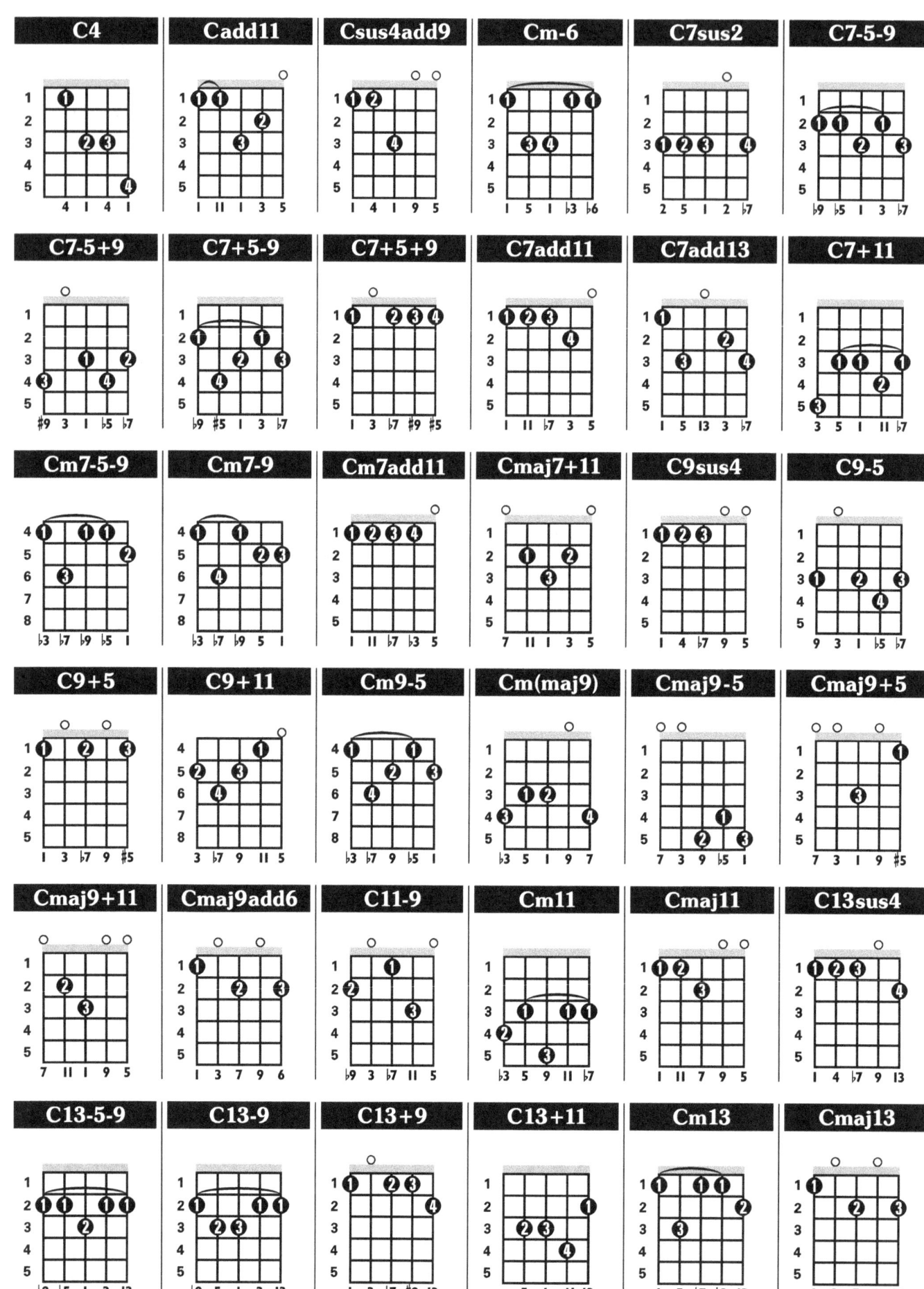

C#/ D♭ Chords

D♭
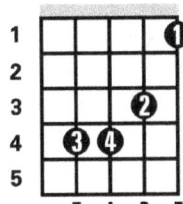
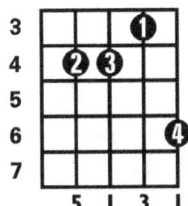
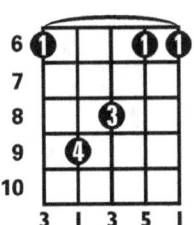

D♭m
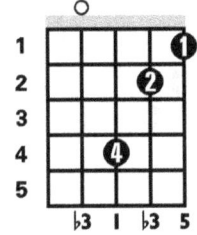
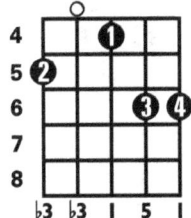
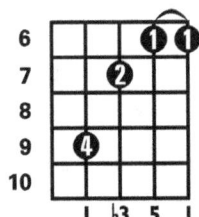

D♭7
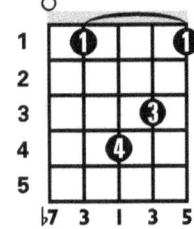
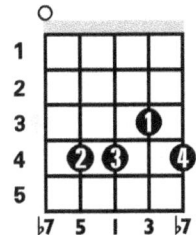
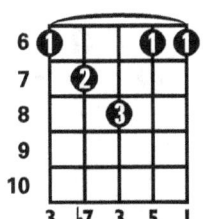

D♭m7
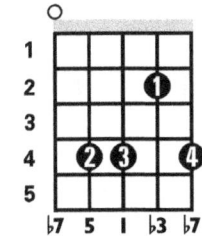
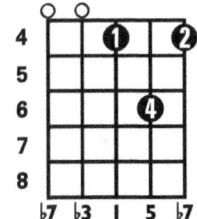
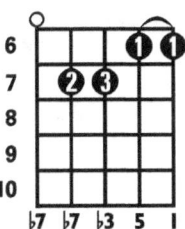

D♭5
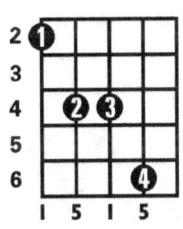
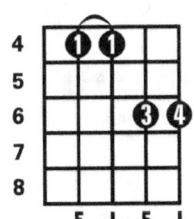
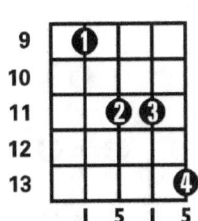

D♭6
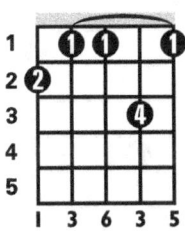
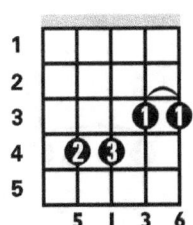
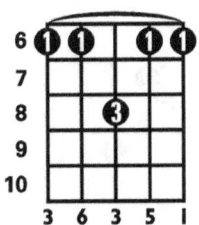

D♭m6
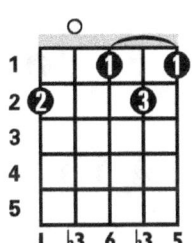
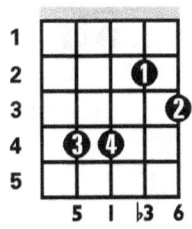
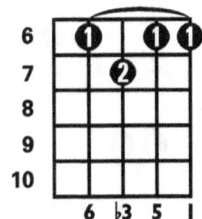

D♭maj7
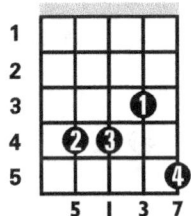
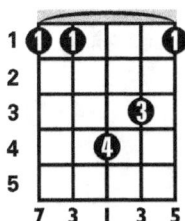
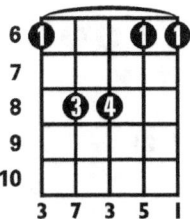

C#/ D♭ Chords

D♭°	D♭°7	D♭-5	D♭+
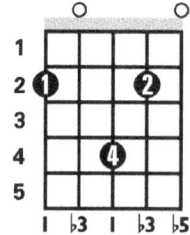	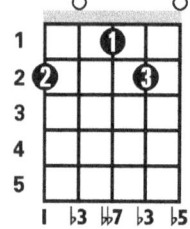	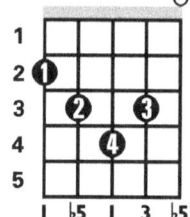	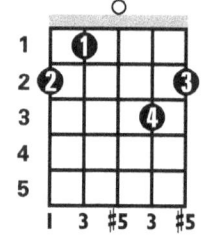
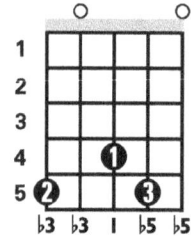	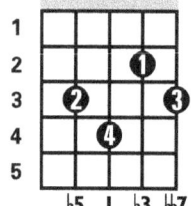	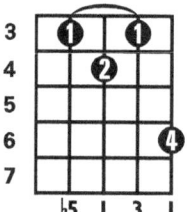	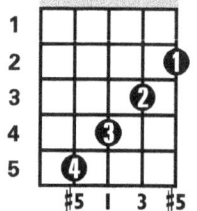
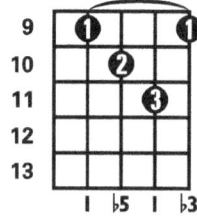	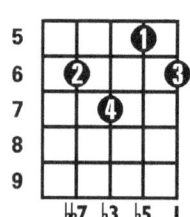	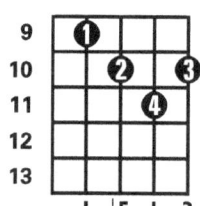	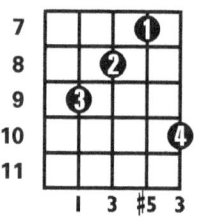

D♭sus2	D♭sus4	D♭7sus4	D♭m7-5
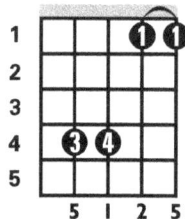	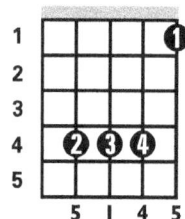	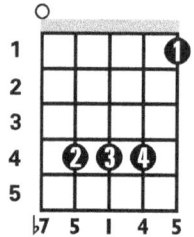	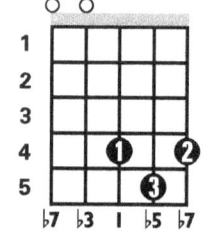
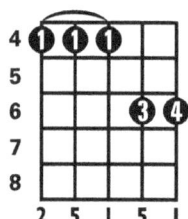	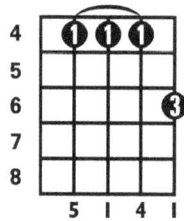	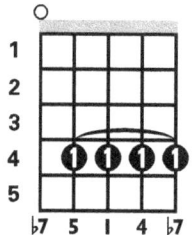	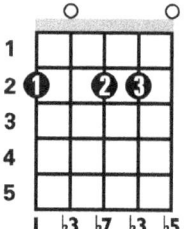
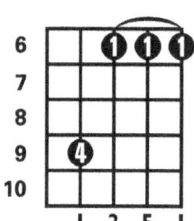	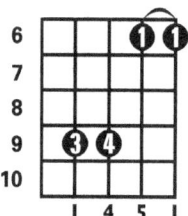	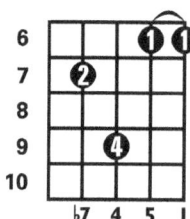	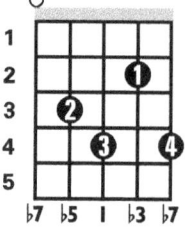

C#/ D♭ Chords

D♭add9
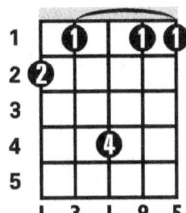
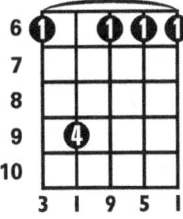
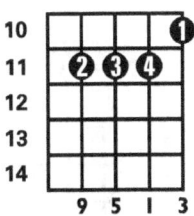

D♭madd9
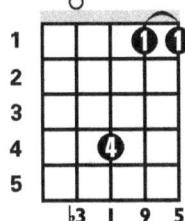
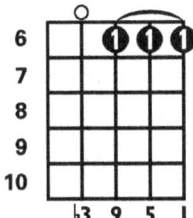
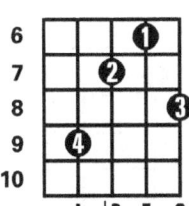

D♭6add9
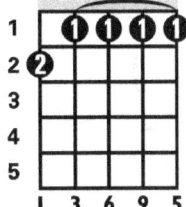
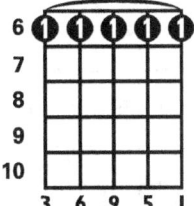
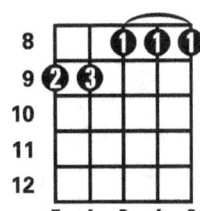

D♭m6add9
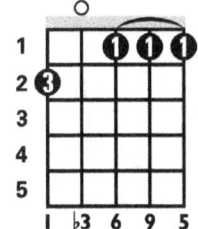
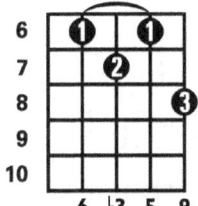
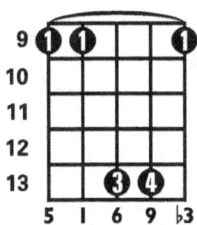

D♭7-5
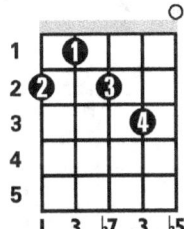
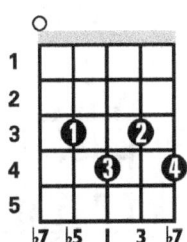
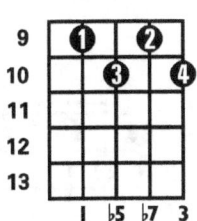

D♭7+5
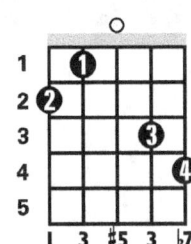
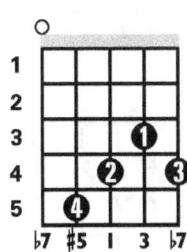
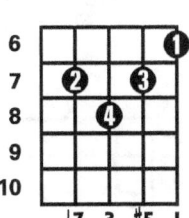

D♭7-9
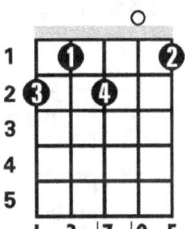
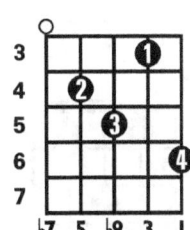
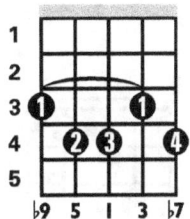

D♭7+9
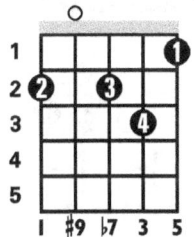
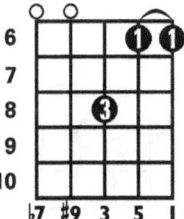
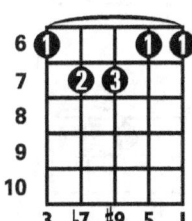

C#/ D♭ Chords

D♭m(maj7)	D♭maj7-5	D♭maj7+5	D♭9
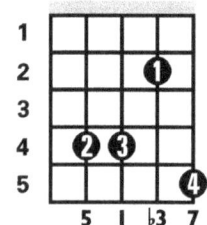	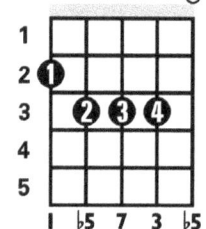	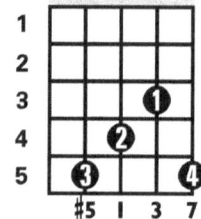	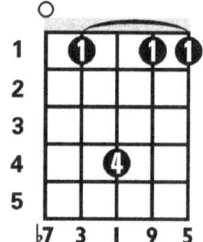
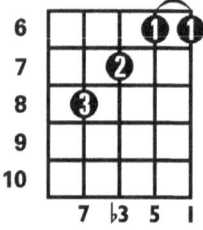	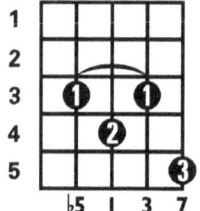	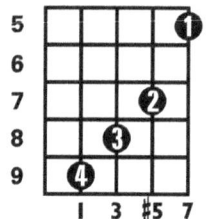	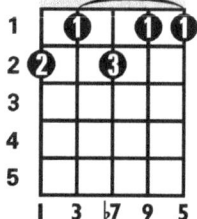
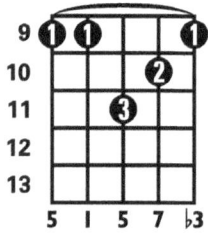	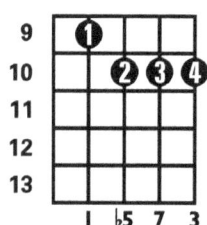	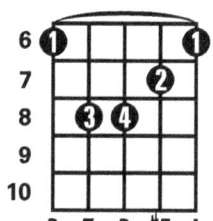	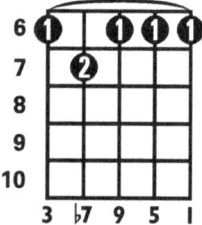

D♭m9	D♭maj9	D♭11	D♭13
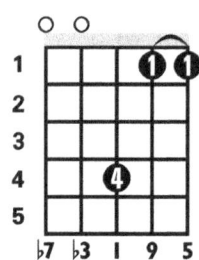	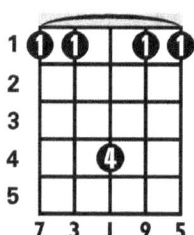	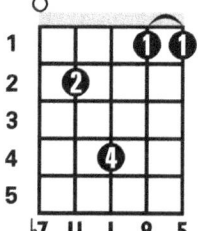	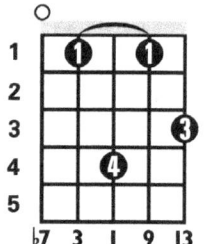
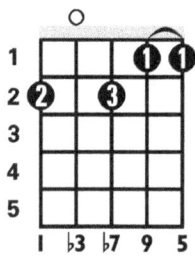	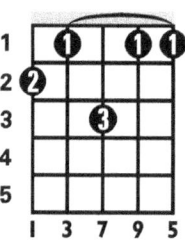	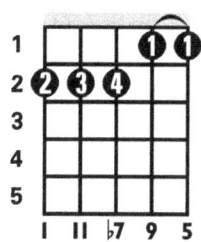	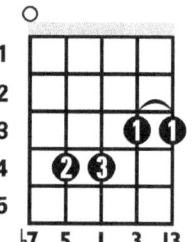
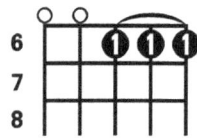	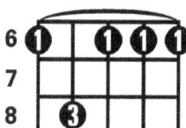	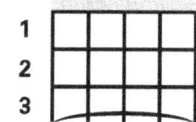	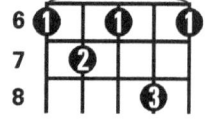

C#/ D♭ Chords (Advanced)

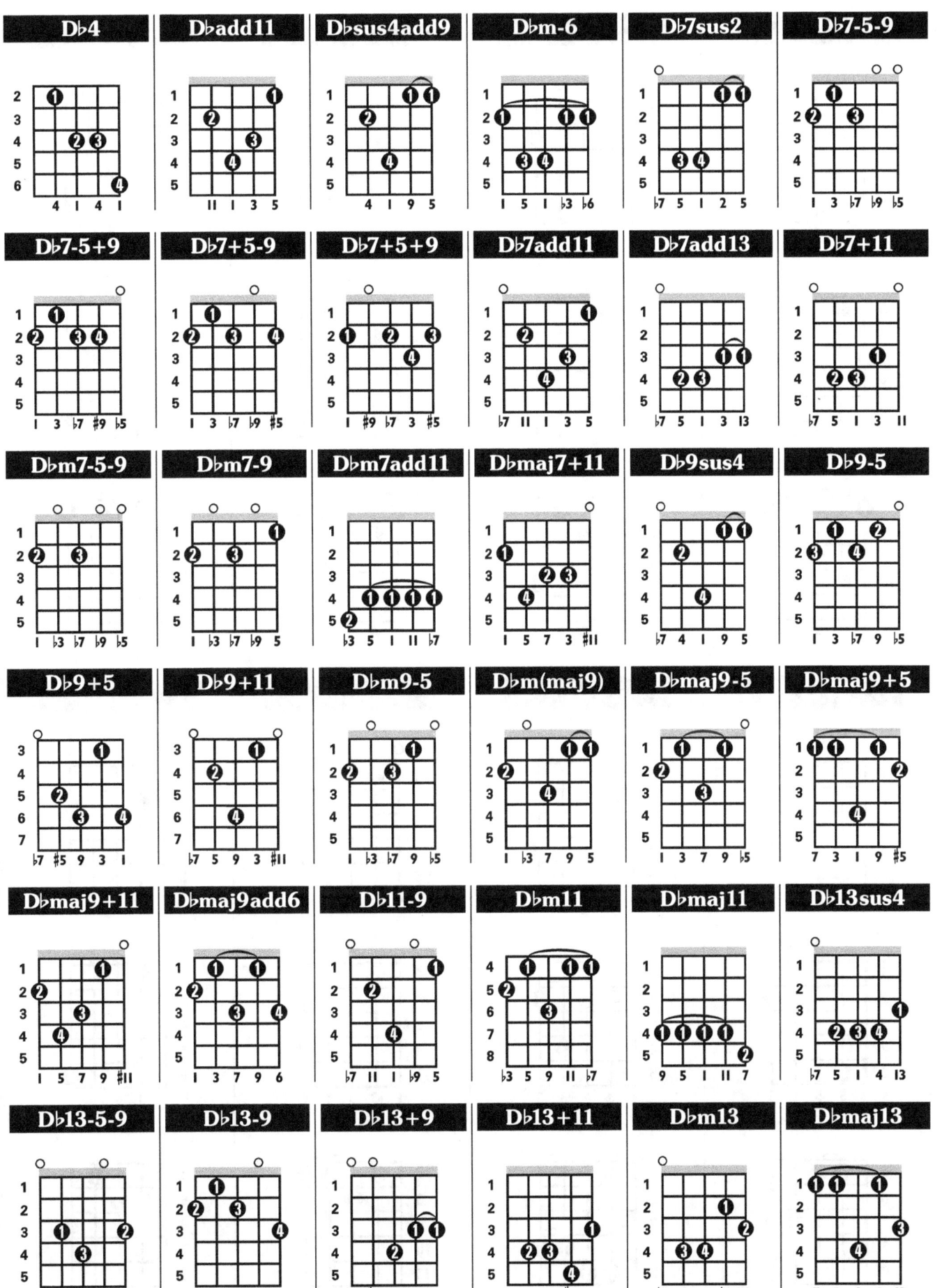

D Chords

D	Dm	D7	Dm7
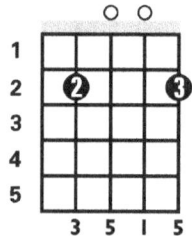	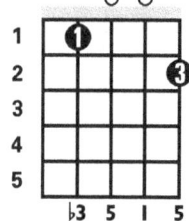	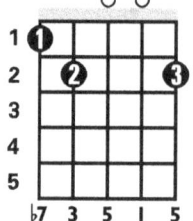	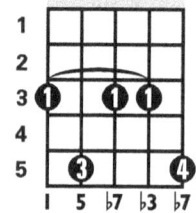
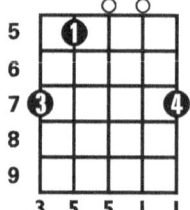	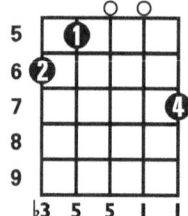	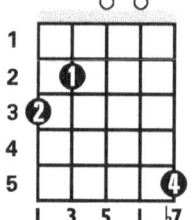	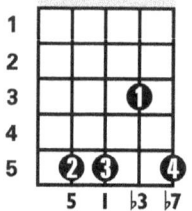
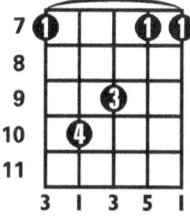	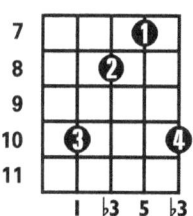	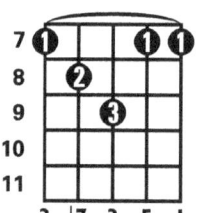	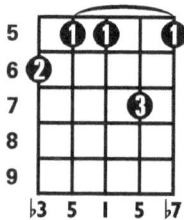

D5	D6	Dm6	Dmaj7
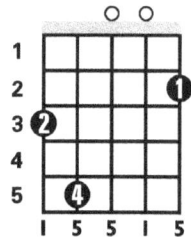	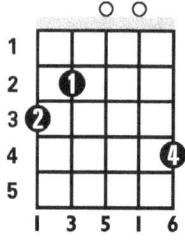	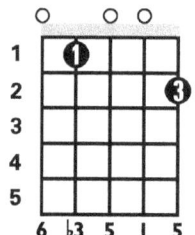	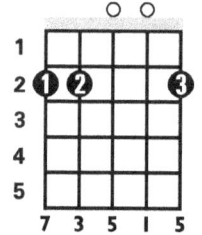
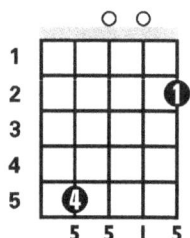	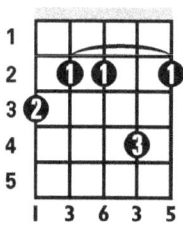	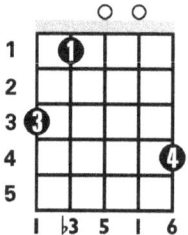	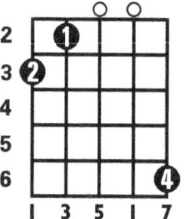
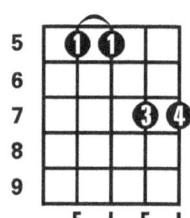	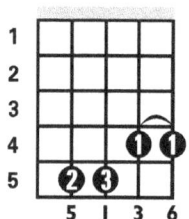	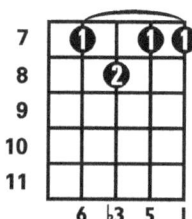	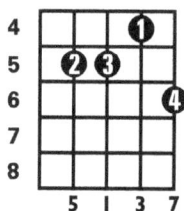

D Chords

D°
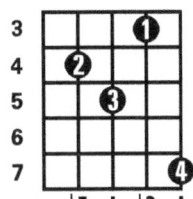
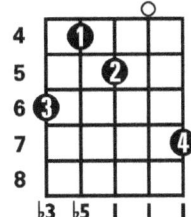
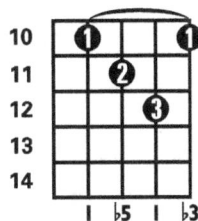

D°7
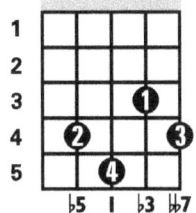
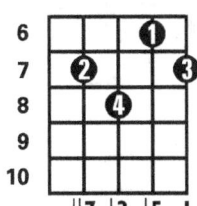

D-5
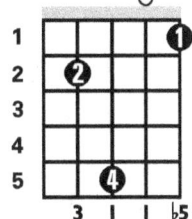
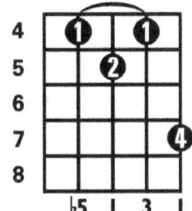
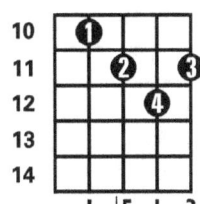

D+
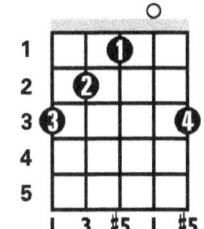
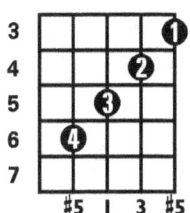
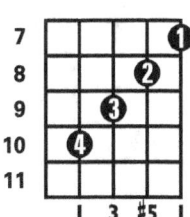

Dsus2
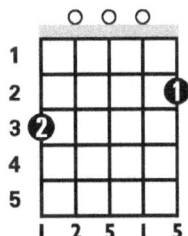
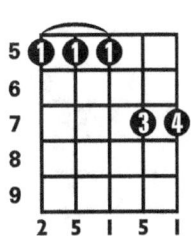
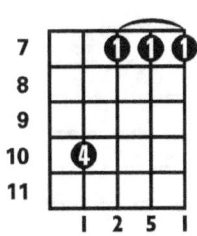

Dsus4
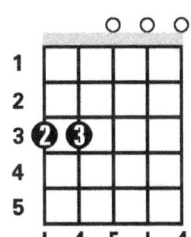
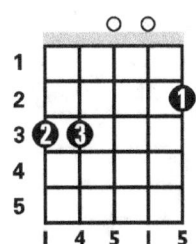
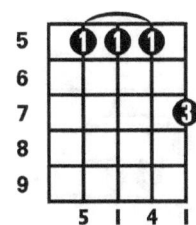

D7sus4
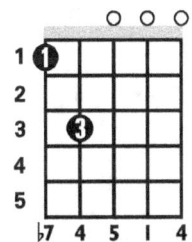
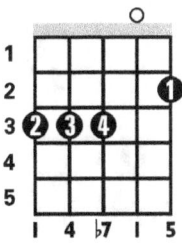
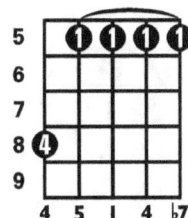

Dm7-5
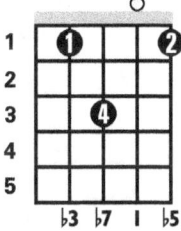
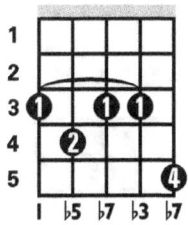
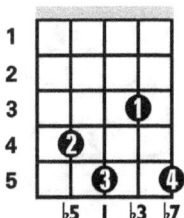

D Chords

Dadd9	Dmadd9	D6add9	Dm6add9
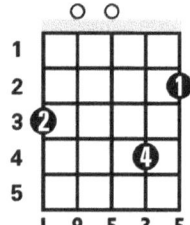	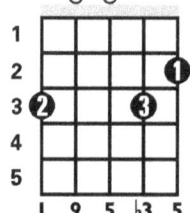	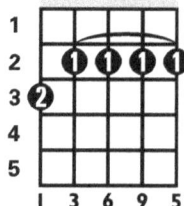	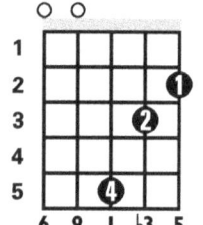
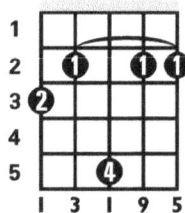	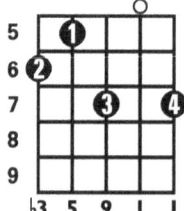	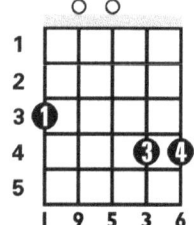	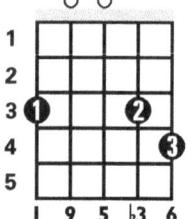
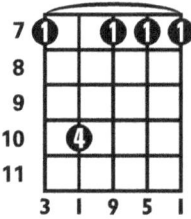	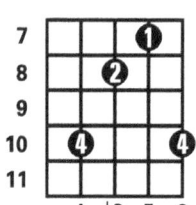	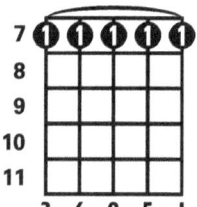	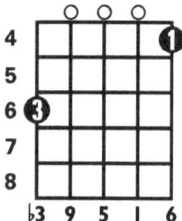

D7-5	D7+5	D7-9	D7+9
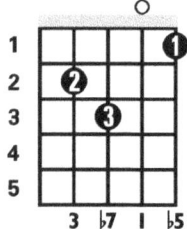	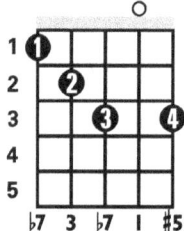	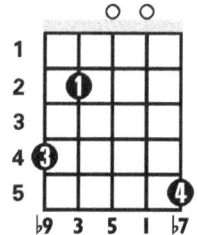	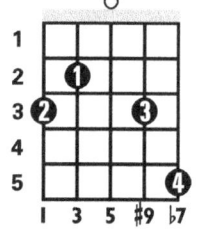
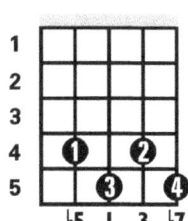	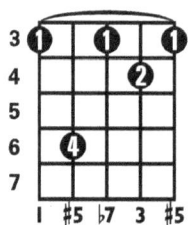	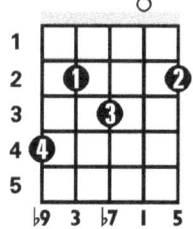	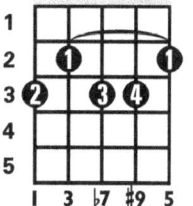
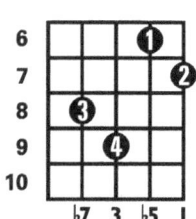	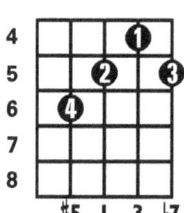	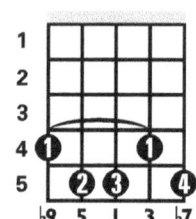	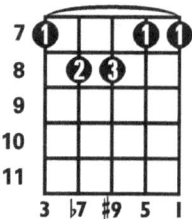

D Chords

Dm(maj7)
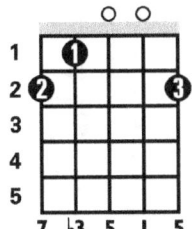
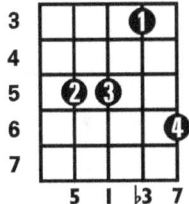
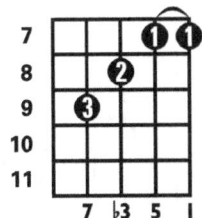

Dmaj7-5
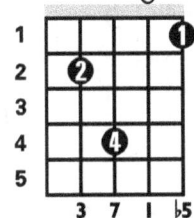
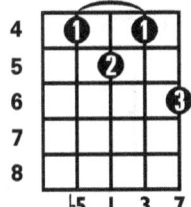
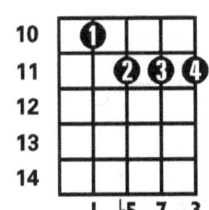

Dmaj7+5
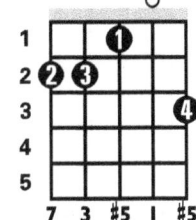
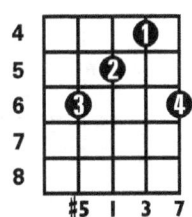
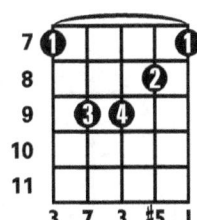

D9
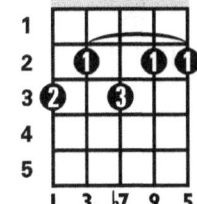
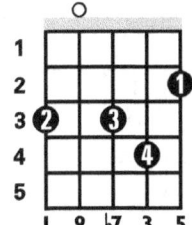
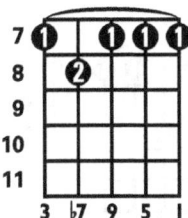

Dm9
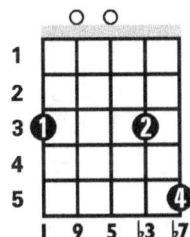
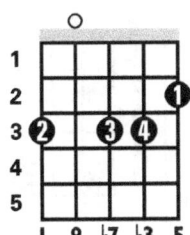
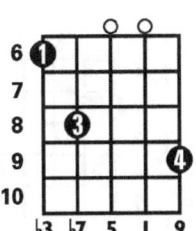

Dmaj9
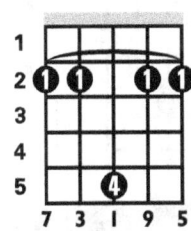
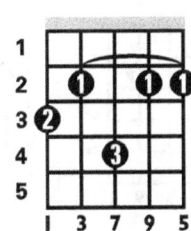
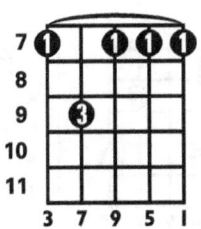

D11
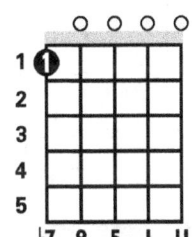
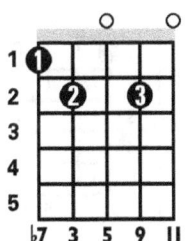
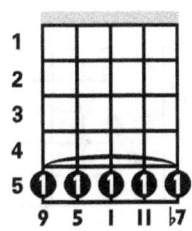

D13
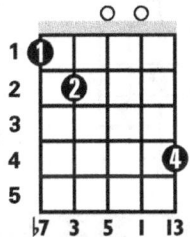
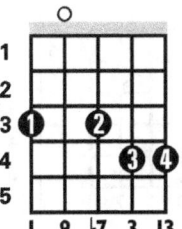
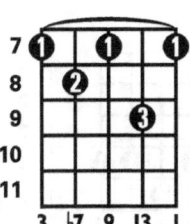

D Chords (Advanced)

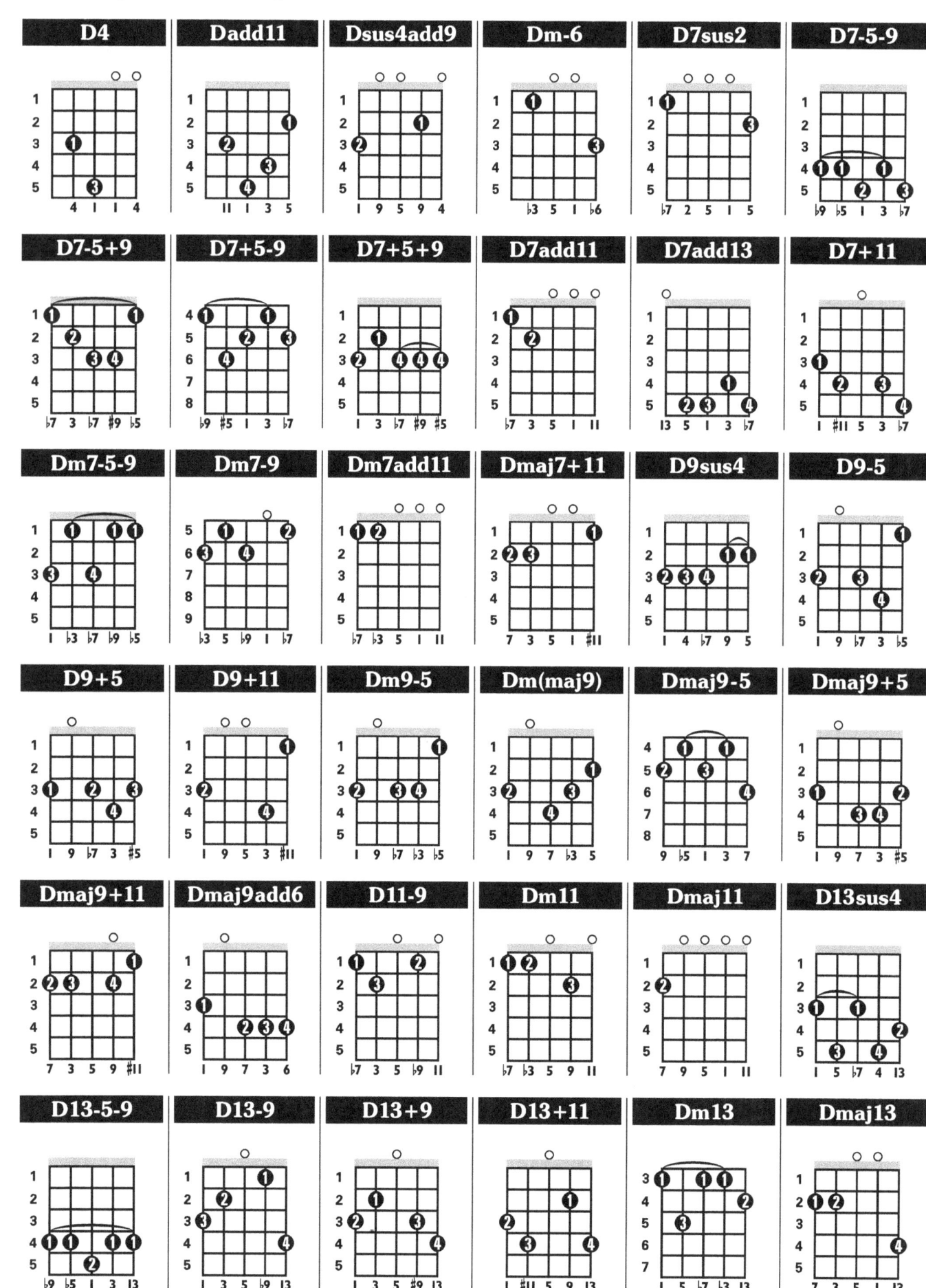

D#/ E♭ Chords

E♭
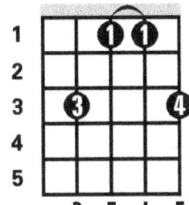
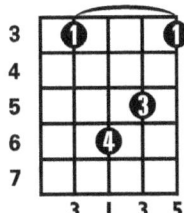
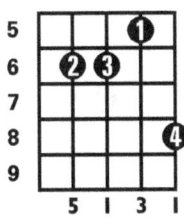

E♭m
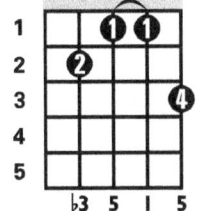
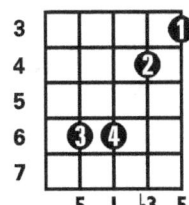
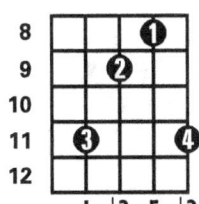

E♭7
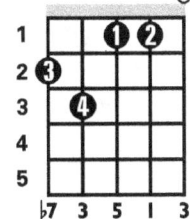
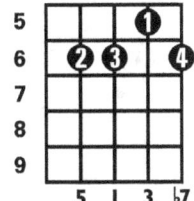
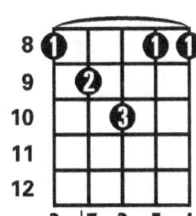

E♭m7
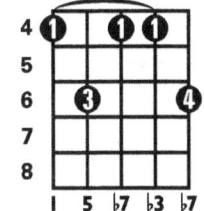
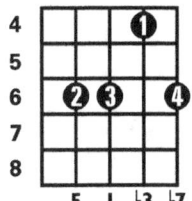
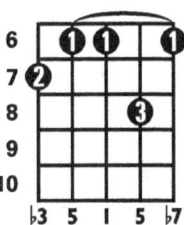

E♭5
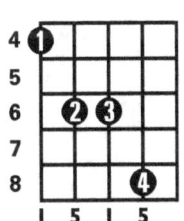
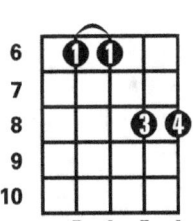
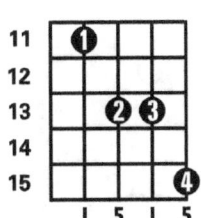

E♭6
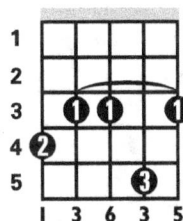
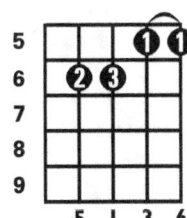
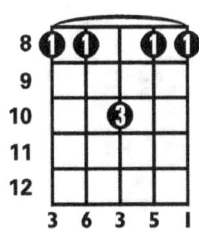

E♭m6
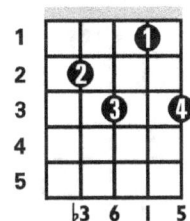
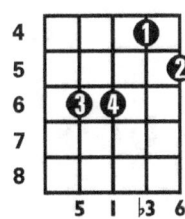
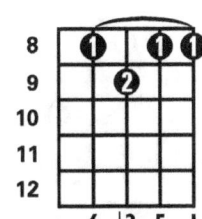

E♭maj7
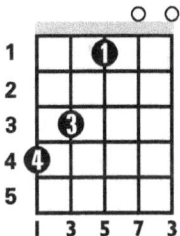
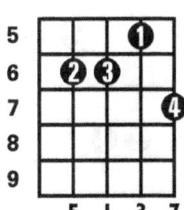
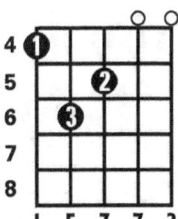

D♯/ E♭ Chords

E♭°	E♭°7	E♭-5	E♭+
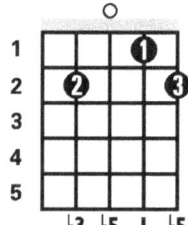	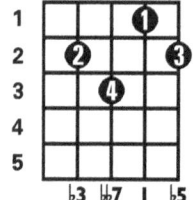	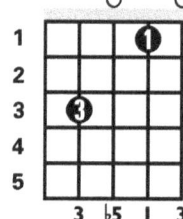	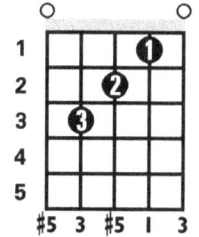
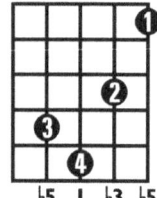	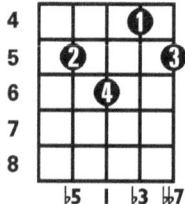	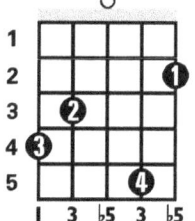	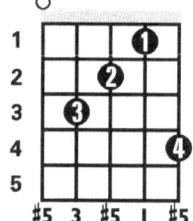
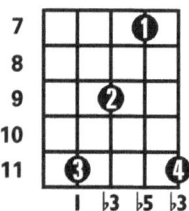	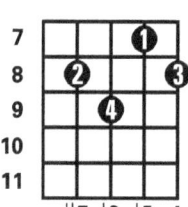	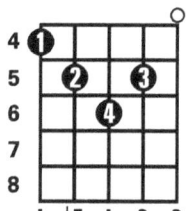	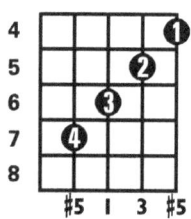

E♭sus2	E♭sus4	E♭7sus4	E♭m7-5
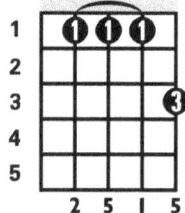	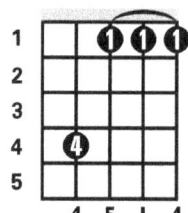	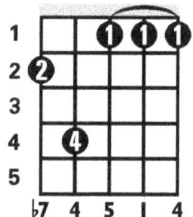	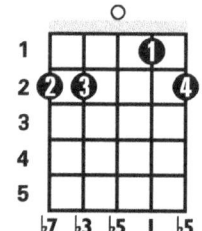
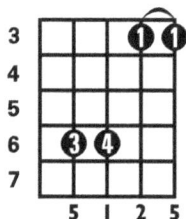	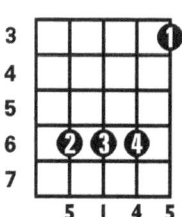	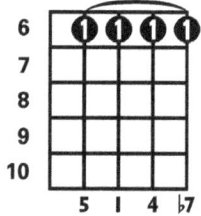	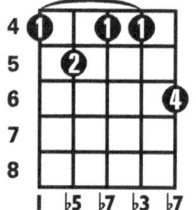
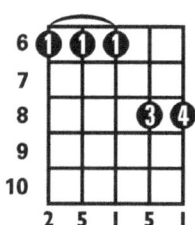	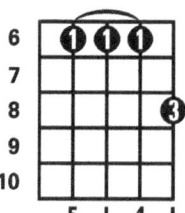	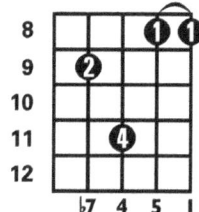	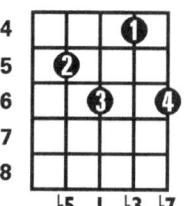

D#/ E♭ Chords

E♭add9
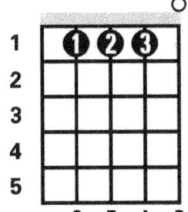
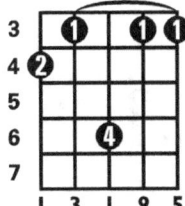
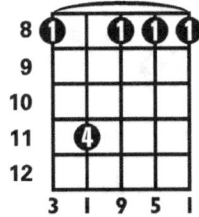

E♭madd9
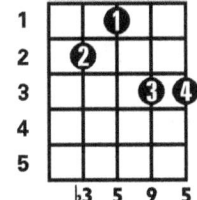
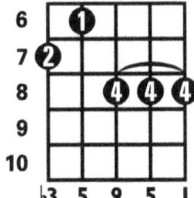
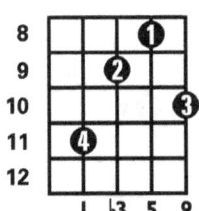

E♭6add9
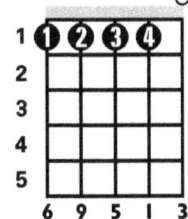
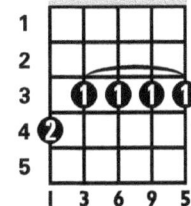
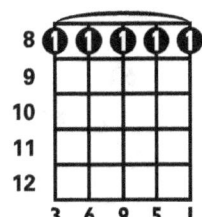

E♭m6add9
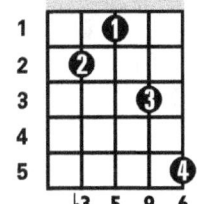
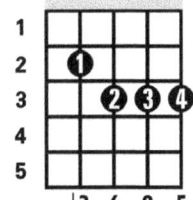
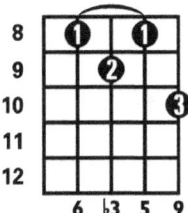

E♭7-5
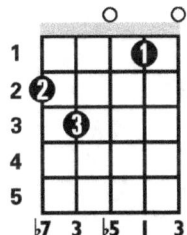
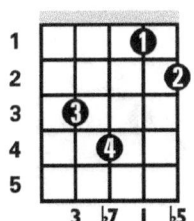
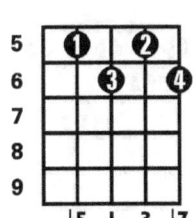

E♭7+5
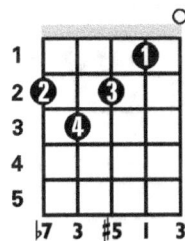
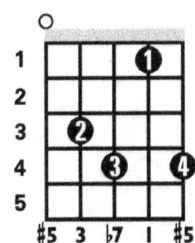
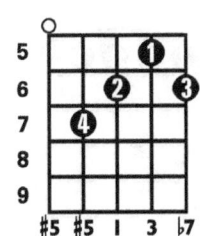

E♭7-9
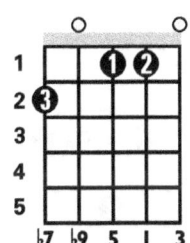
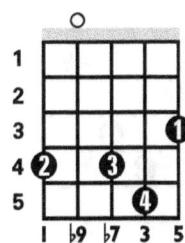
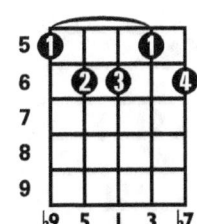

E♭7+9
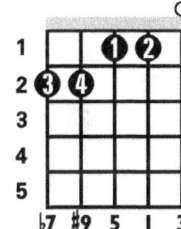
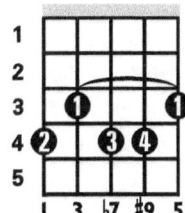
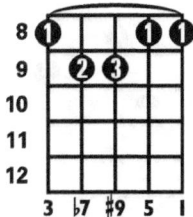

D#/ E♭ Chords

E♭m(maj7)
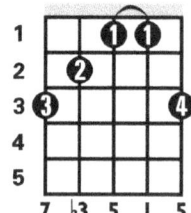
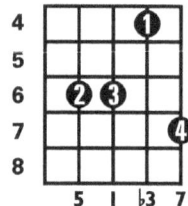
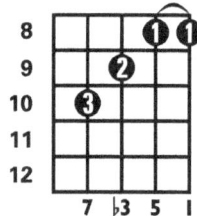

E♭maj7-5
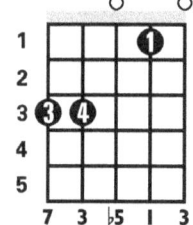
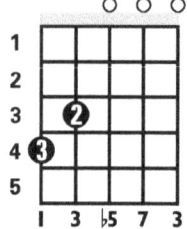
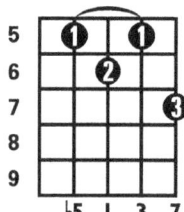

E♭maj7+5
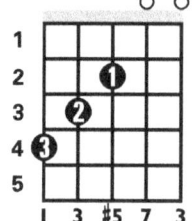
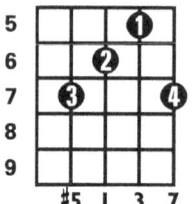
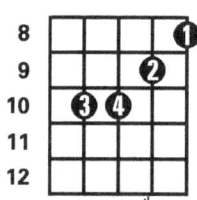

E♭9
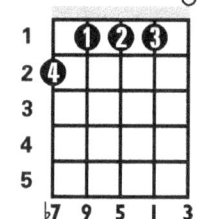
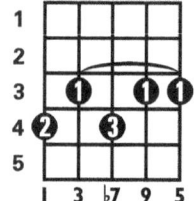
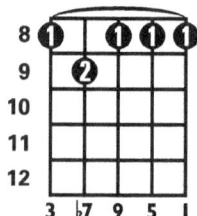

E♭m9
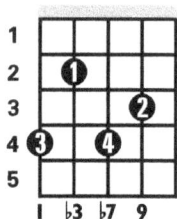
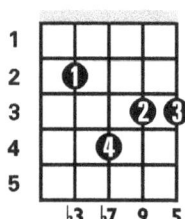
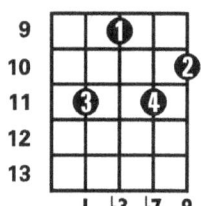

E♭maj9
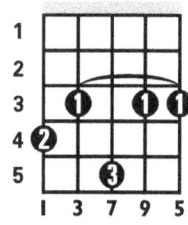
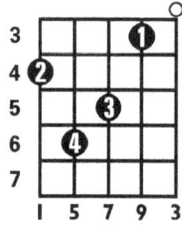
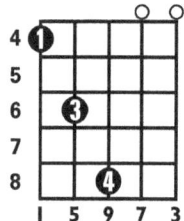

E♭11
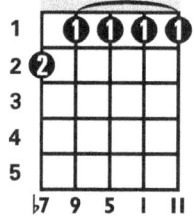
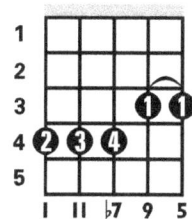
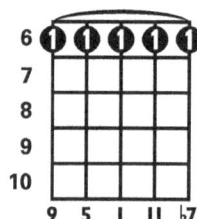

E♭13
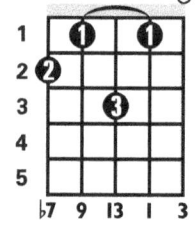
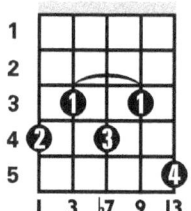
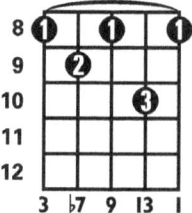

D#/E♭ Chords (Advanced)

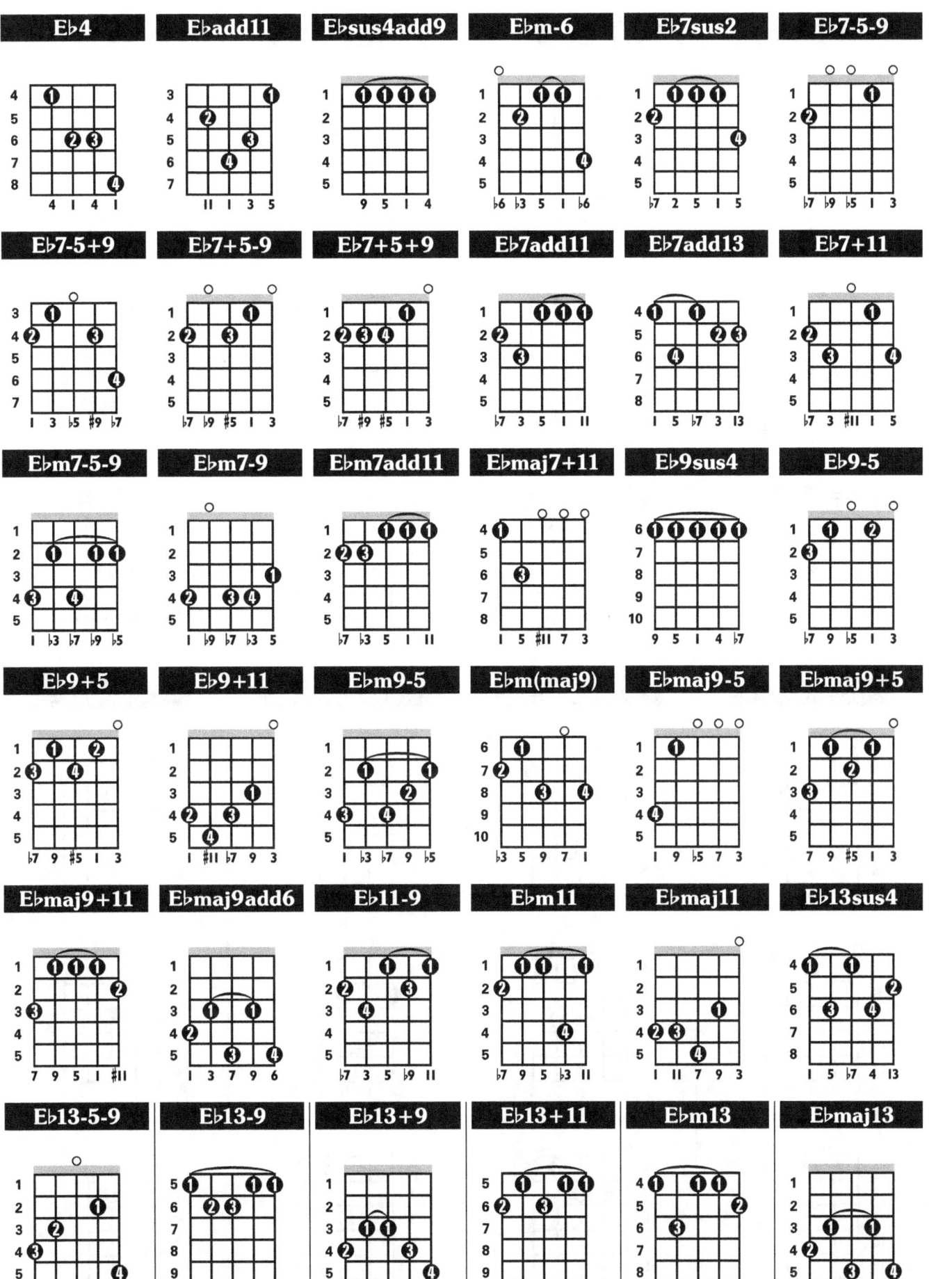

E Chords

E
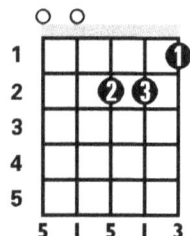
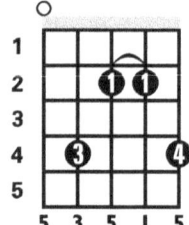
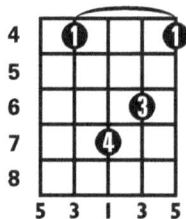

Em
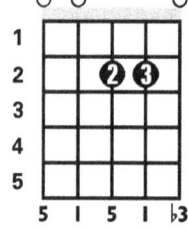
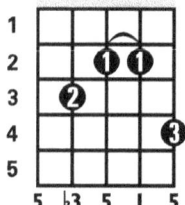
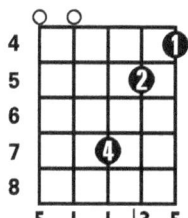

E7
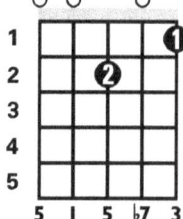
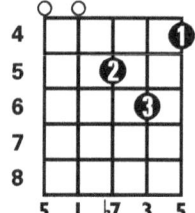
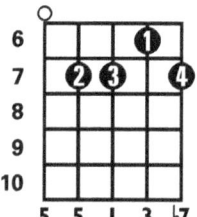

Em7
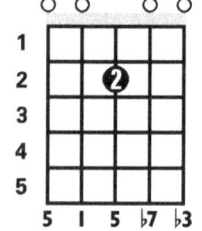
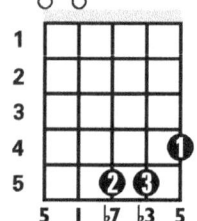
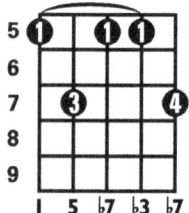

E5
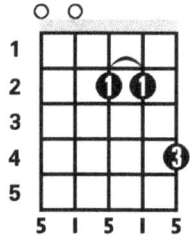
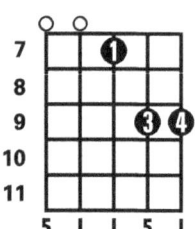
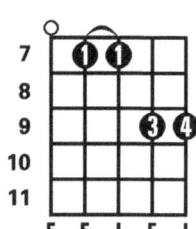

E6
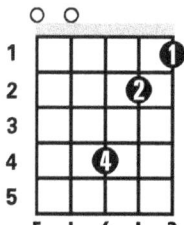
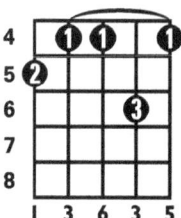
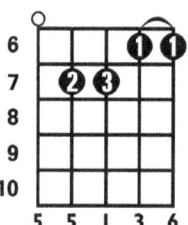

Em6
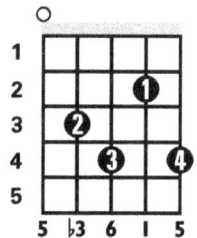
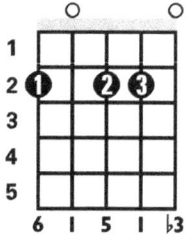
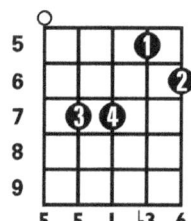

Emaj7
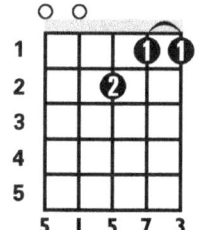
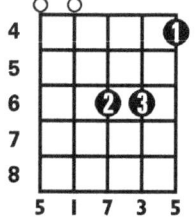
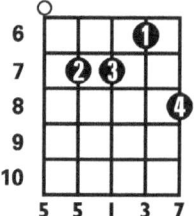

E Chords

E°
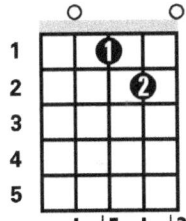
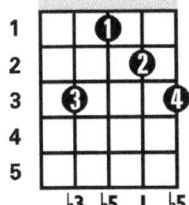
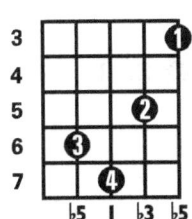

E°7
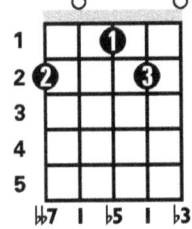
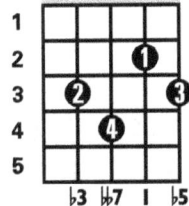
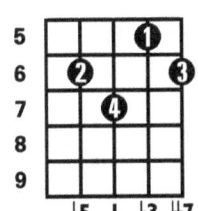

E-5
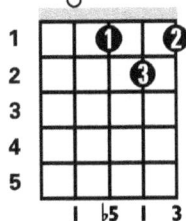
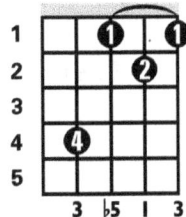
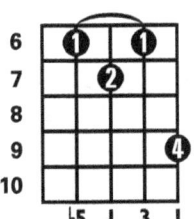

E+
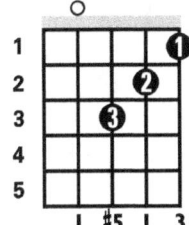
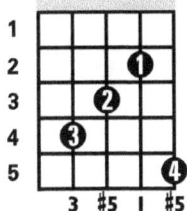
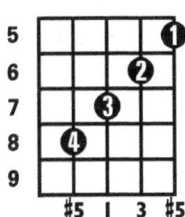

Esus2
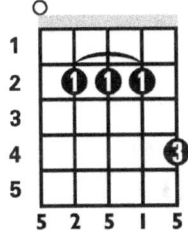
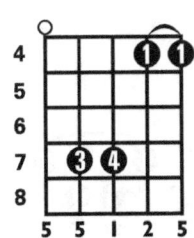
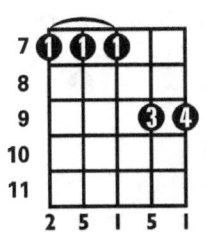

Esus4
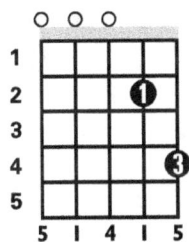
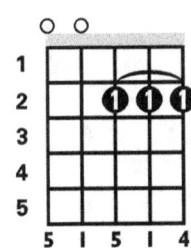
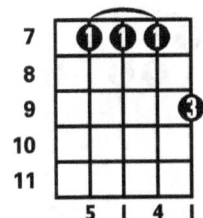

E7sus4
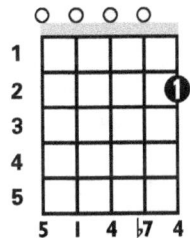
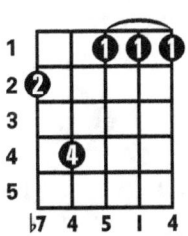
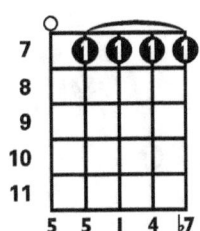

Em7-5
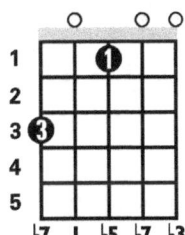
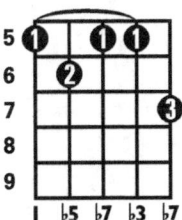
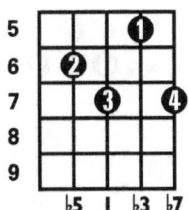

E Chords

Eadd9	Emadd9	E6add9	Em6add9
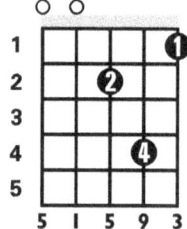	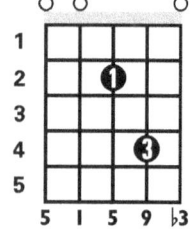	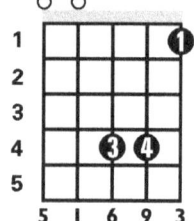	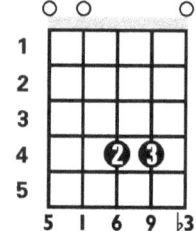
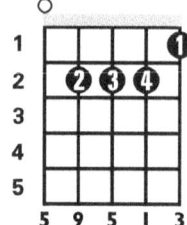	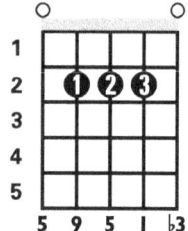	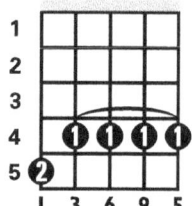	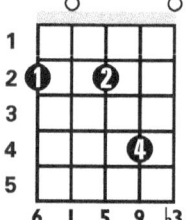
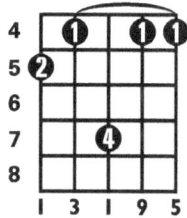	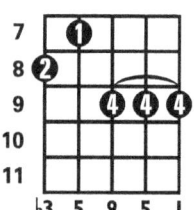	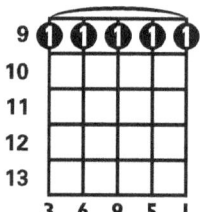	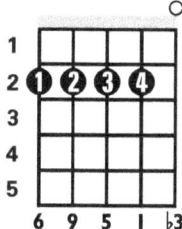

E7-5	E7+5	E7-9	E7+9
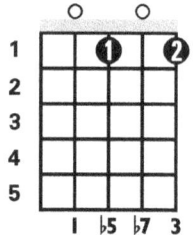	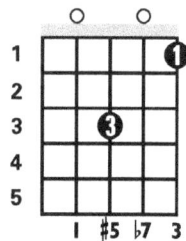	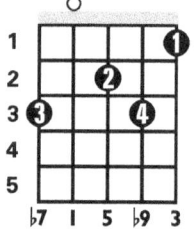	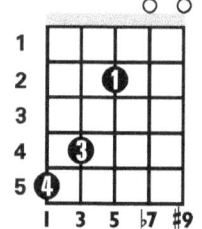
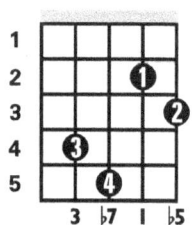	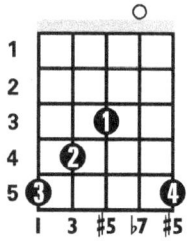	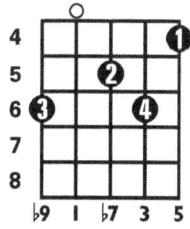	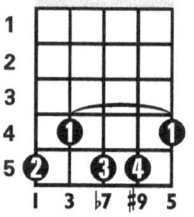
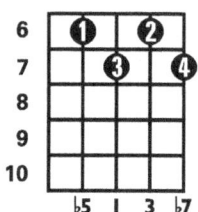	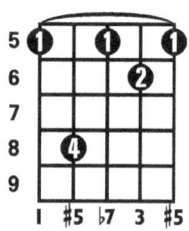	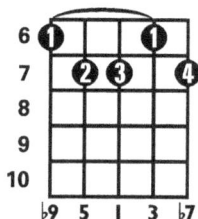	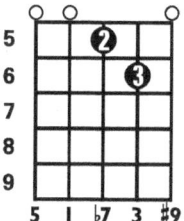

E Chords

Em(maj7)
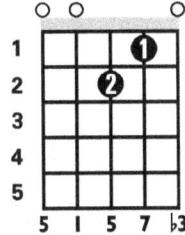
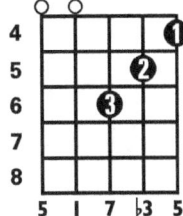
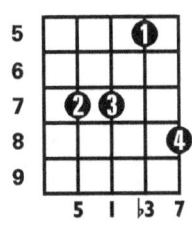

Emaj7-5
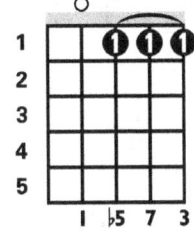
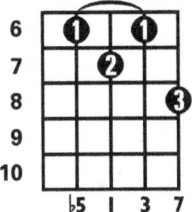
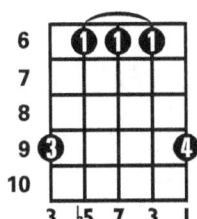

Emaj7+5
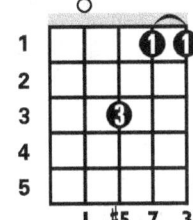
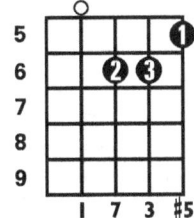
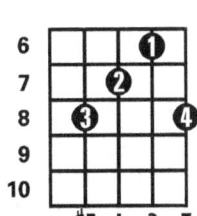

E9
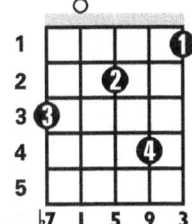
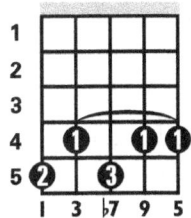
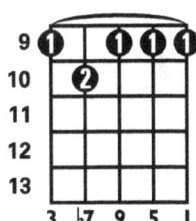

Em9
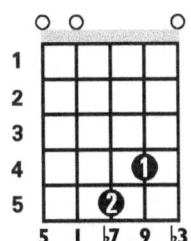
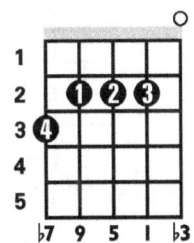
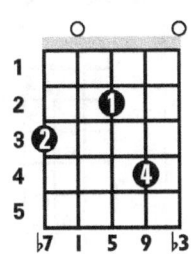

Emaj9
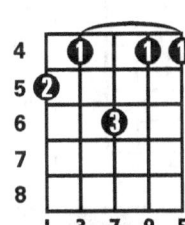
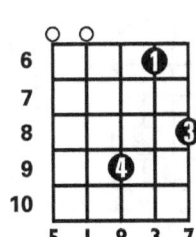
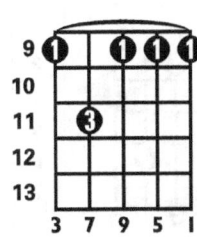

E11
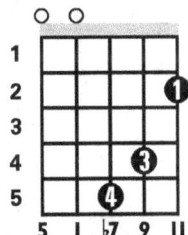
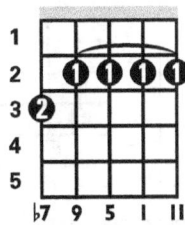
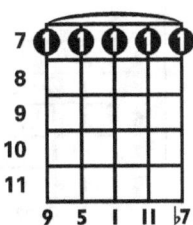

E13
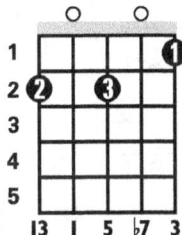
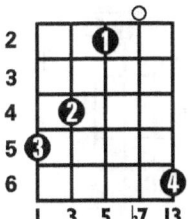
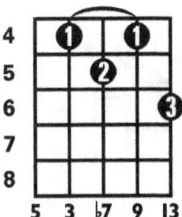

E Chords (Advanced)

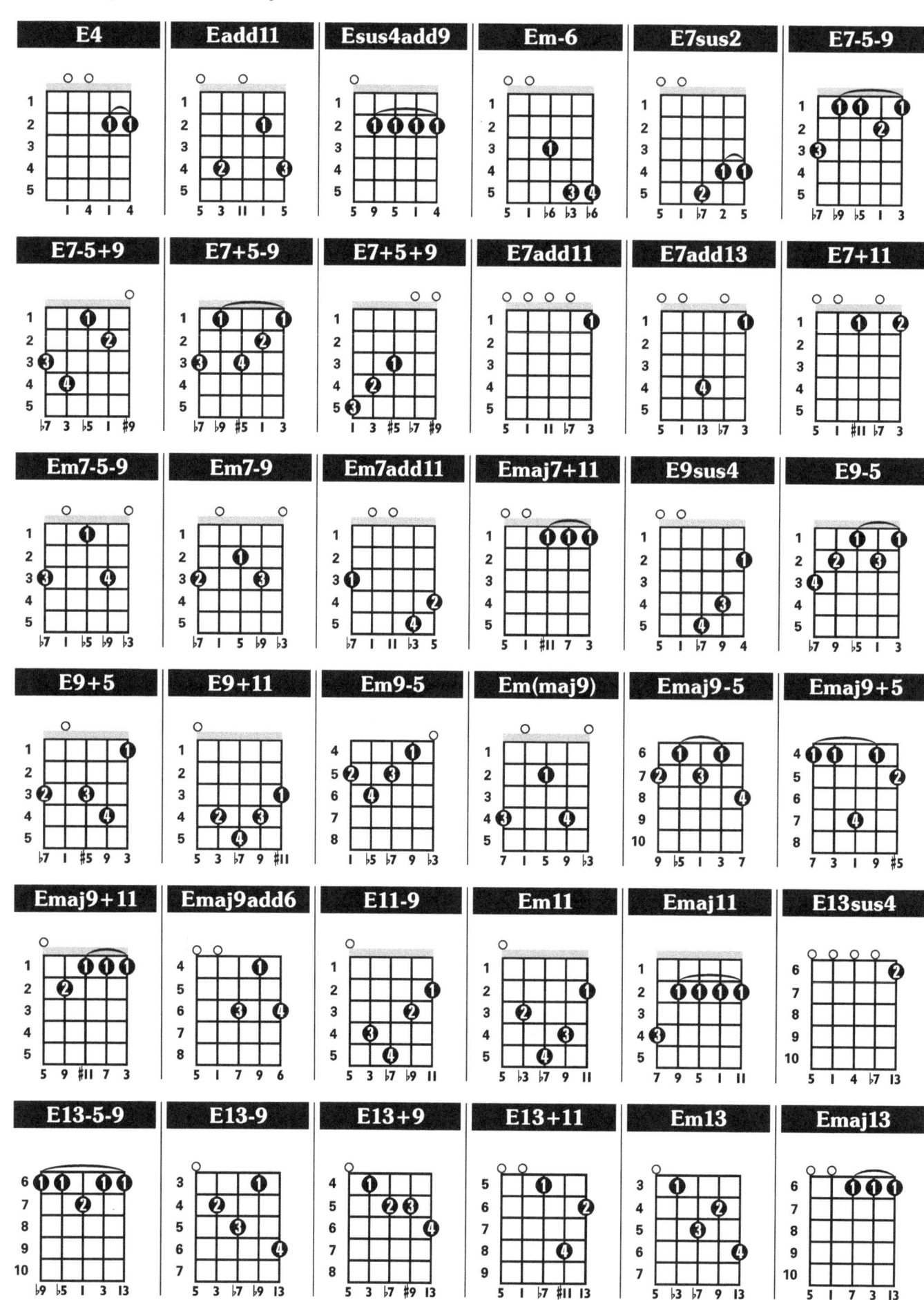

F Chords

F
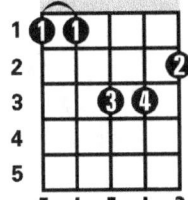
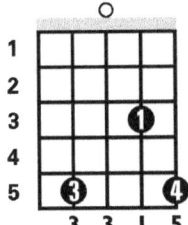
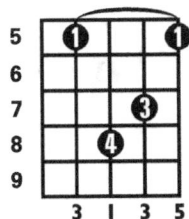

Fm
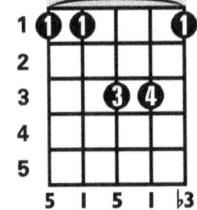
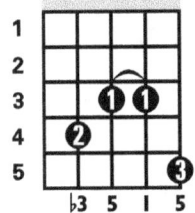
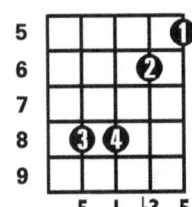

F7
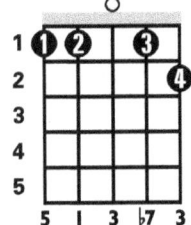
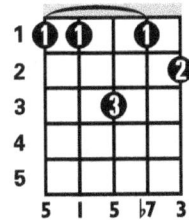
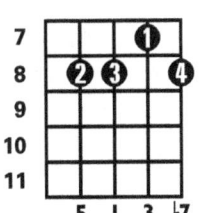

Fm7
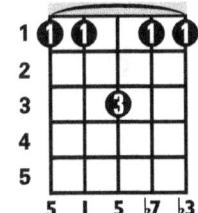
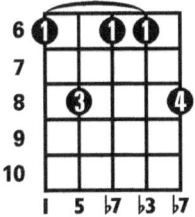
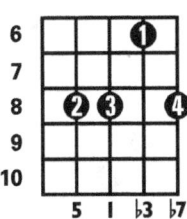

F5
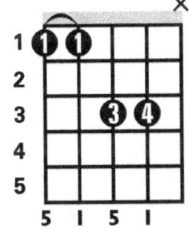
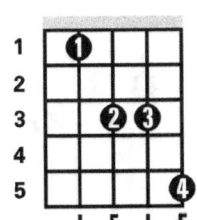
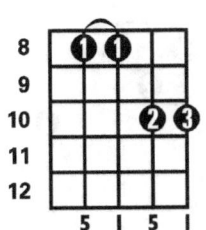

F6
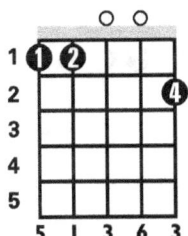
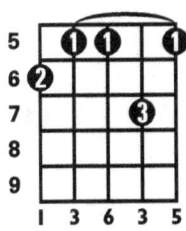
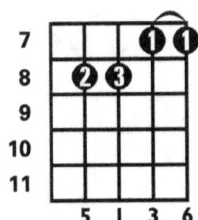

Fm6
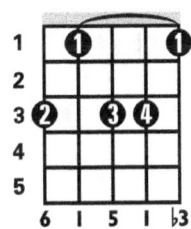
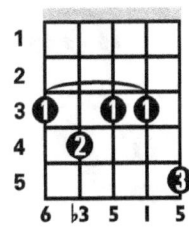
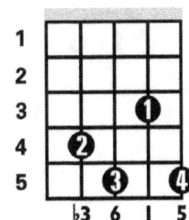

Fmaj7
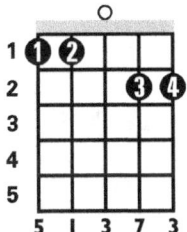
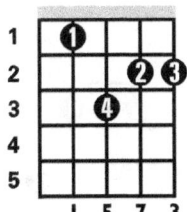
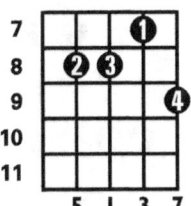

F Chords

F°	F°7	F-5	F+
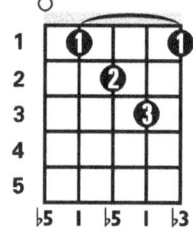	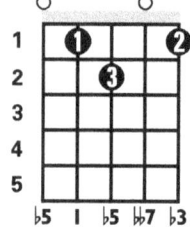	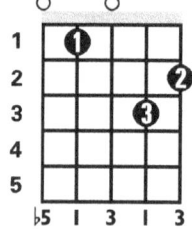	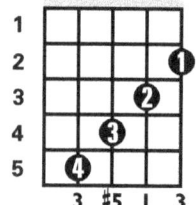
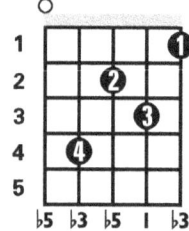	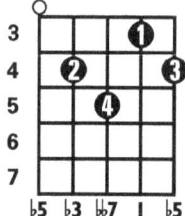	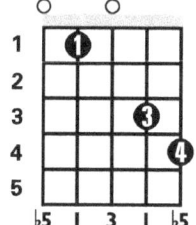	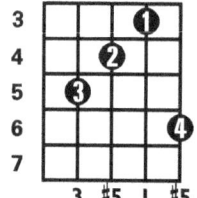
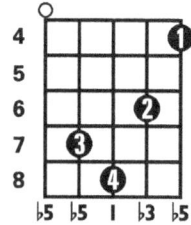	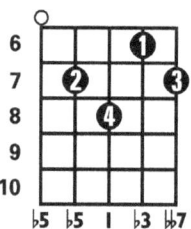	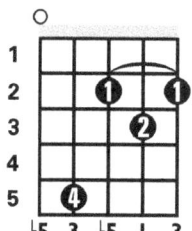	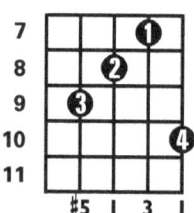

Fsus2	Fsus4	F7sus4	Fm7-5
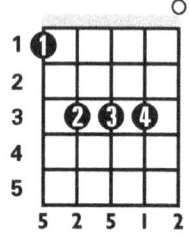	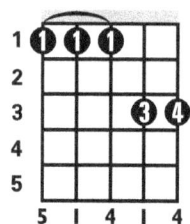	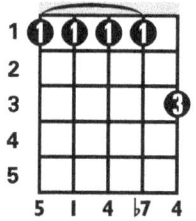	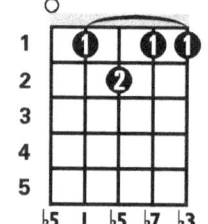
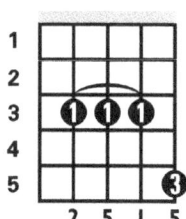	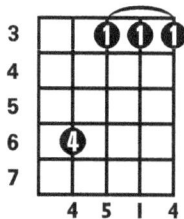	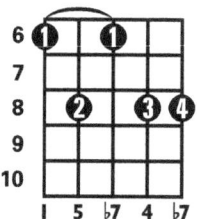	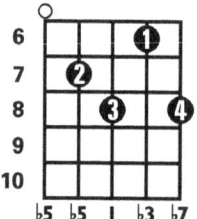
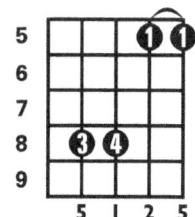	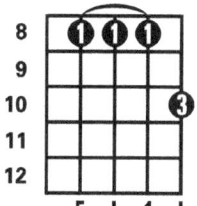	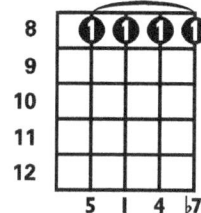	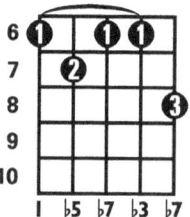

F Chords

Fadd9
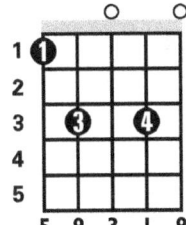
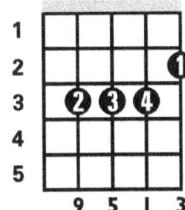
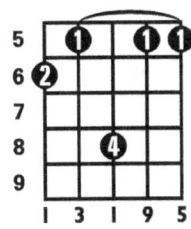

Fmadd9
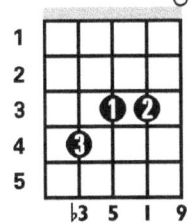
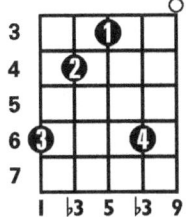
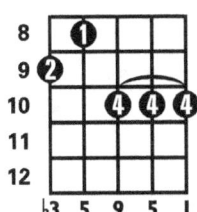

F6add9
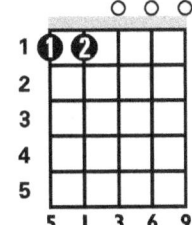
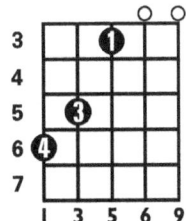
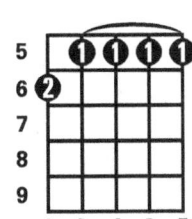

Fm6add9
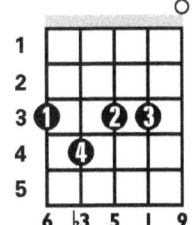
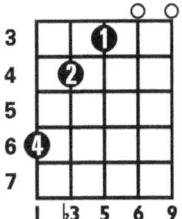
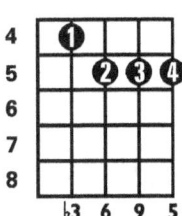

F7-5
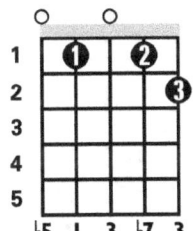
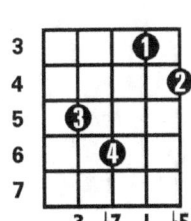
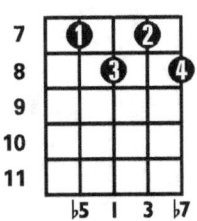

F7+5
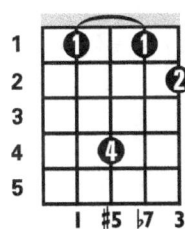
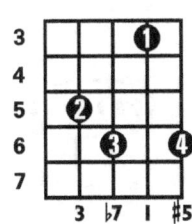
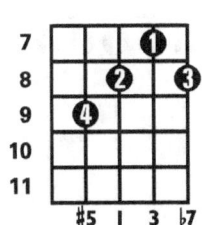

F7-9
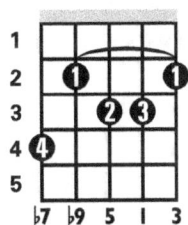
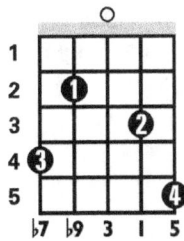
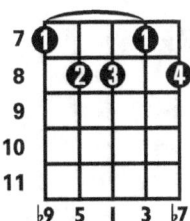

F7+9
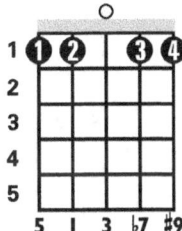
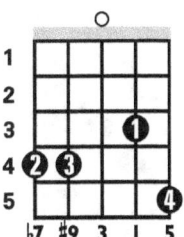
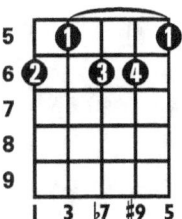

F Chords

Fm(maj7)	Fmaj7-5	Fmaj7+5	F9
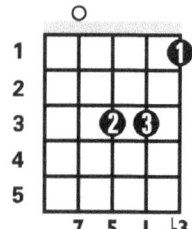	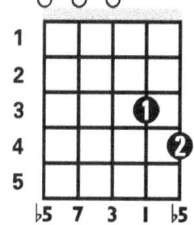	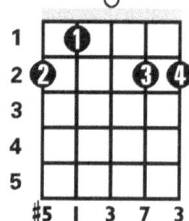	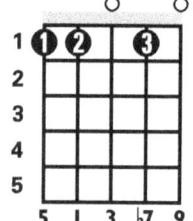
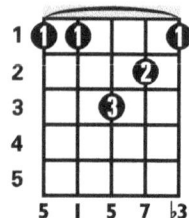	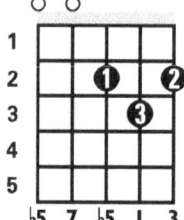	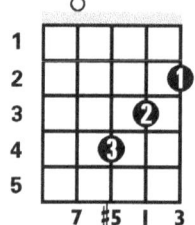	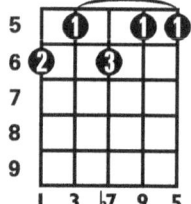
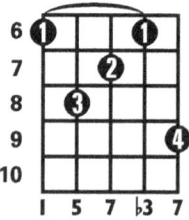	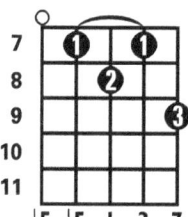	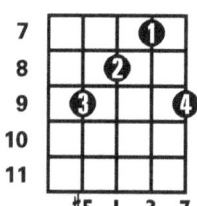	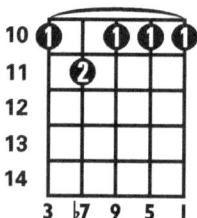

Fm9	Fmaj9	F11	F13
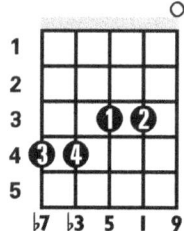	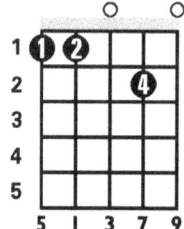	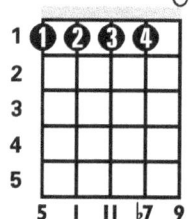	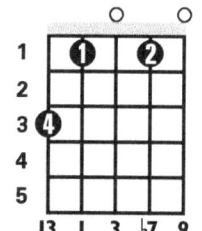
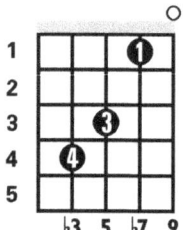	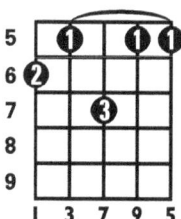	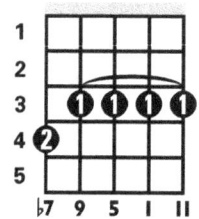	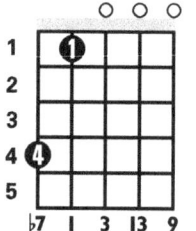
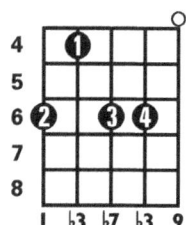	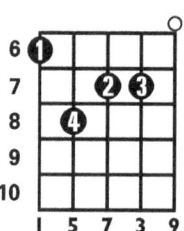	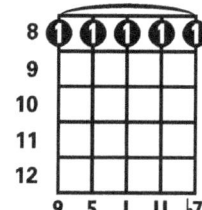	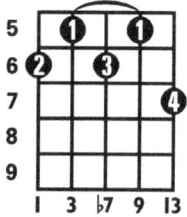

F Chords (Advanced)

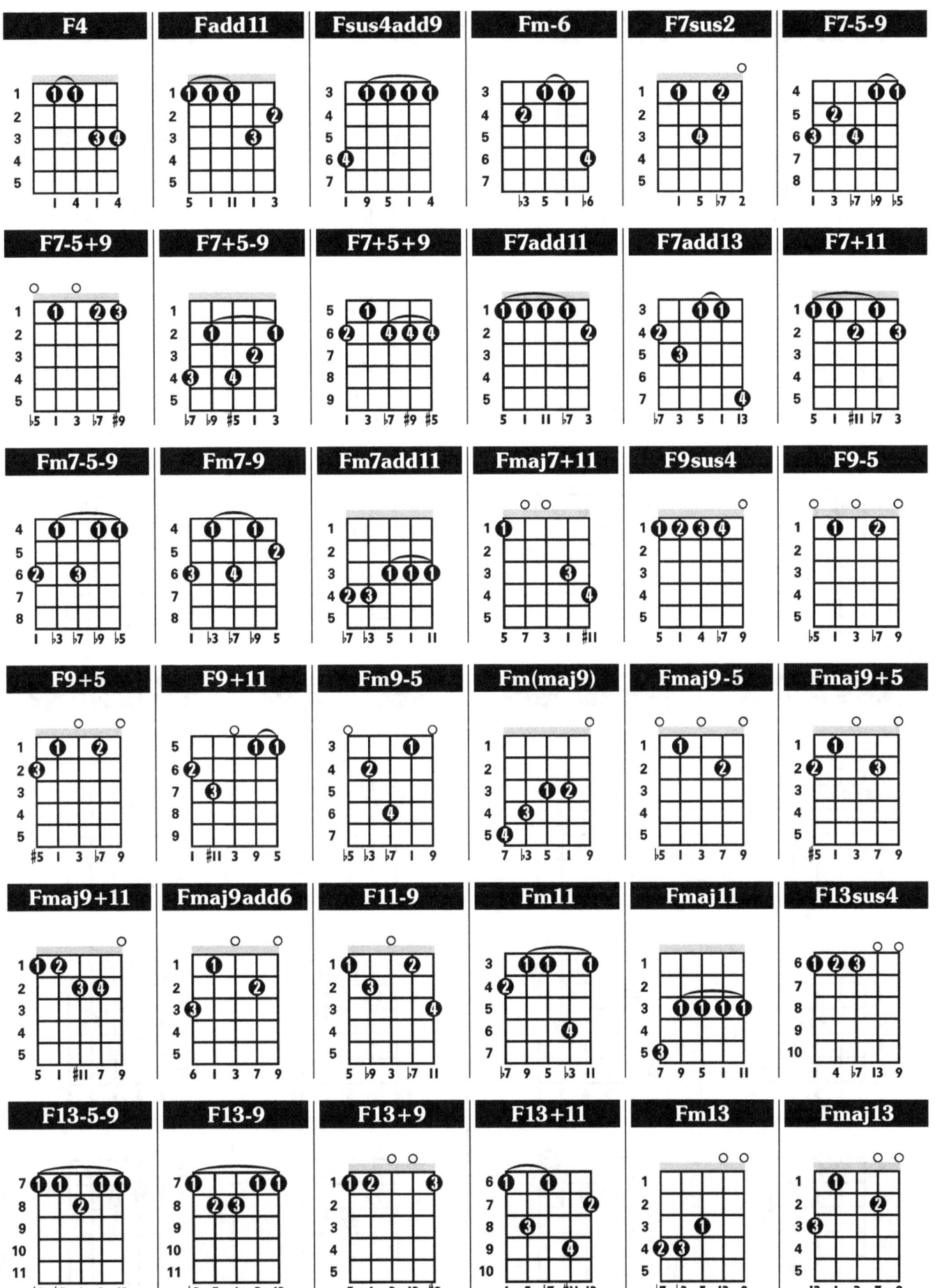

F#/G♭ Chords

F#	F#m	F#7	F#m7
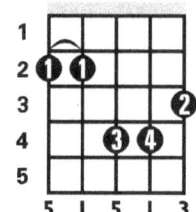	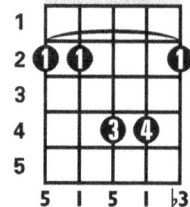	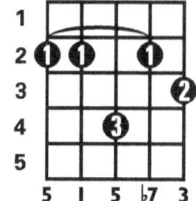	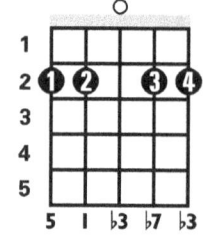
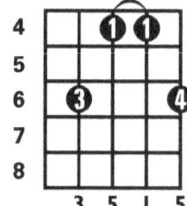	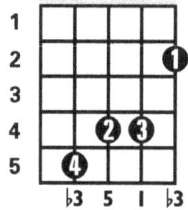	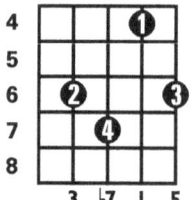	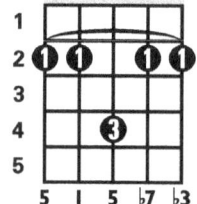
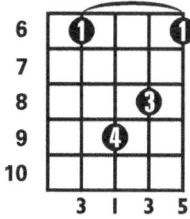	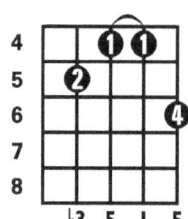	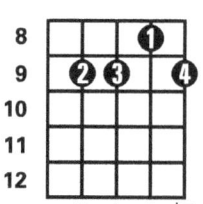	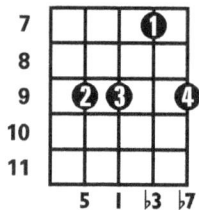

F#5	F#6	F#m6	F#maj7
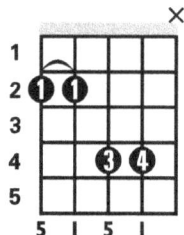	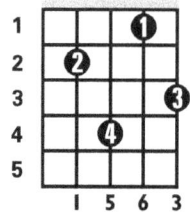	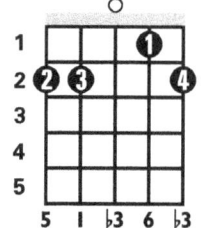	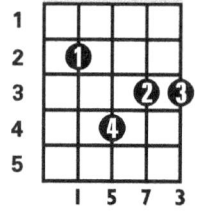
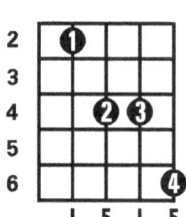	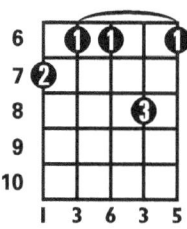	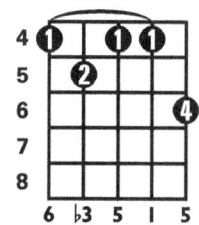	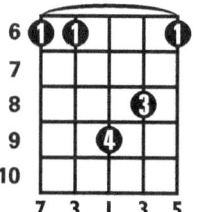
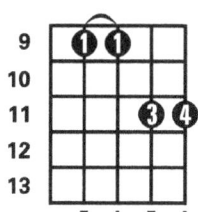	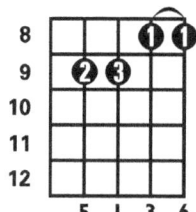	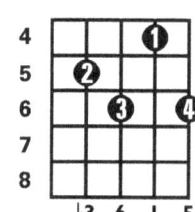	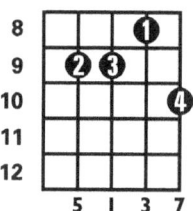

F#/G♭ Chords

F#°	F#°7	F#-5	F#+
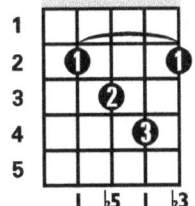	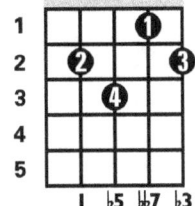	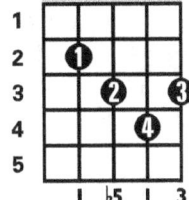	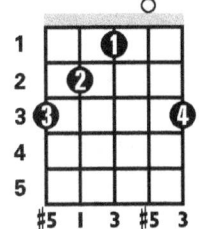
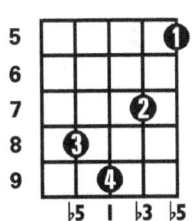	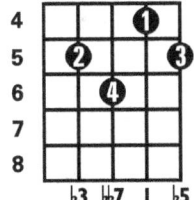	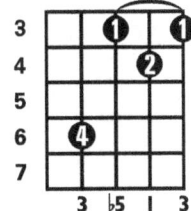	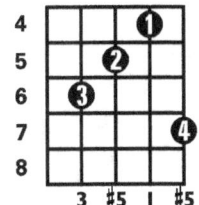
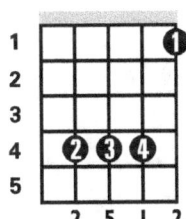	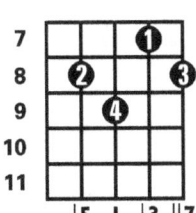	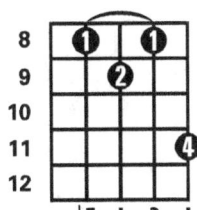	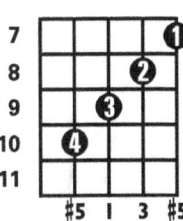

F#sus2	F#sus4	F#7sus4	F#m7-5
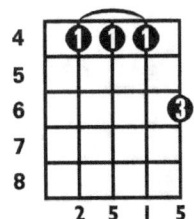	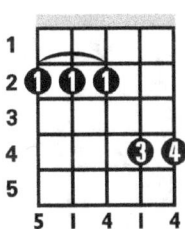	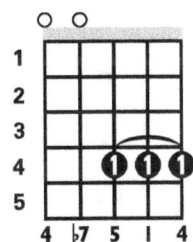	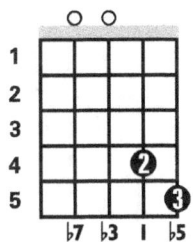
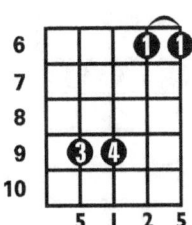	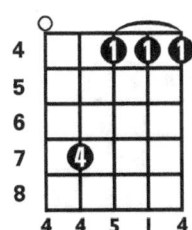	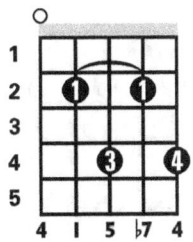	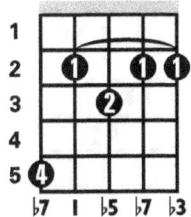
	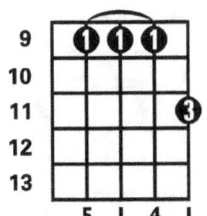	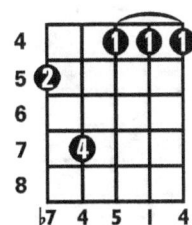	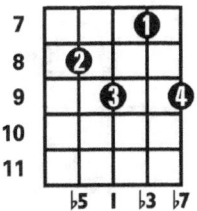

F#/G♭ Chords

F#add9
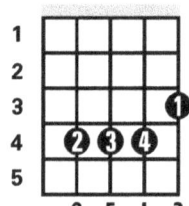
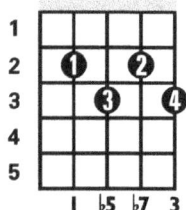
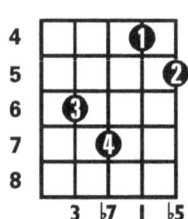

F#madd9
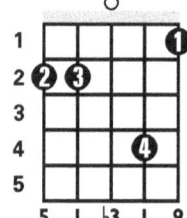
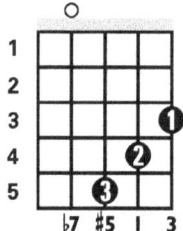
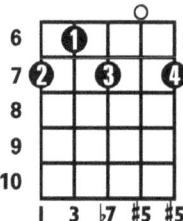

F#6add9
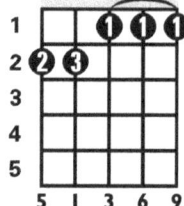
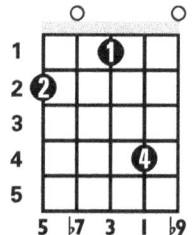
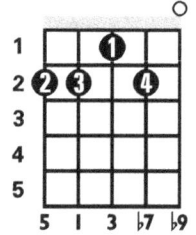

F#m6add9
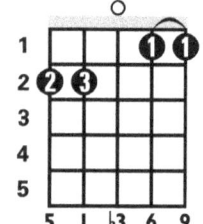
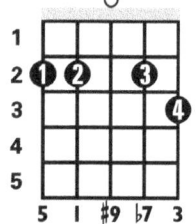
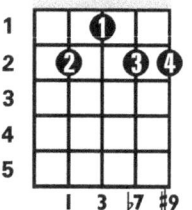

F#7-5
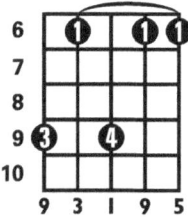
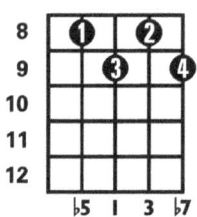
(third diagram)

F#7+5
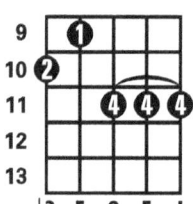
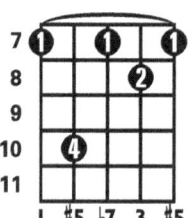

F#7-9
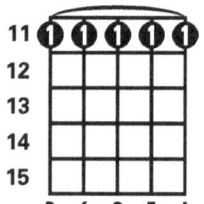
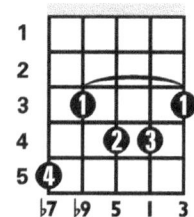

F#7+9
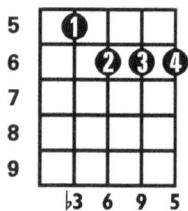
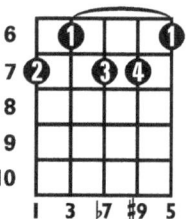

44

F#/G♭ Chords

F#m(maj7)
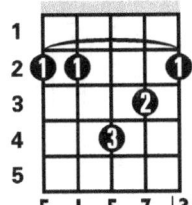
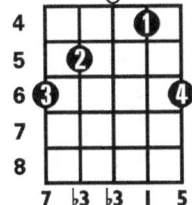
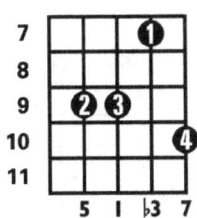

F#maj7-5
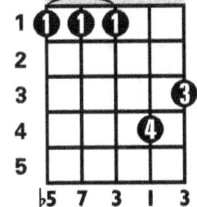
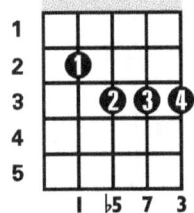
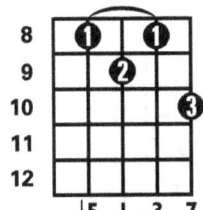

F#maj7+5
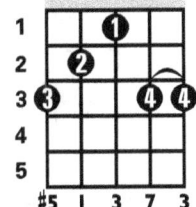
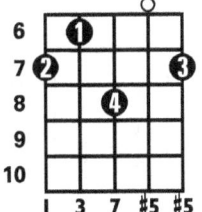
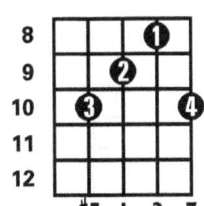

F#9
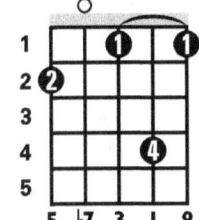
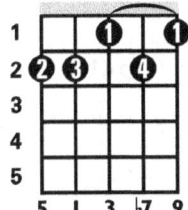
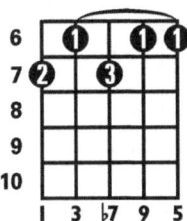

F#m9
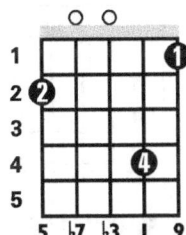
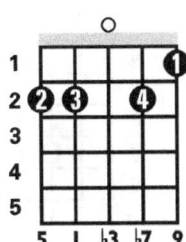
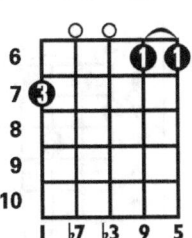

F#maj9
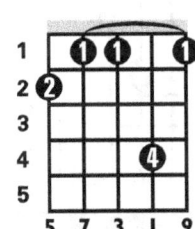
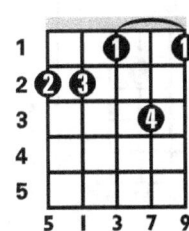
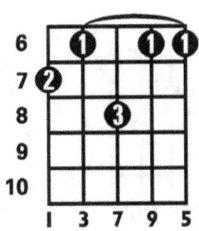

F#11
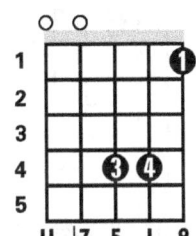
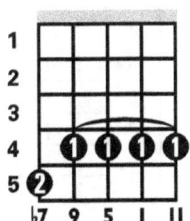
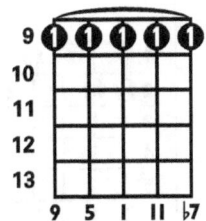

F#13
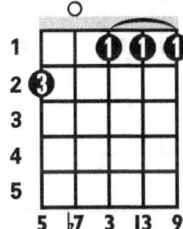
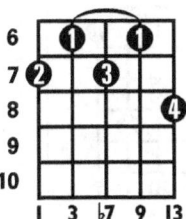
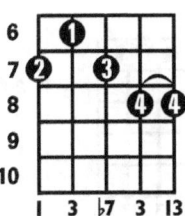

F#/G♭ Chords (Advanced)

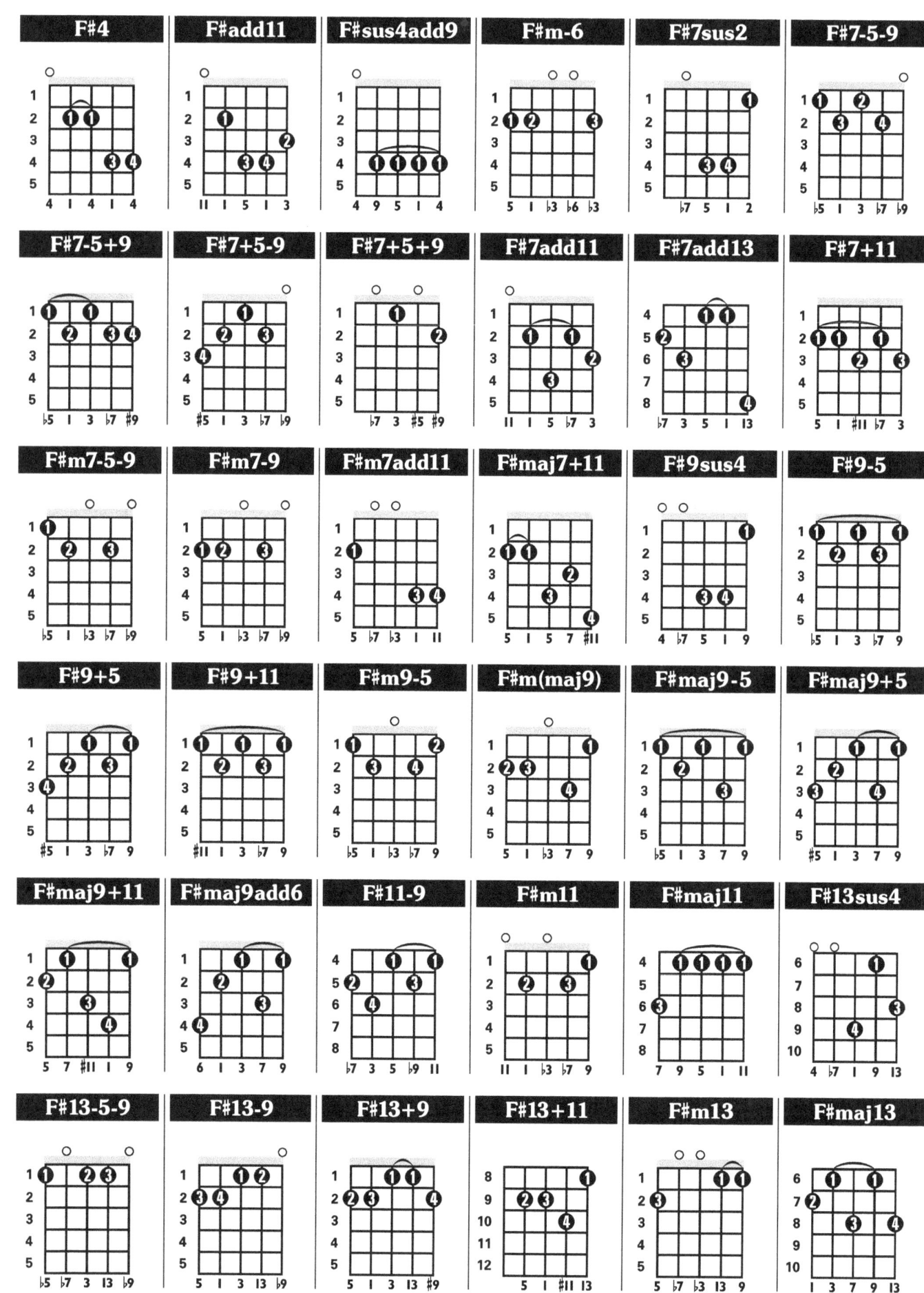

G Chords

G
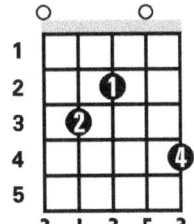
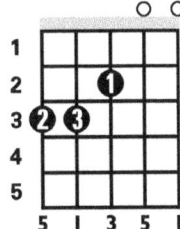
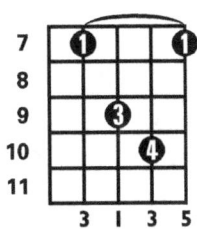

Gm
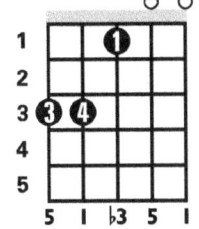
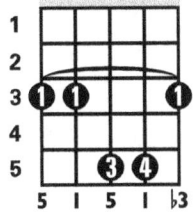
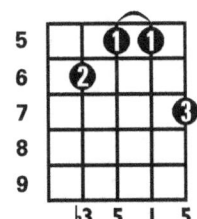

G7
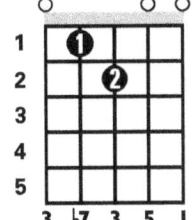
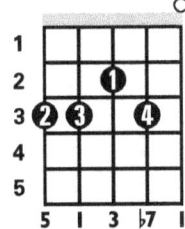
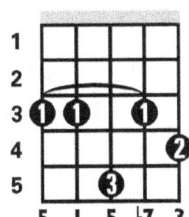

Gm7
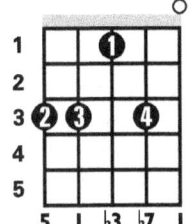
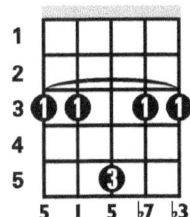
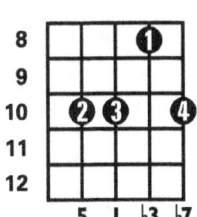

G5
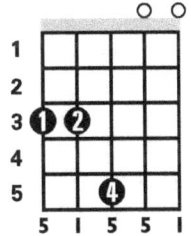
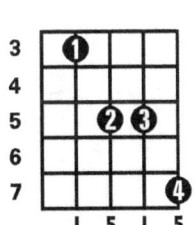
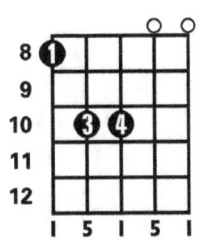

G6
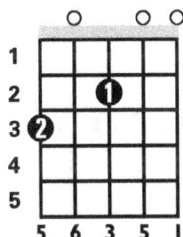
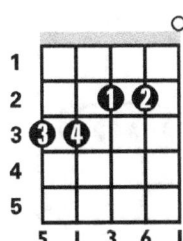
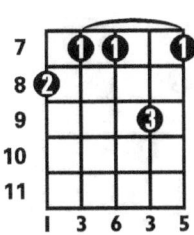

Gm6
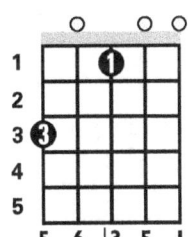
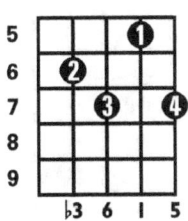
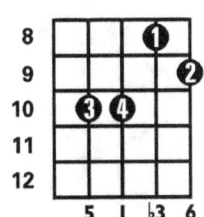

Gmaj7
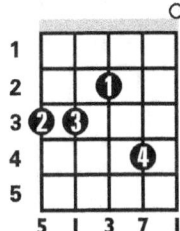
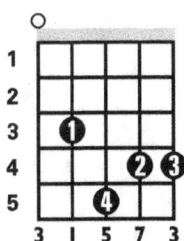
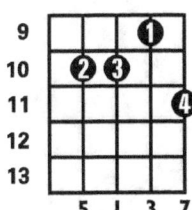

G Chords

G°
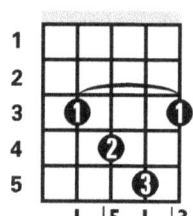
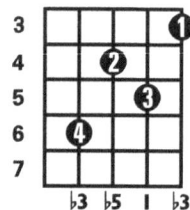
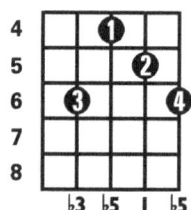

G°7
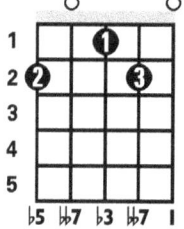
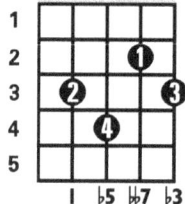
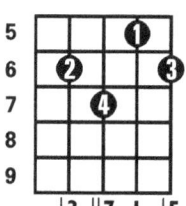

G-5
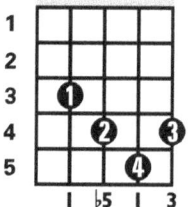
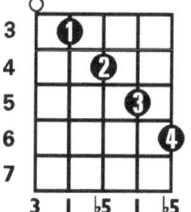
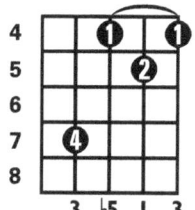

G+
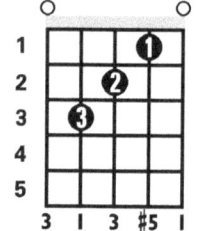
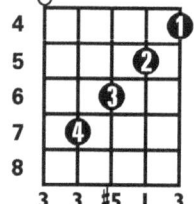
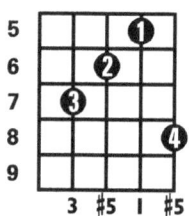

Gsus2
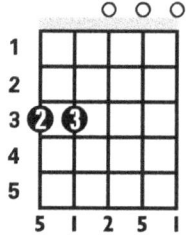
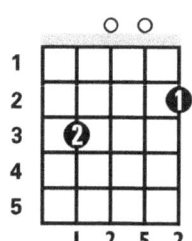
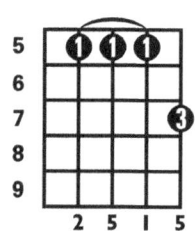

Gsus4
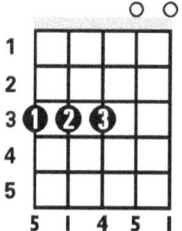
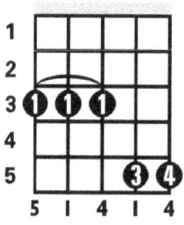
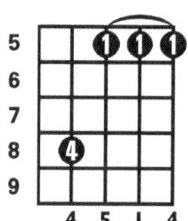

G7sus4
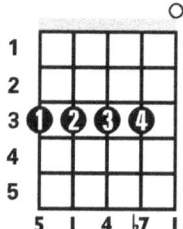
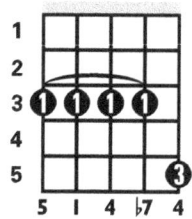
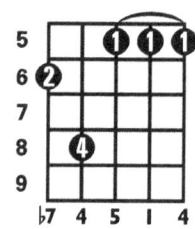

Gm7-5
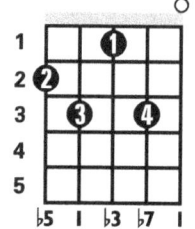
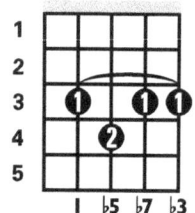
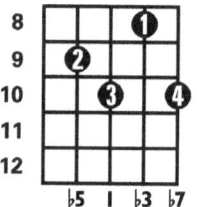

G Chords

Gadd9
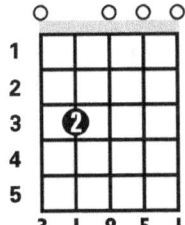
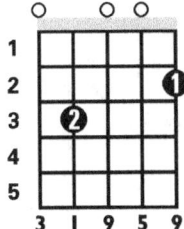
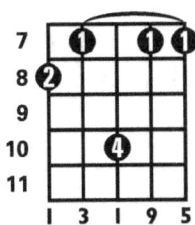

Gmadd9
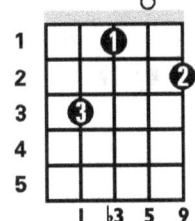
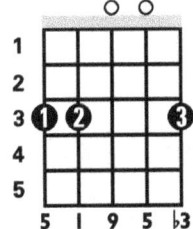
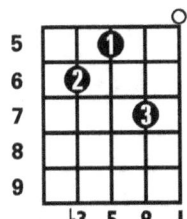

G6add9
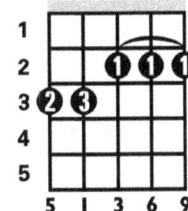
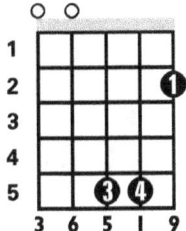
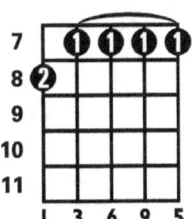

Gm6add9
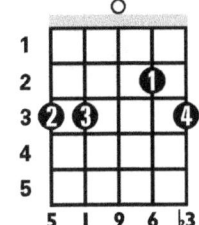
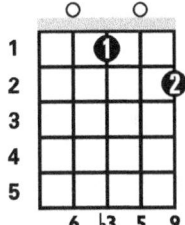
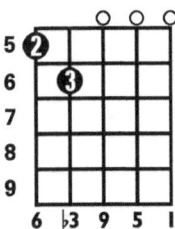

G7-5
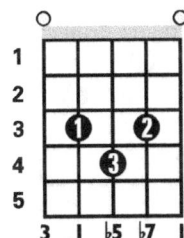
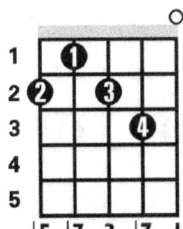
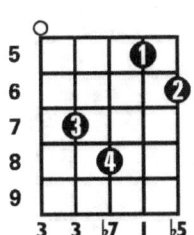

G7+5
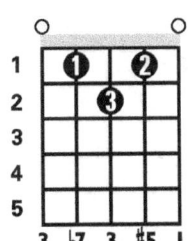
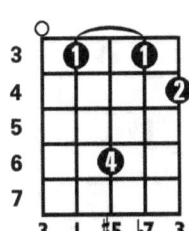
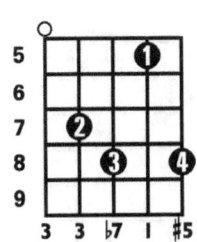

G7-9
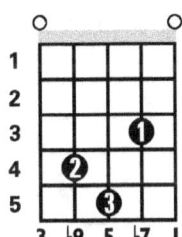
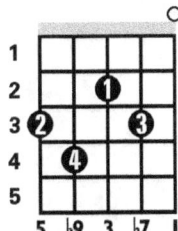
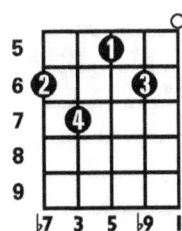

G7+9
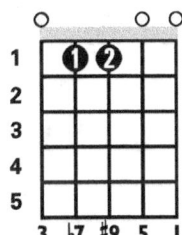
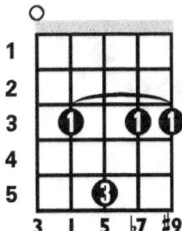
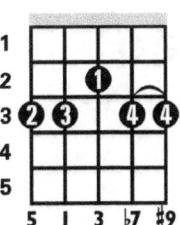

49

G Chords

Gm(maj7)	Gmaj7-5	Gmaj7+5	G9
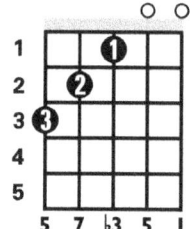	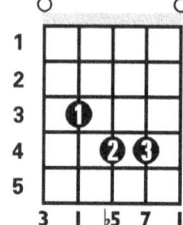	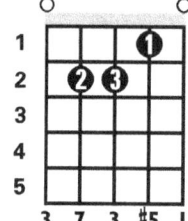	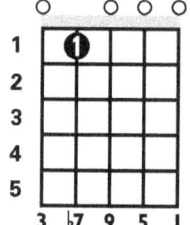
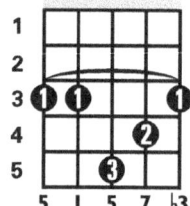	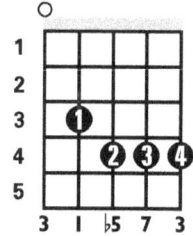	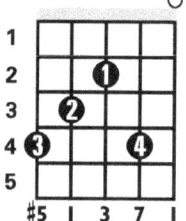	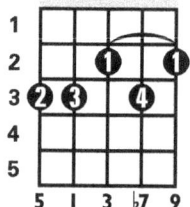
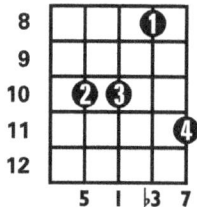	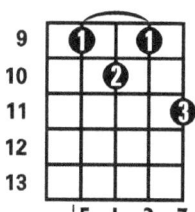	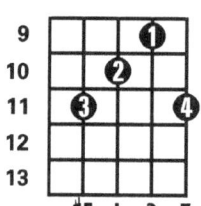	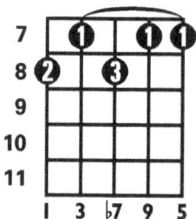

Gm9	Gmaj9	G11	G13
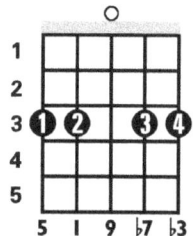	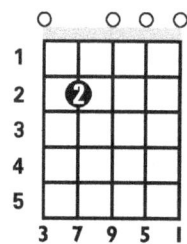	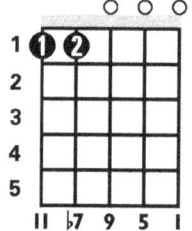	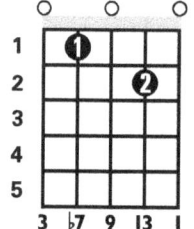
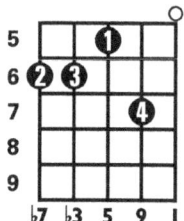	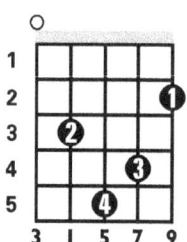	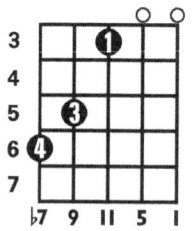	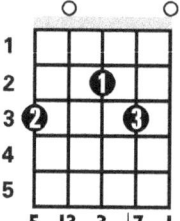
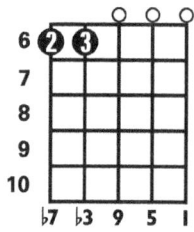	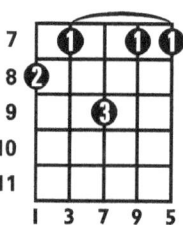	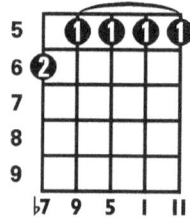	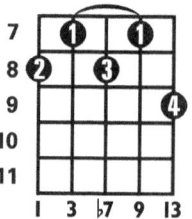

G Chords (Advanced)

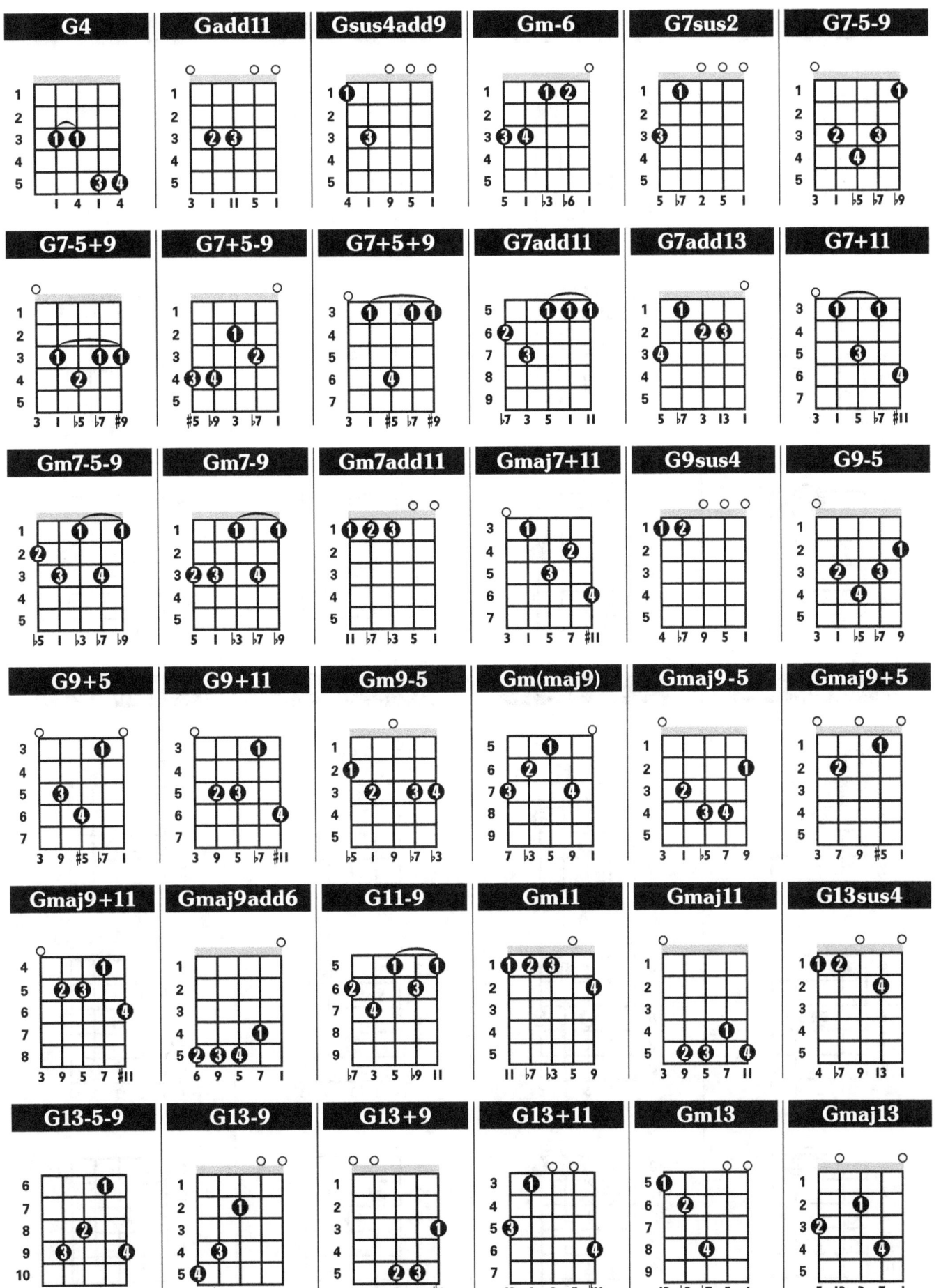

G# / A♭ Chords

A♭
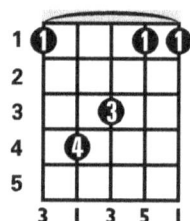
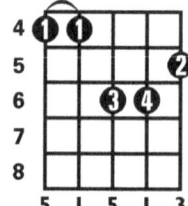
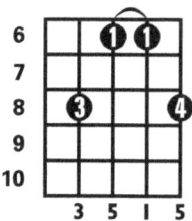

A♭m
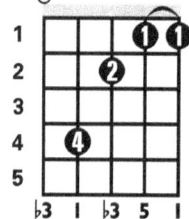
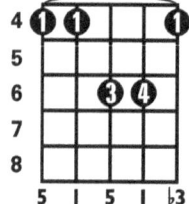
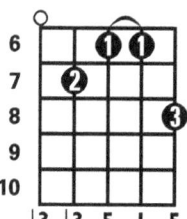

A♭7
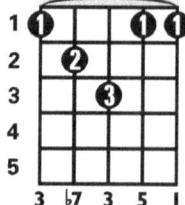
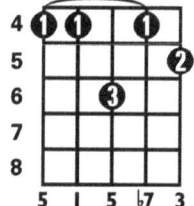
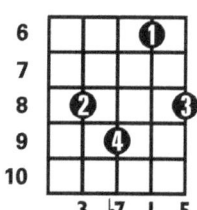

A♭m7
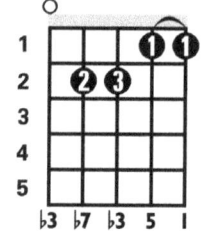
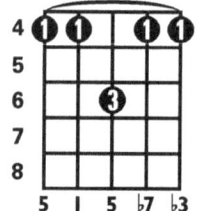
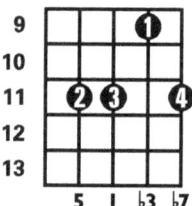

A♭5
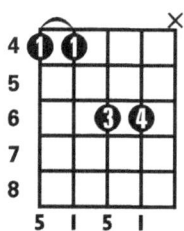
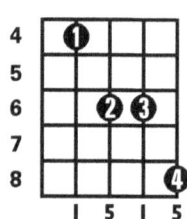
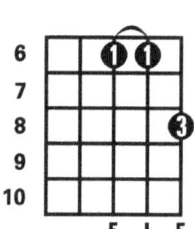

A♭6
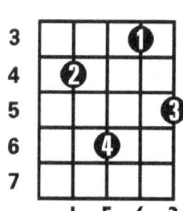
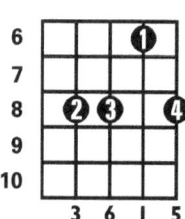
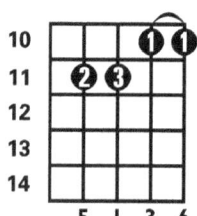

A♭m6
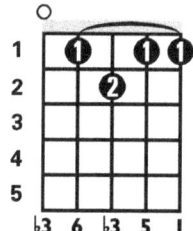
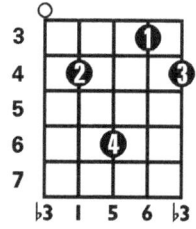
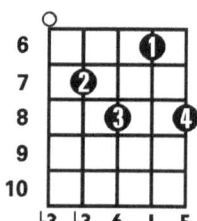

A♭maj7
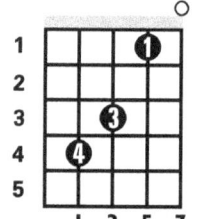
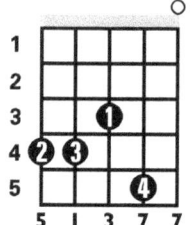
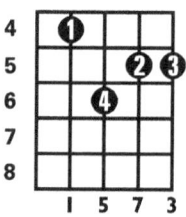

G#/A♭ Chords

A♭°
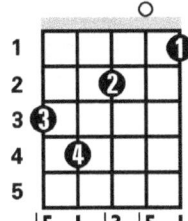
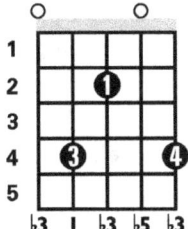
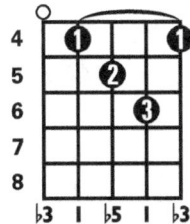

A♭°7
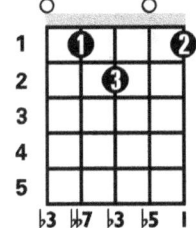
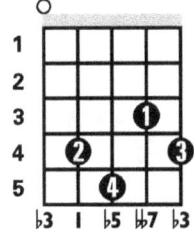
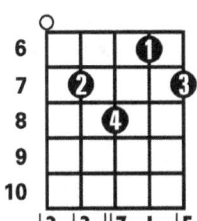

A♭-5
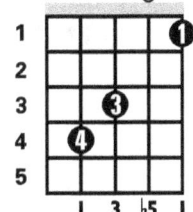
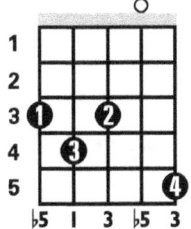
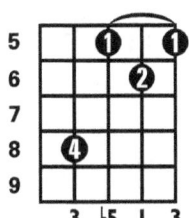

A♭+
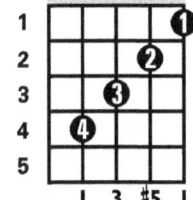
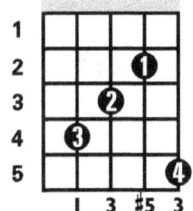
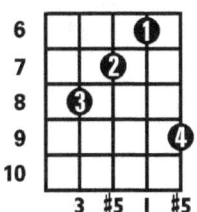

A♭sus2
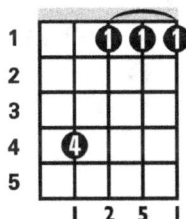
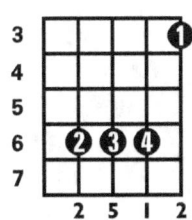
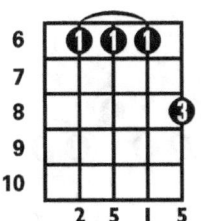

A♭sus4
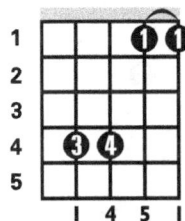
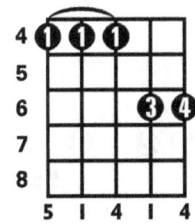
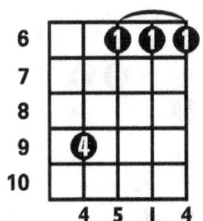

A♭7sus4
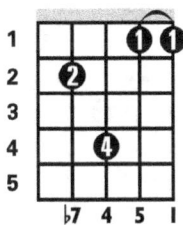
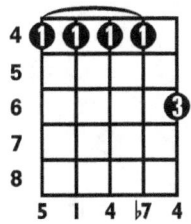
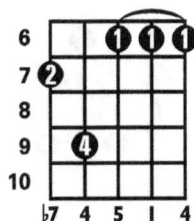

A♭m7-5
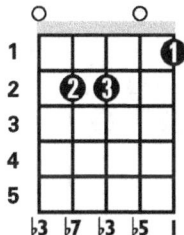
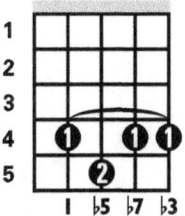
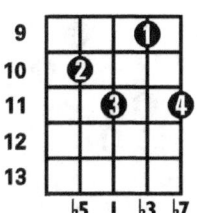

G# / A♭ Chords

A♭add9
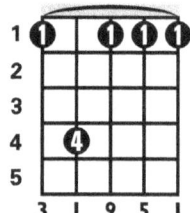
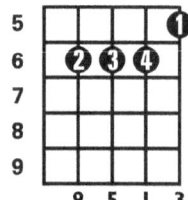
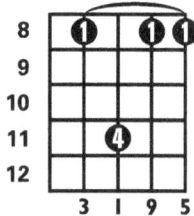

A♭madd9
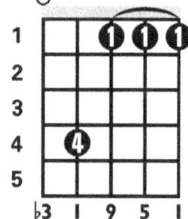
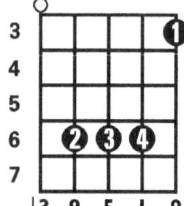
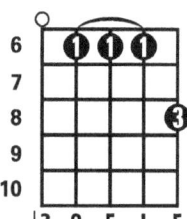

A♭6add9
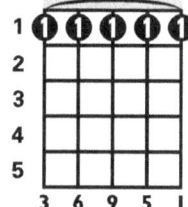
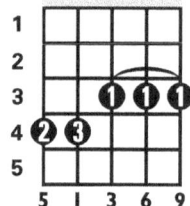
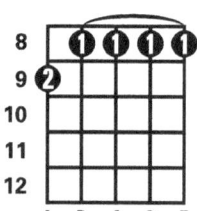

A♭m6add9
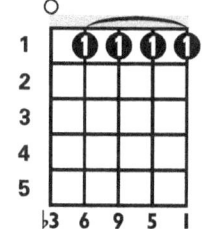
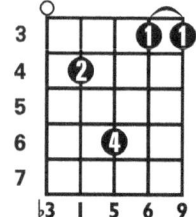
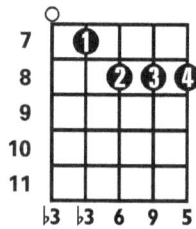

A♭7-5
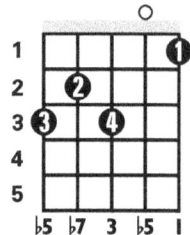
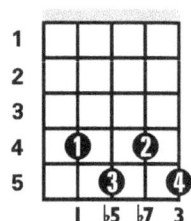
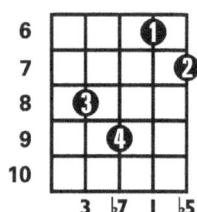

A♭7+5
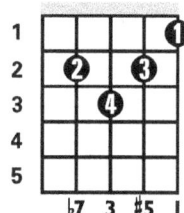
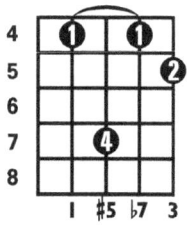
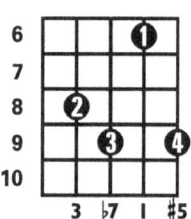

A♭7-9
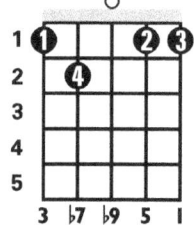
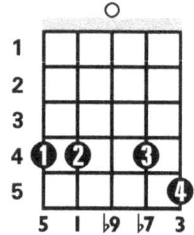
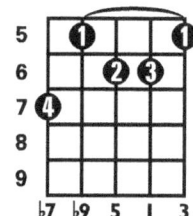

A♭7+9
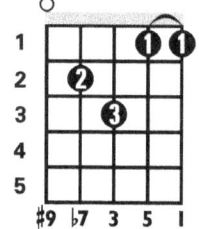
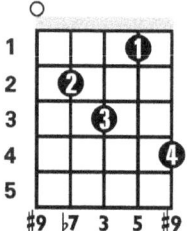
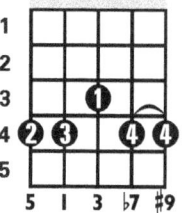

G#/A♭ Chords

A♭m(maj7)
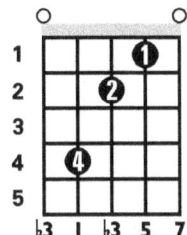
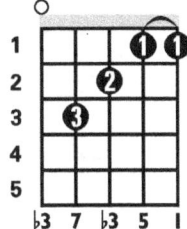
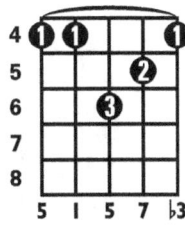

A♭maj7-5
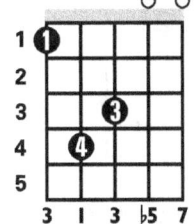
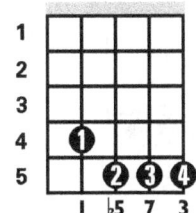
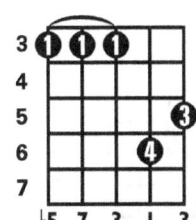

A♭maj7+5
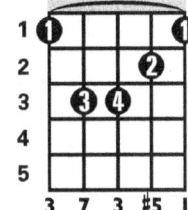
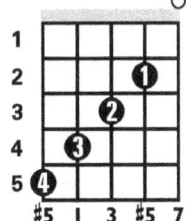
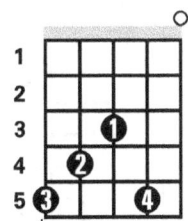

A♭9
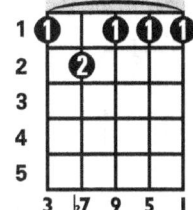
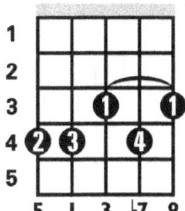
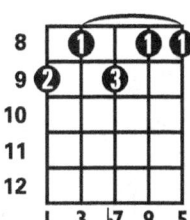

A♭m9
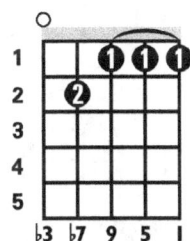
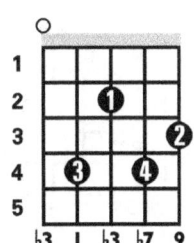
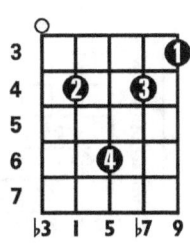

A♭maj9
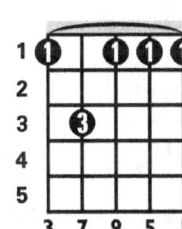
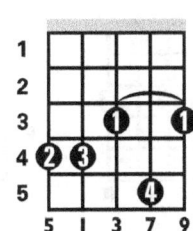
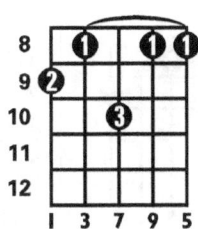

A♭11
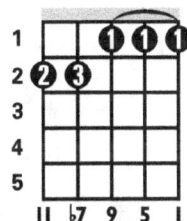
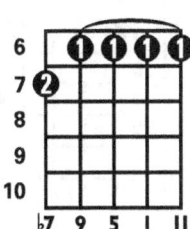
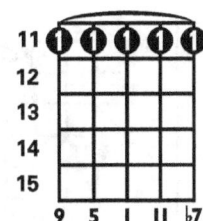

A♭13
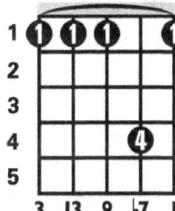
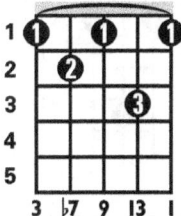
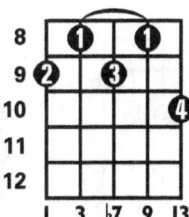

G♯ / A♭ Chords (Advanced)

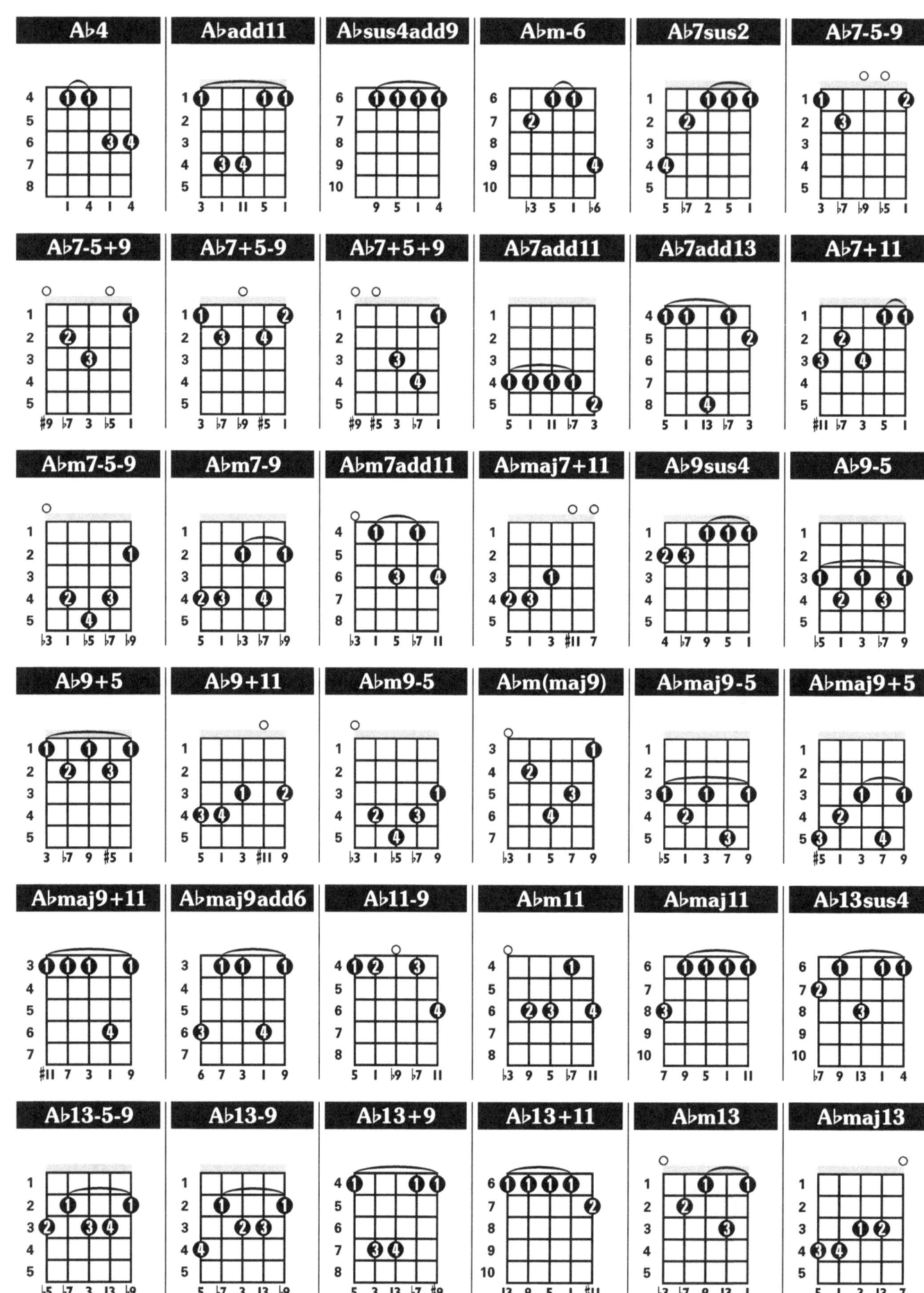

A Chords

A
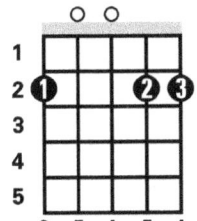
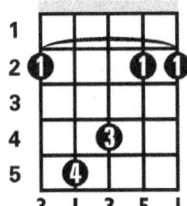
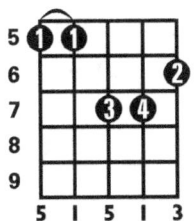

Am
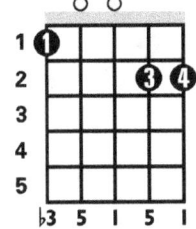
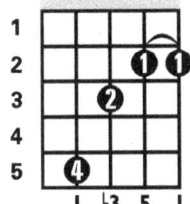
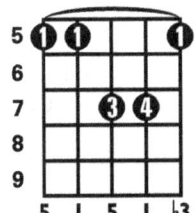

A7
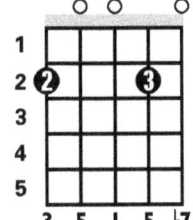
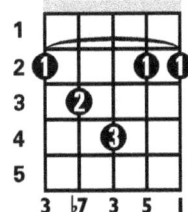
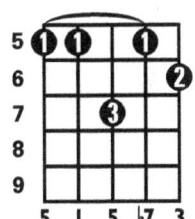

Am7
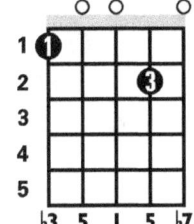
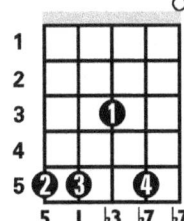
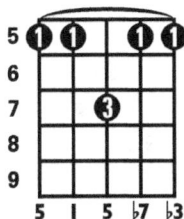

A5
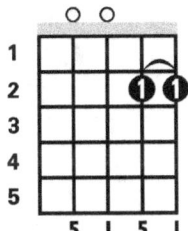
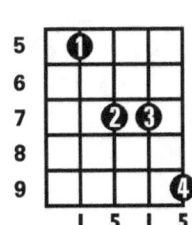
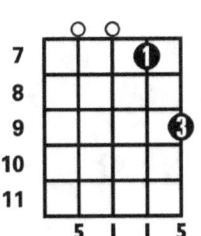

A6
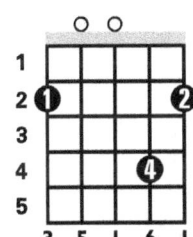
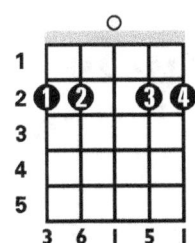
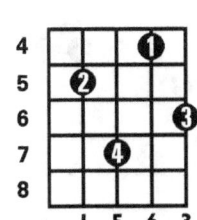

Am6
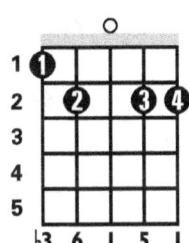
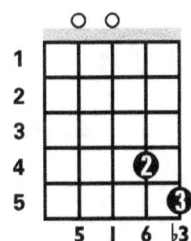
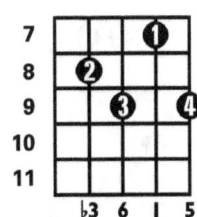

Amaj7
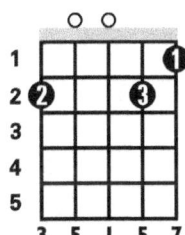
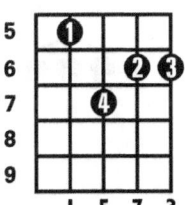
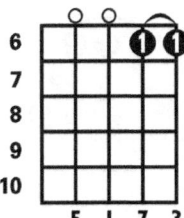

A Chords

A°	A°7	A-5	A+
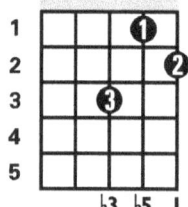	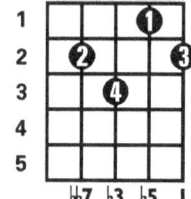	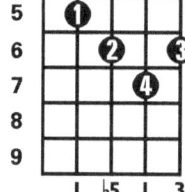	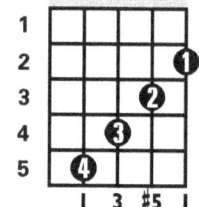
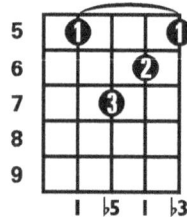	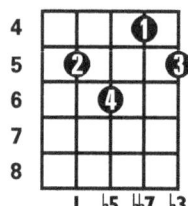	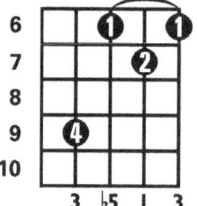	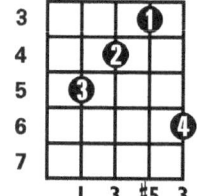
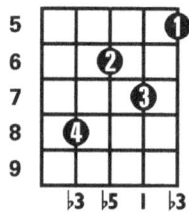	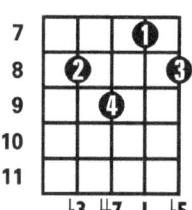	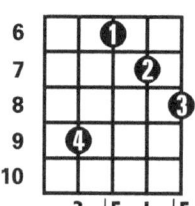	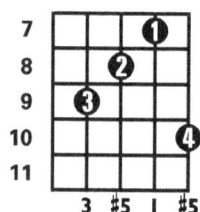

Asus2	Asus4	A7sus4	Am7-5
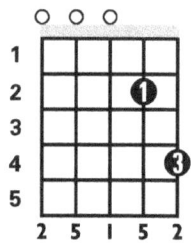	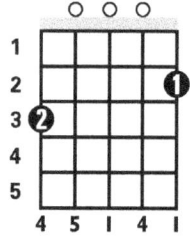	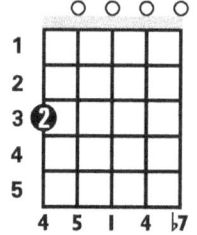	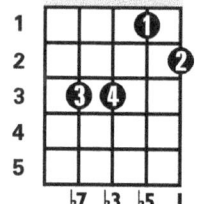
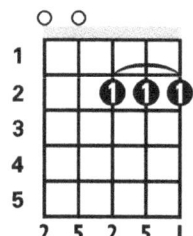	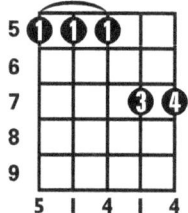	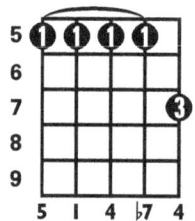	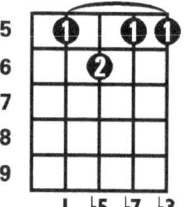
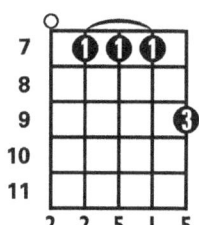	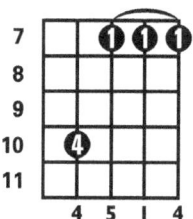	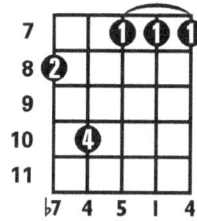	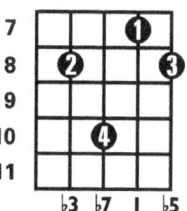

A Chords

Aadd9	Amadd9	A6add9	Am6add9
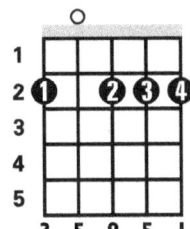	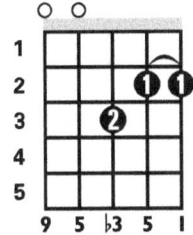	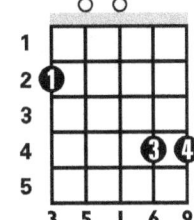	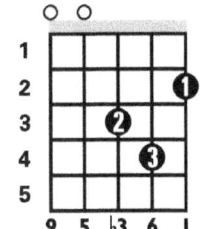
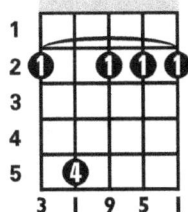	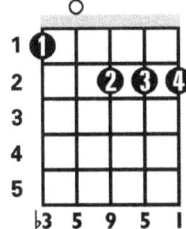	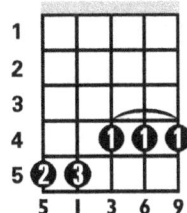	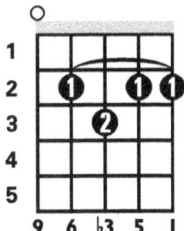
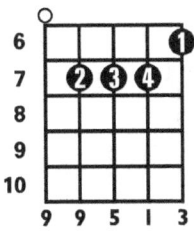	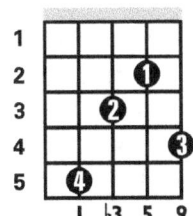	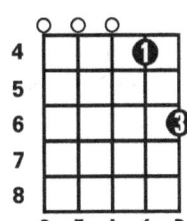	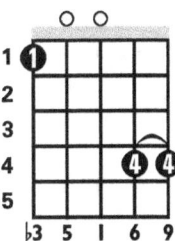

A7-5	A7+5	A7-9	A7+9
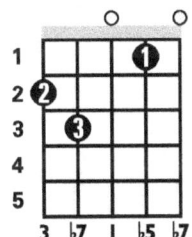	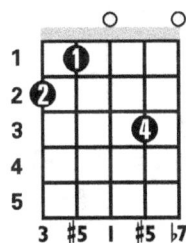	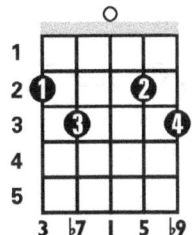	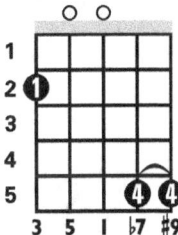
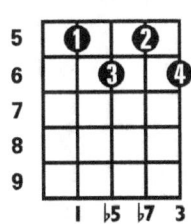	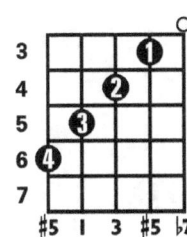	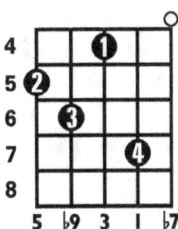	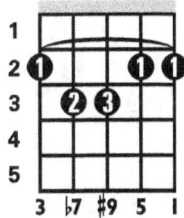
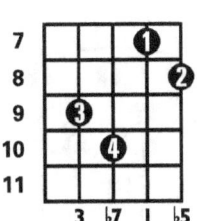	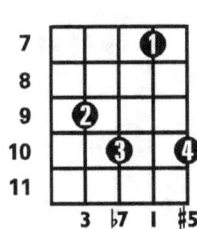	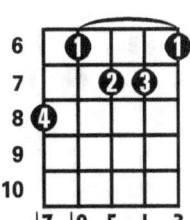	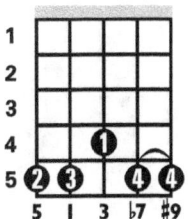

A Chords

Am(maj7)
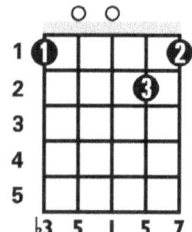
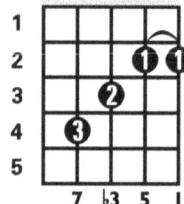
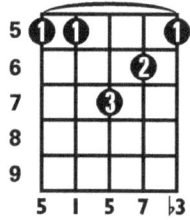

Amaj7-5
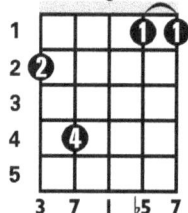
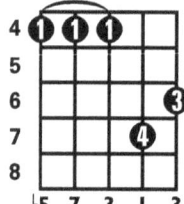
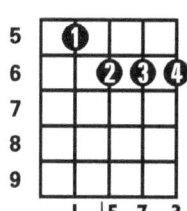

Amaj7+5
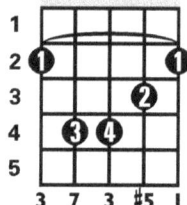
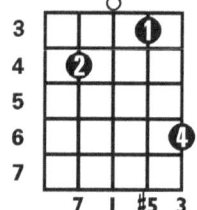
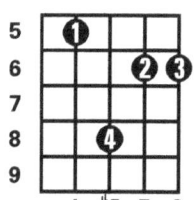

A9
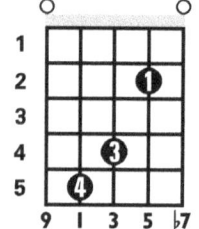
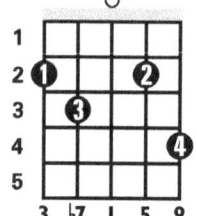
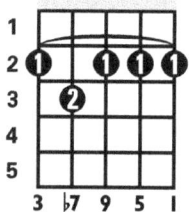

Am9
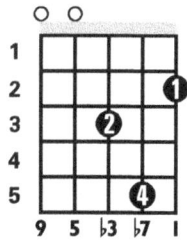
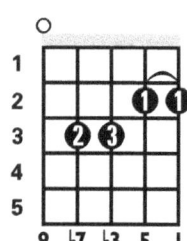
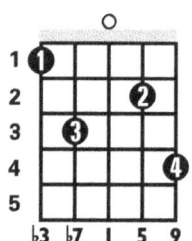

Amaj9
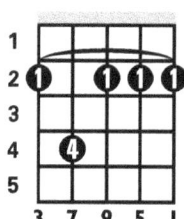
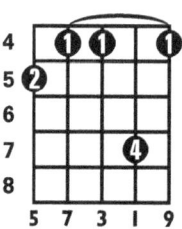
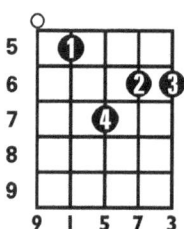

A11
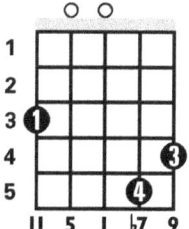
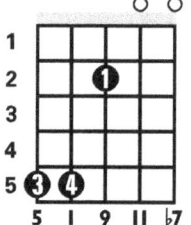
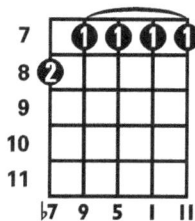

A13
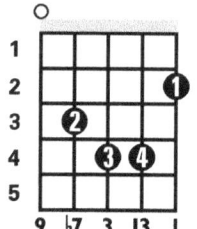
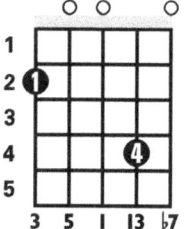
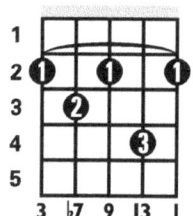

A Chords (Advanced)

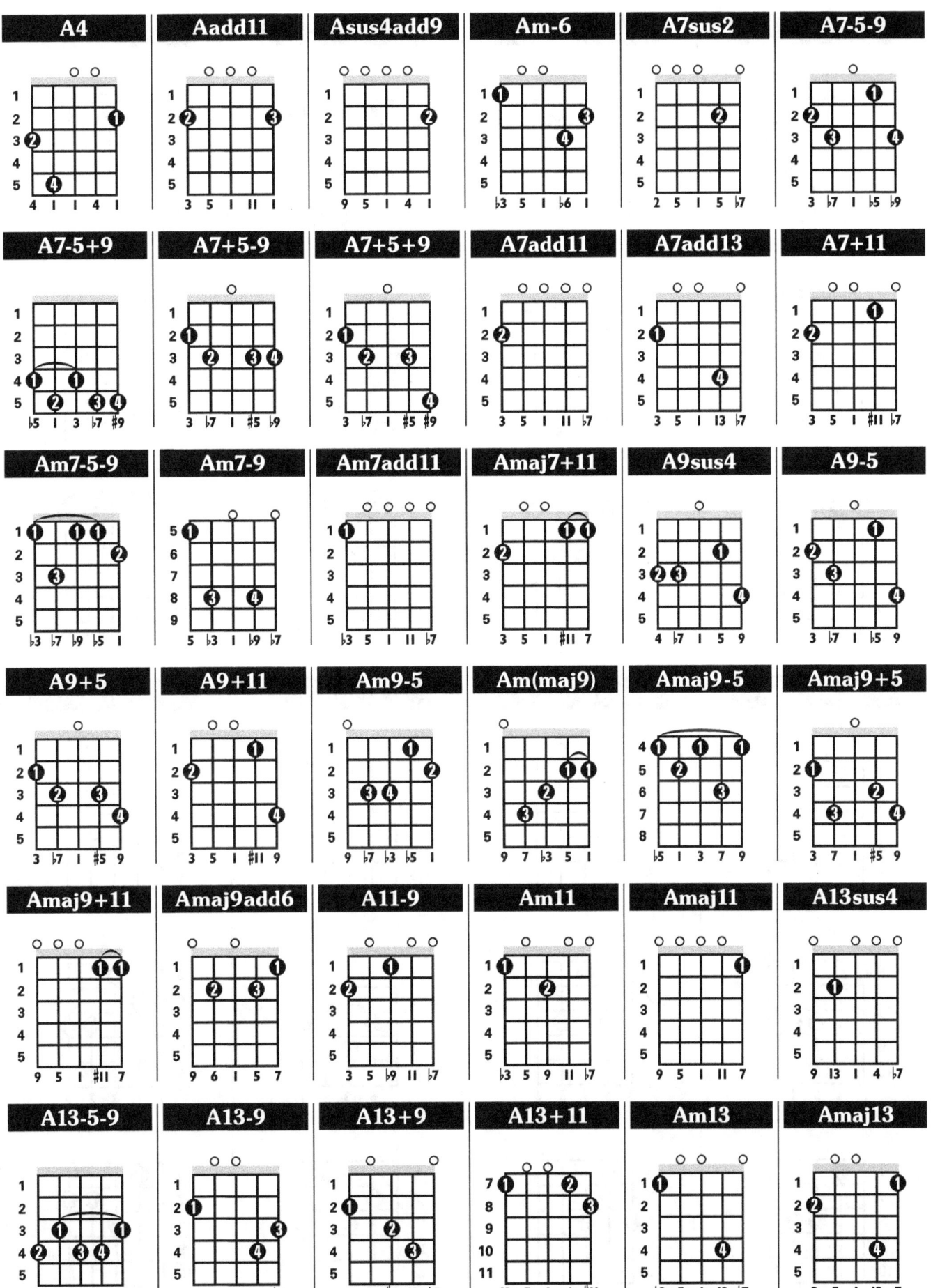

A♯ / B♭ Chords

B♭	B♭m	B♭7	B♭m7
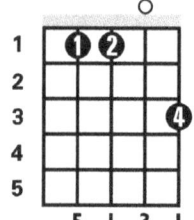	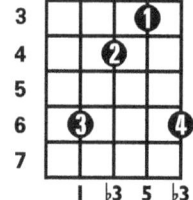	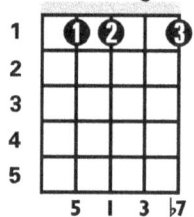	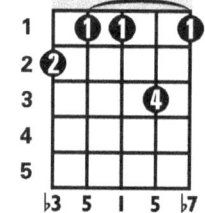
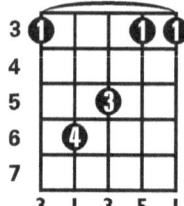	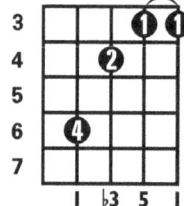	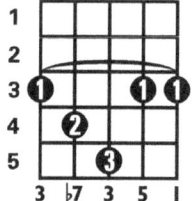	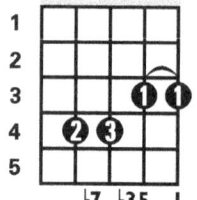
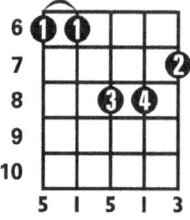	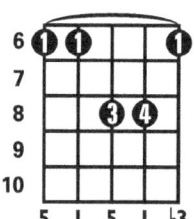	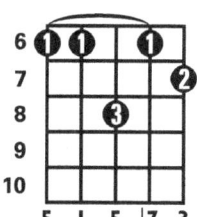	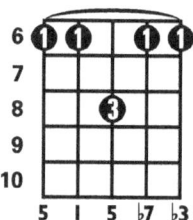

B♭5	B♭6	B♭m6	B♭maj7
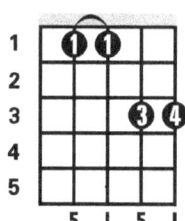	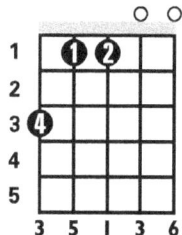	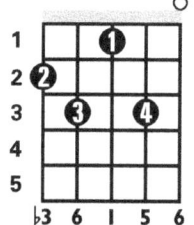	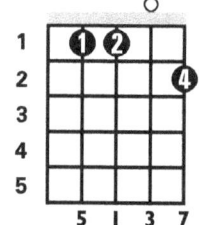
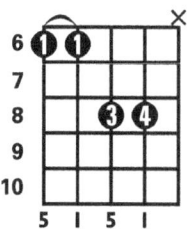	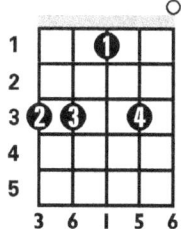	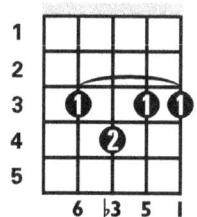	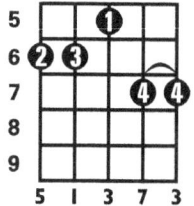
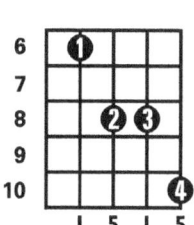	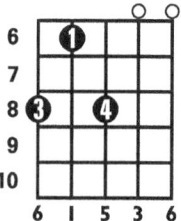	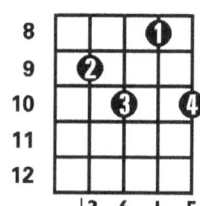	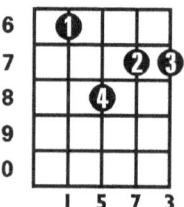

A#/ Bb Chords

Bb°
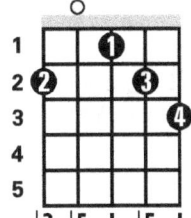
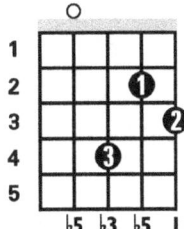
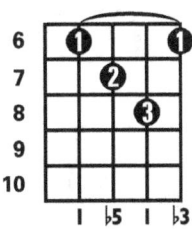

Bb°7
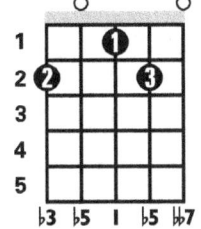
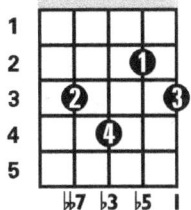
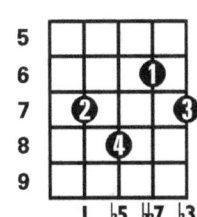

Bb-5
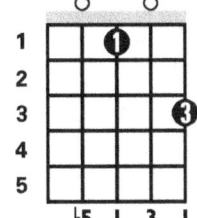
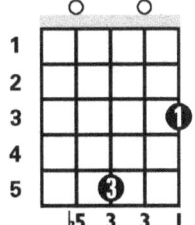
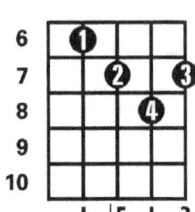

Bb+
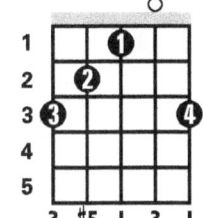
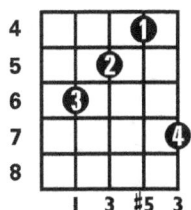
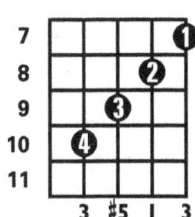

Bbsus2
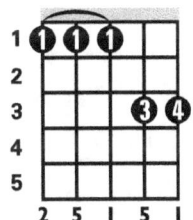
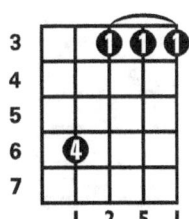
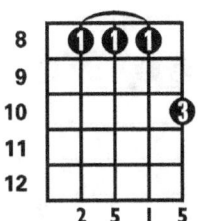

Bbsus4
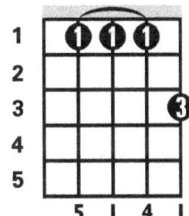
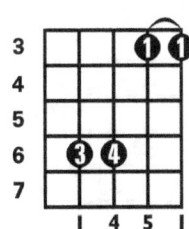
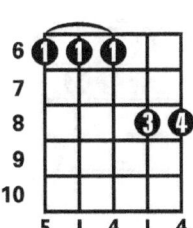

Bb7sus4
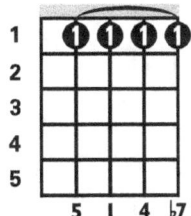
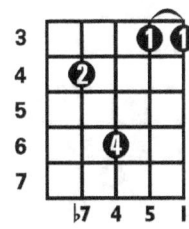
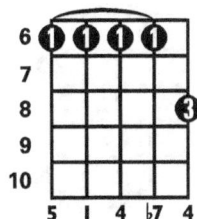

Bbm7-5
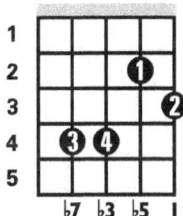
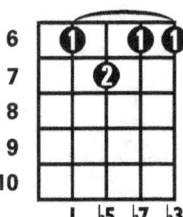
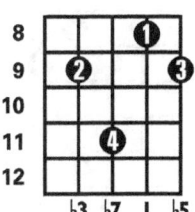

A♯ / B♭ Chords

B♭add9	B♭madd9	B♭6add9	B♭m6add9
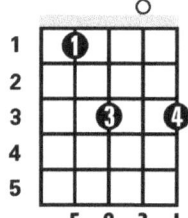	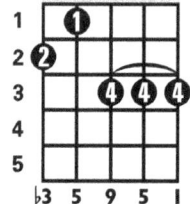	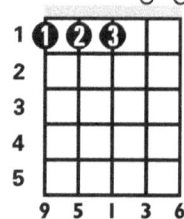	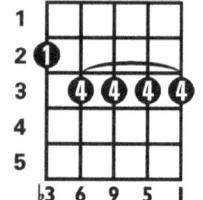
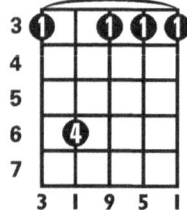	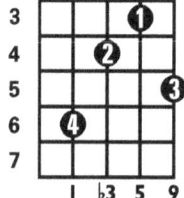	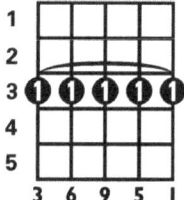	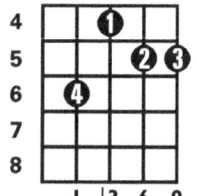
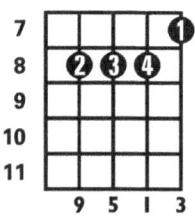	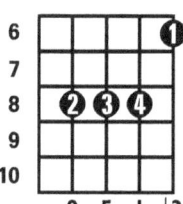	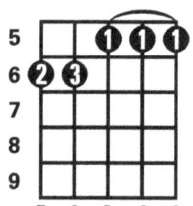	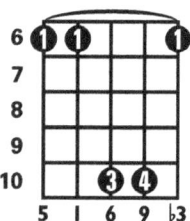

B♭7-5	B♭7+5	B♭7-9	B♭7+9
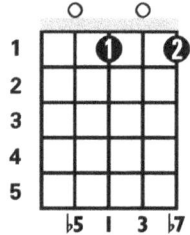	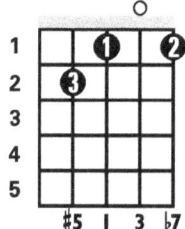	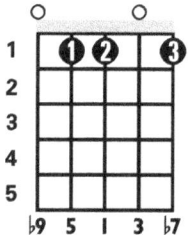	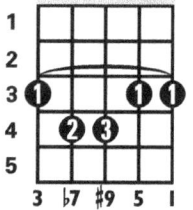
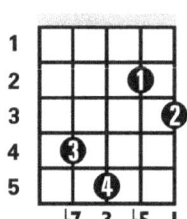	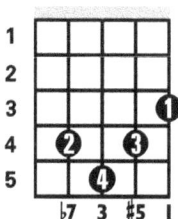	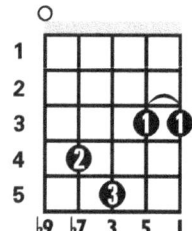	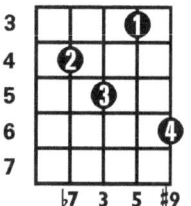
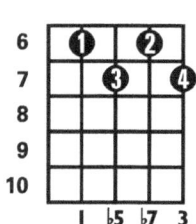	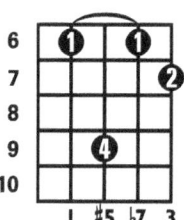	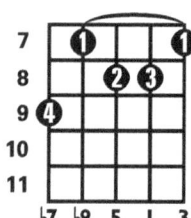	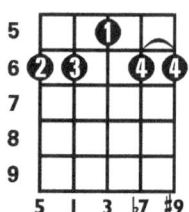

A#/B♭ Chords

B♭m(maj7)
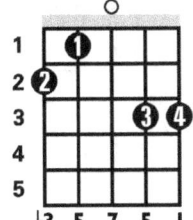
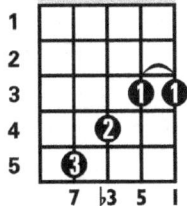
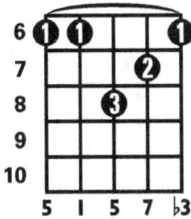

B♭maj7-5
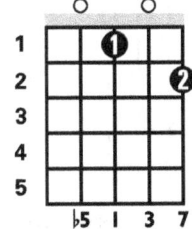
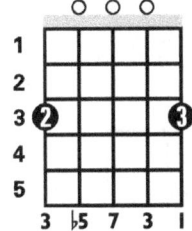
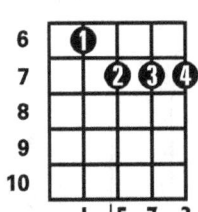

B♭maj7+5
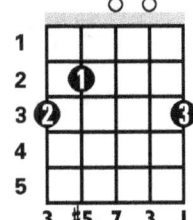
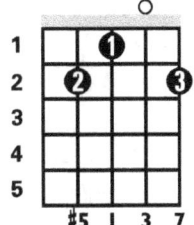
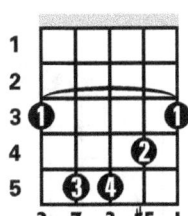

B♭9
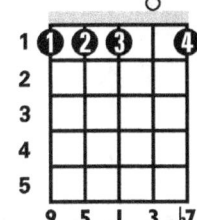
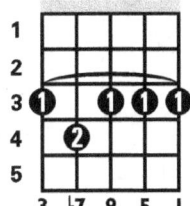
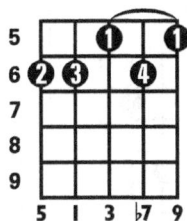

B♭m9
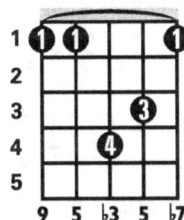
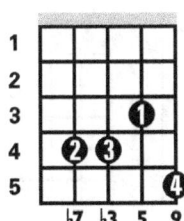
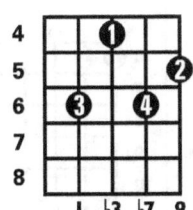

B♭maj9
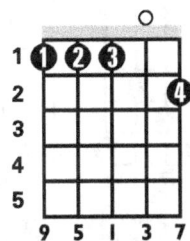
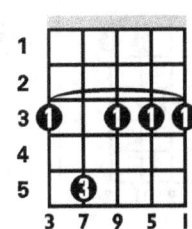
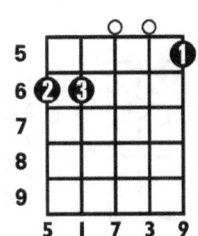

B♭11

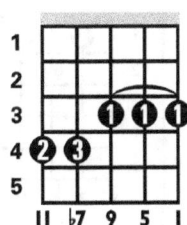
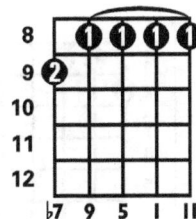

B♭13
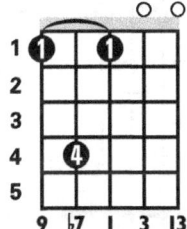
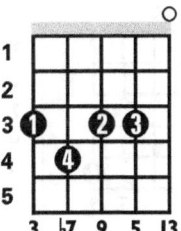
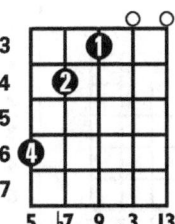

A♯ / B♭ Chords (Advanced)

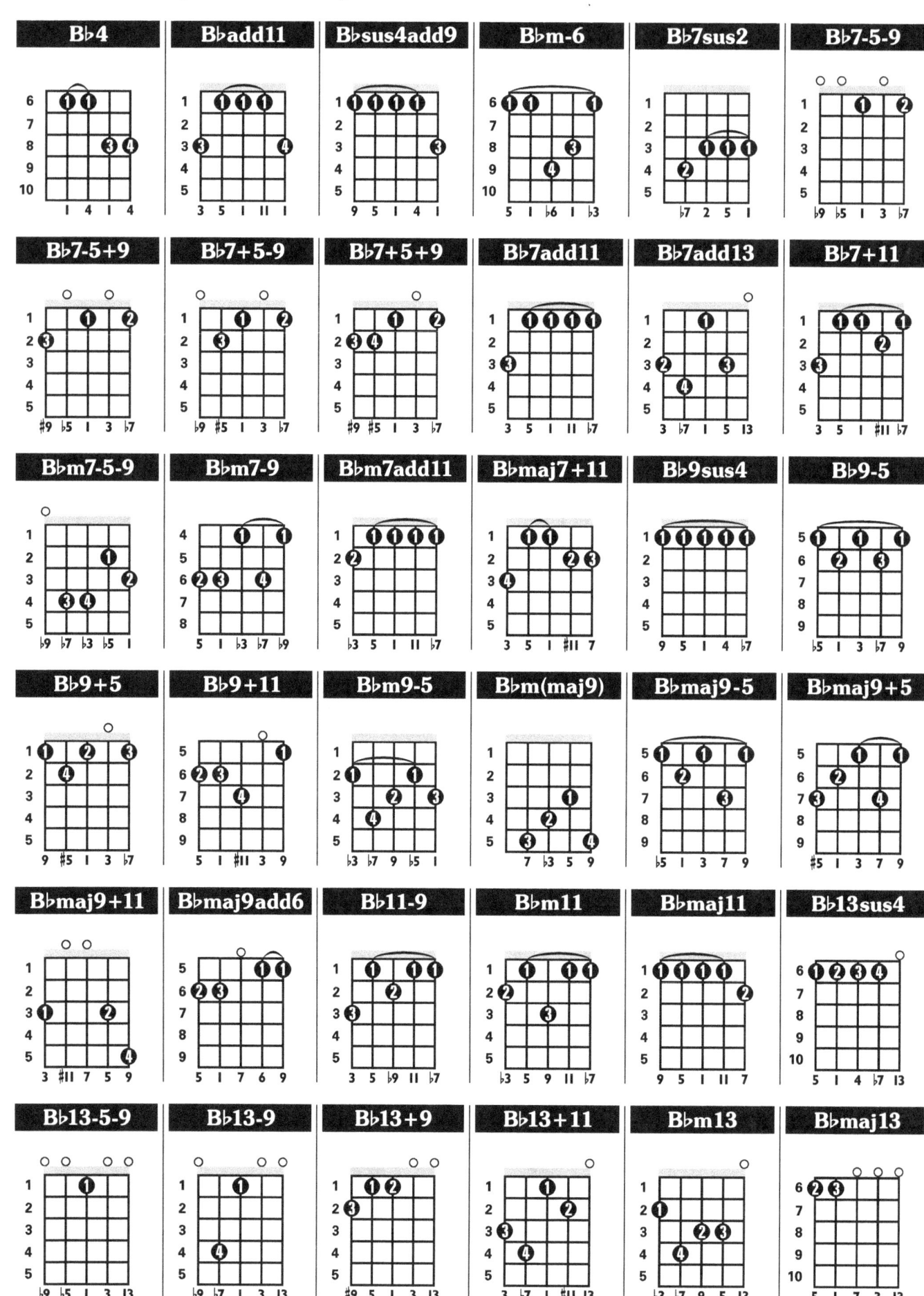

B Chords

B
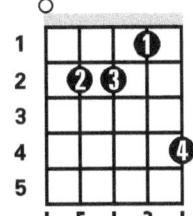
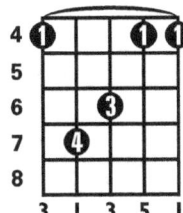
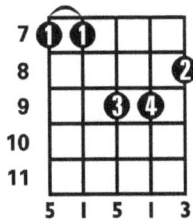

Bm
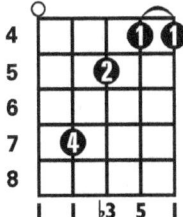
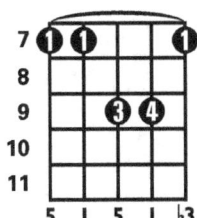

B7
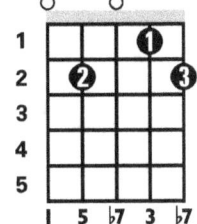
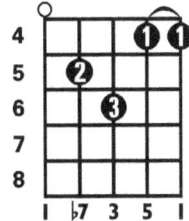
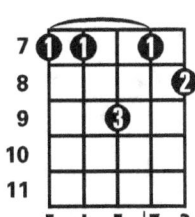

Bm7
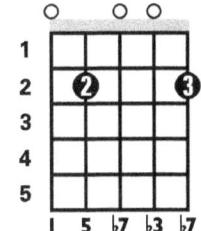
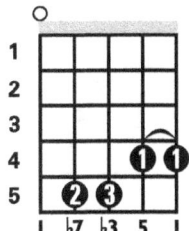
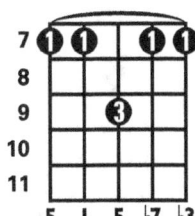

B5
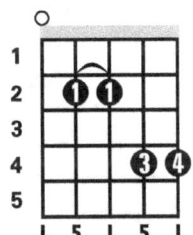
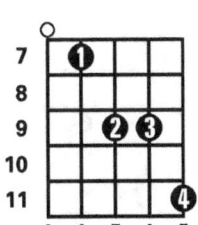
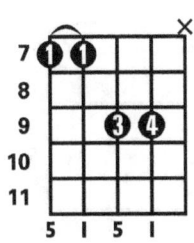

B6
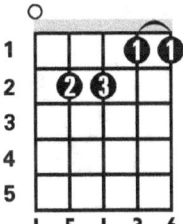
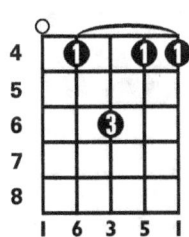
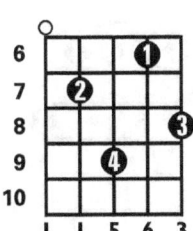

Bm6
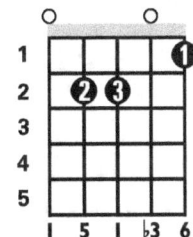
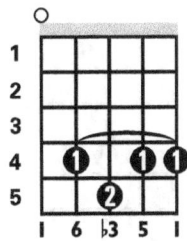
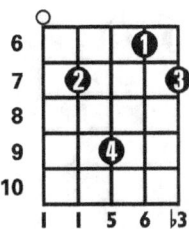

Bmaj7
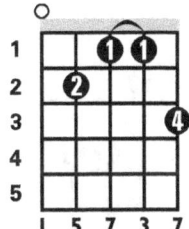
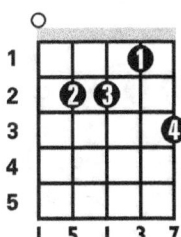
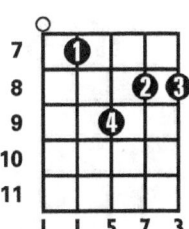

B Chords

B°	B°7	B-5	B+
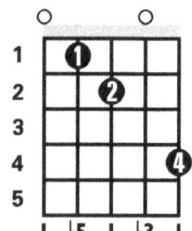	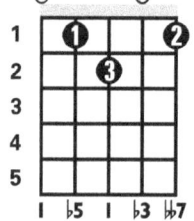	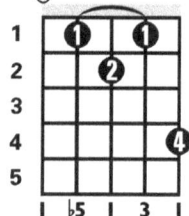	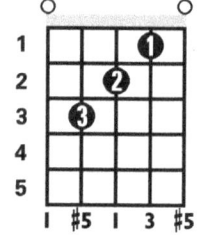
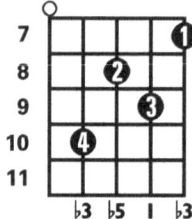	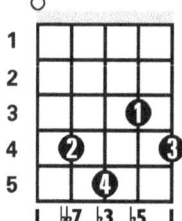	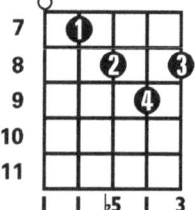	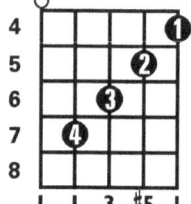
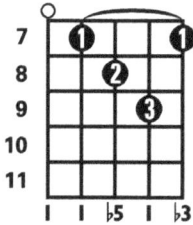	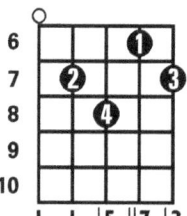	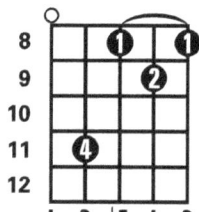	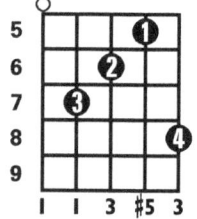

Bsus2	Bsus4	B7sus4	Bm7-5
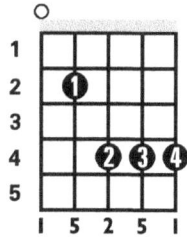	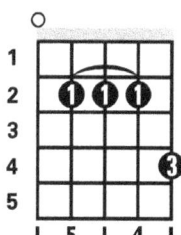	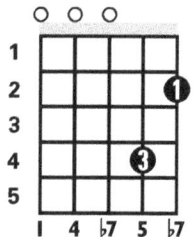	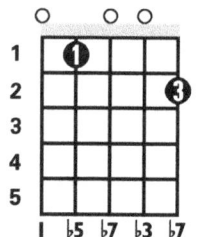
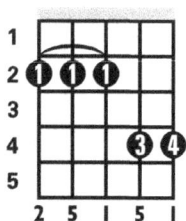	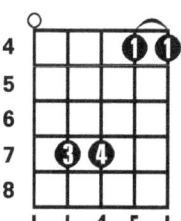	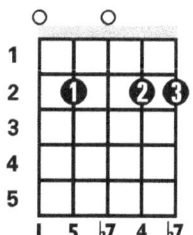	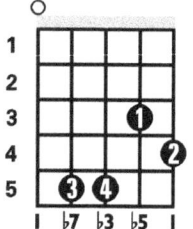
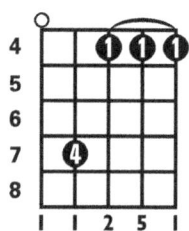	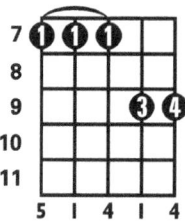	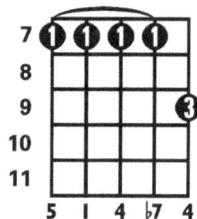	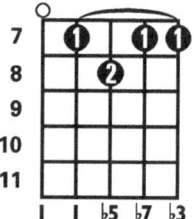

B Chords

Badd9
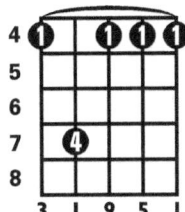
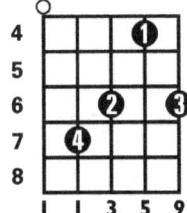
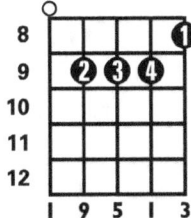

Bmadd9
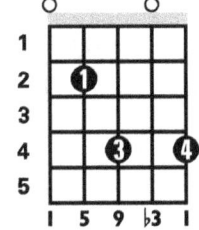
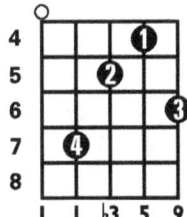
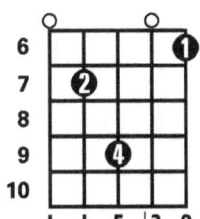

B6add9
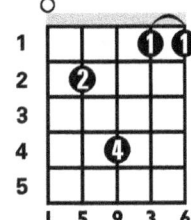
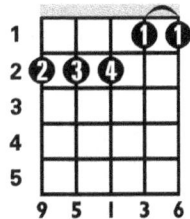
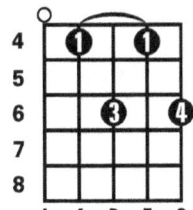

Bm6add9
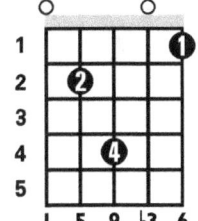
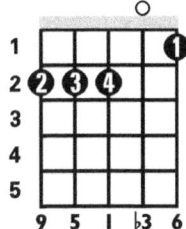
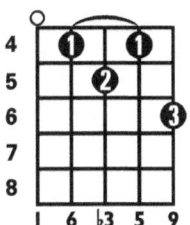

B7-5
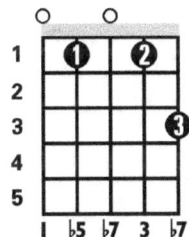
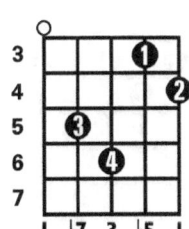
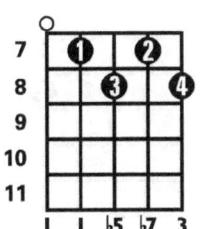

B7+5
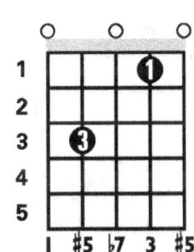
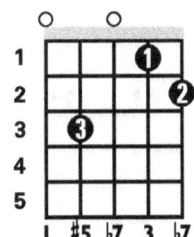
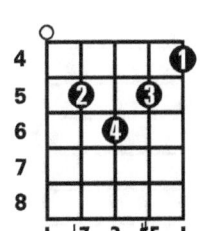

B7-9
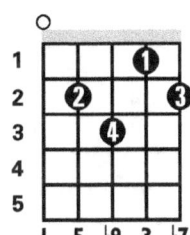
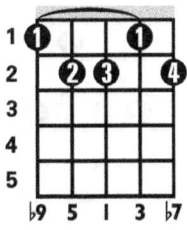
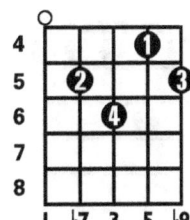

B7+9
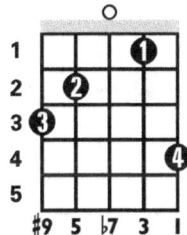
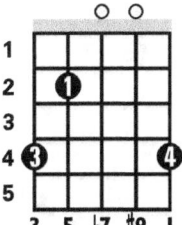
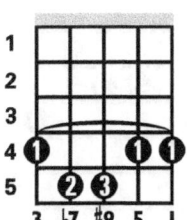

B Chords

Bm(maj7)	Bmaj7-5	Bmaj7+5	B9
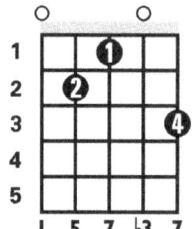	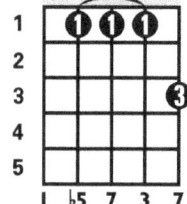	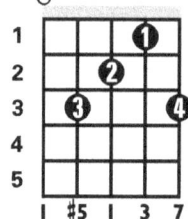	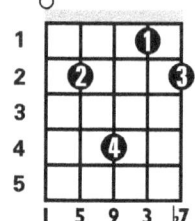
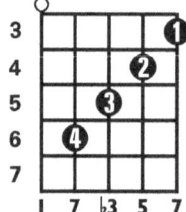	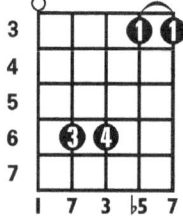	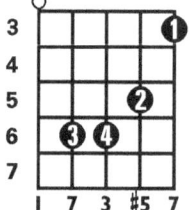	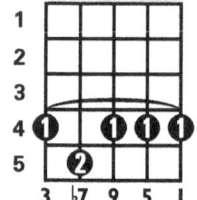
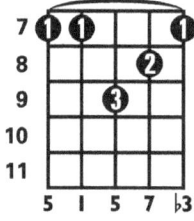	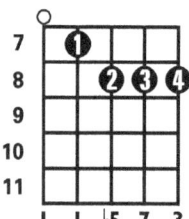	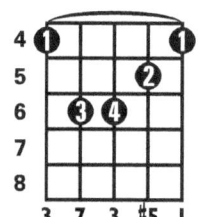	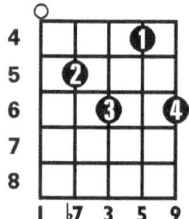

Bm9	Bmaj9	B11	B13
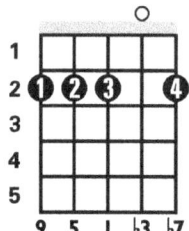	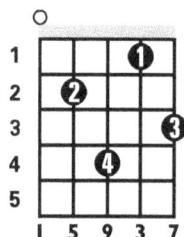	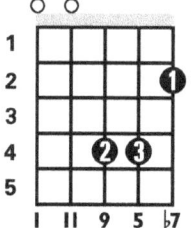	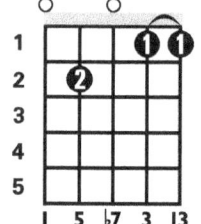
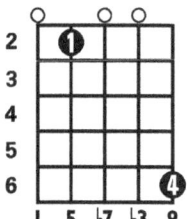	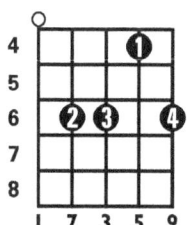	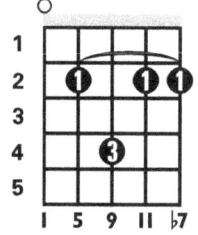	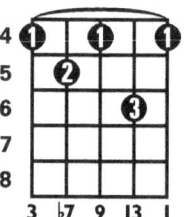
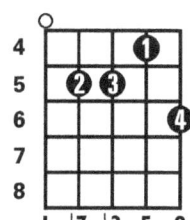	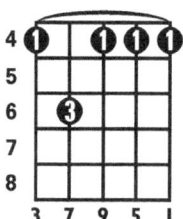	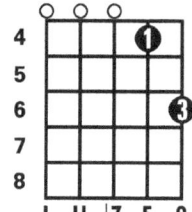	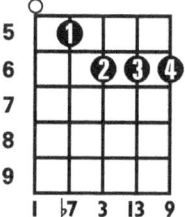

B Chords (Advanced)

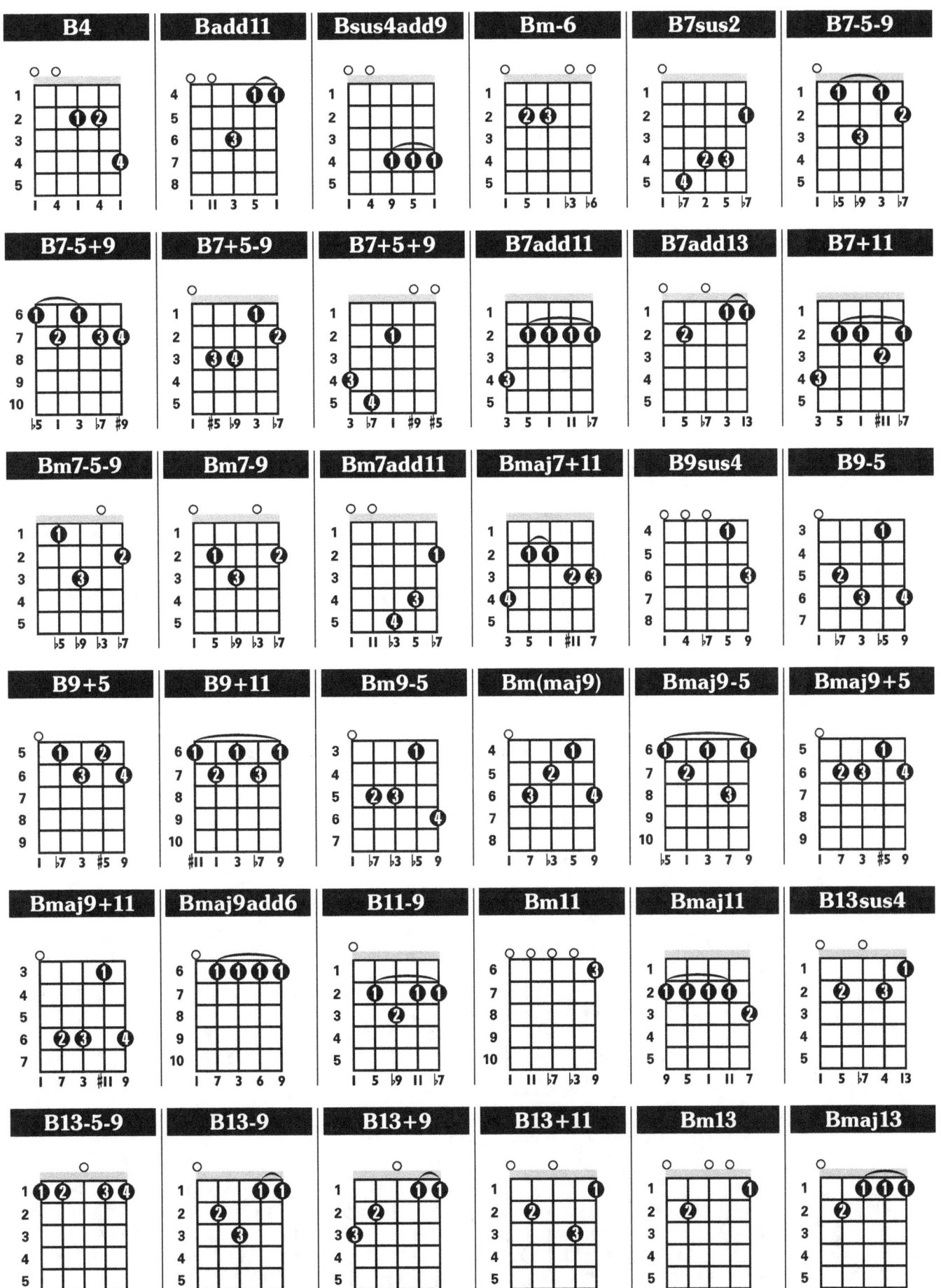

71

Major Slash Chords

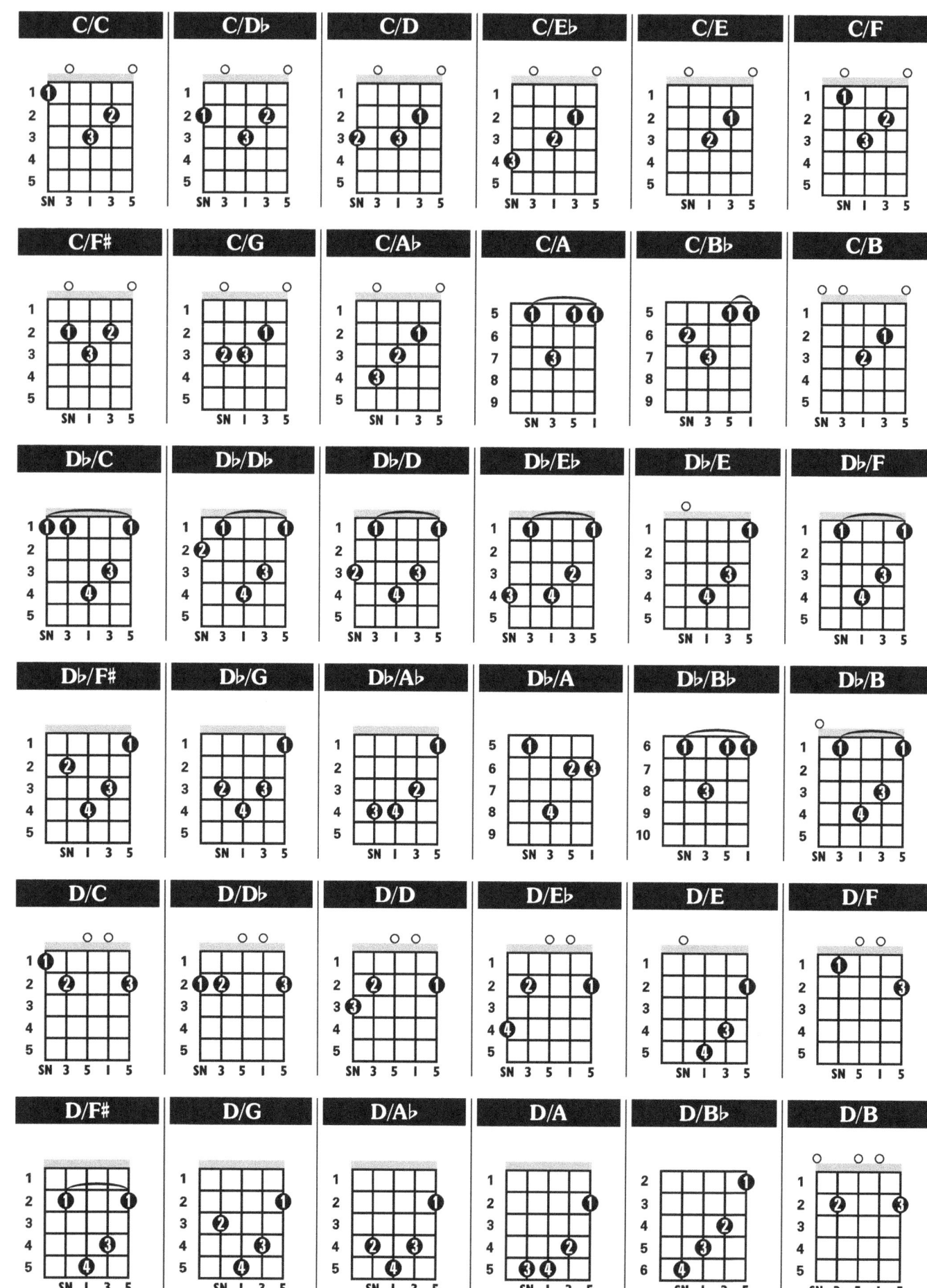

Major Slash Chords

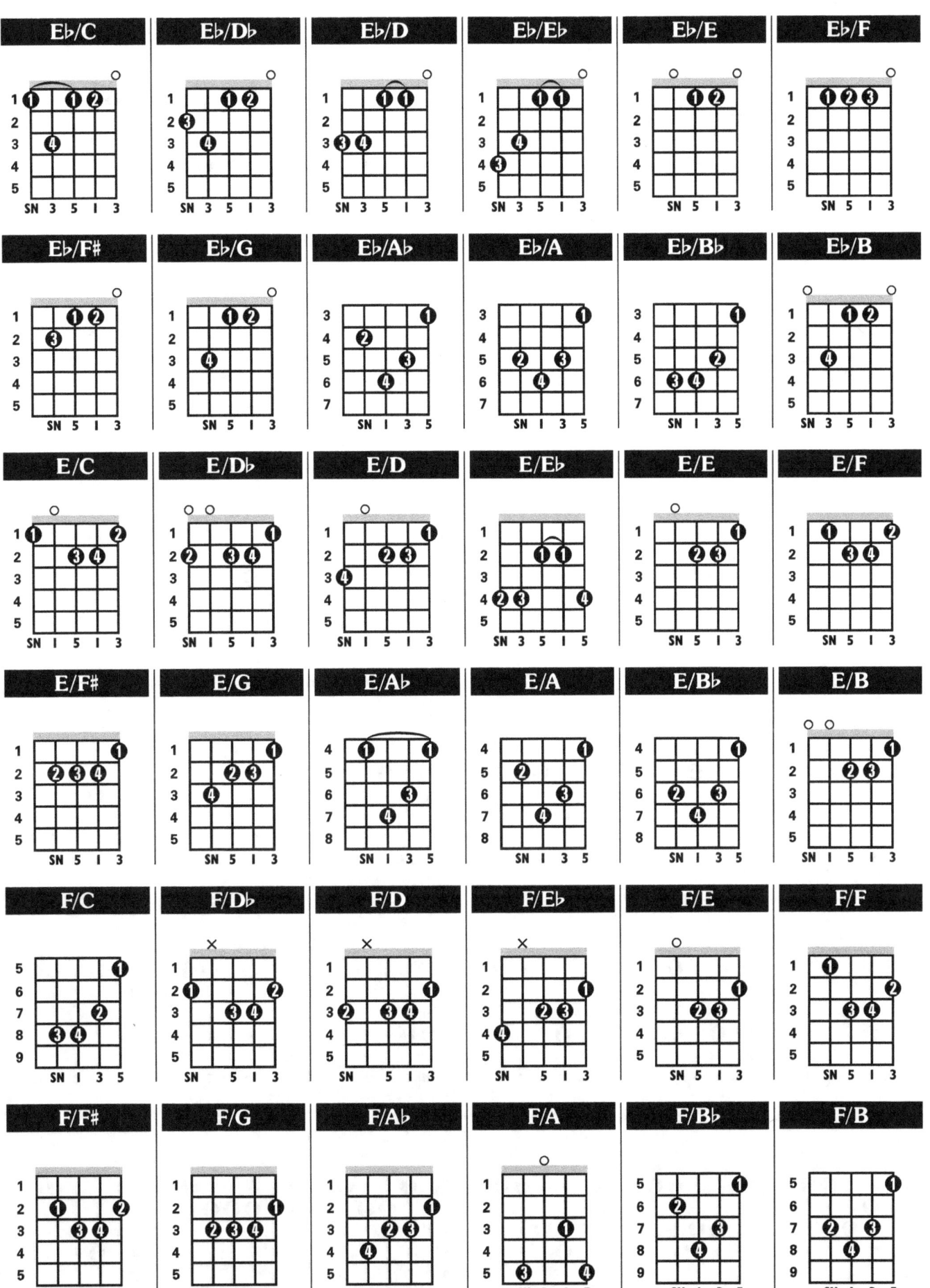

Major Slash Chords

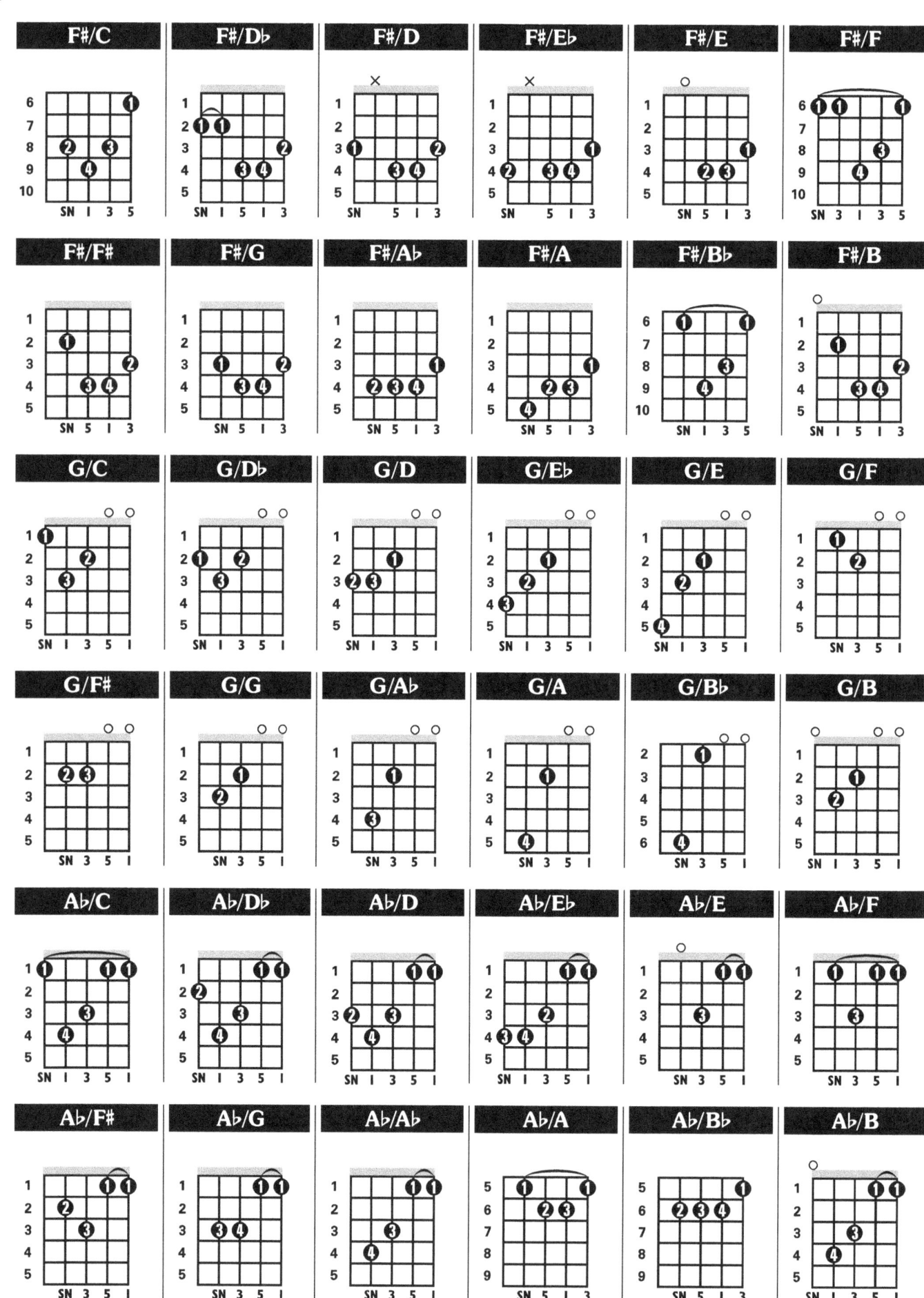

Major Slash Chords

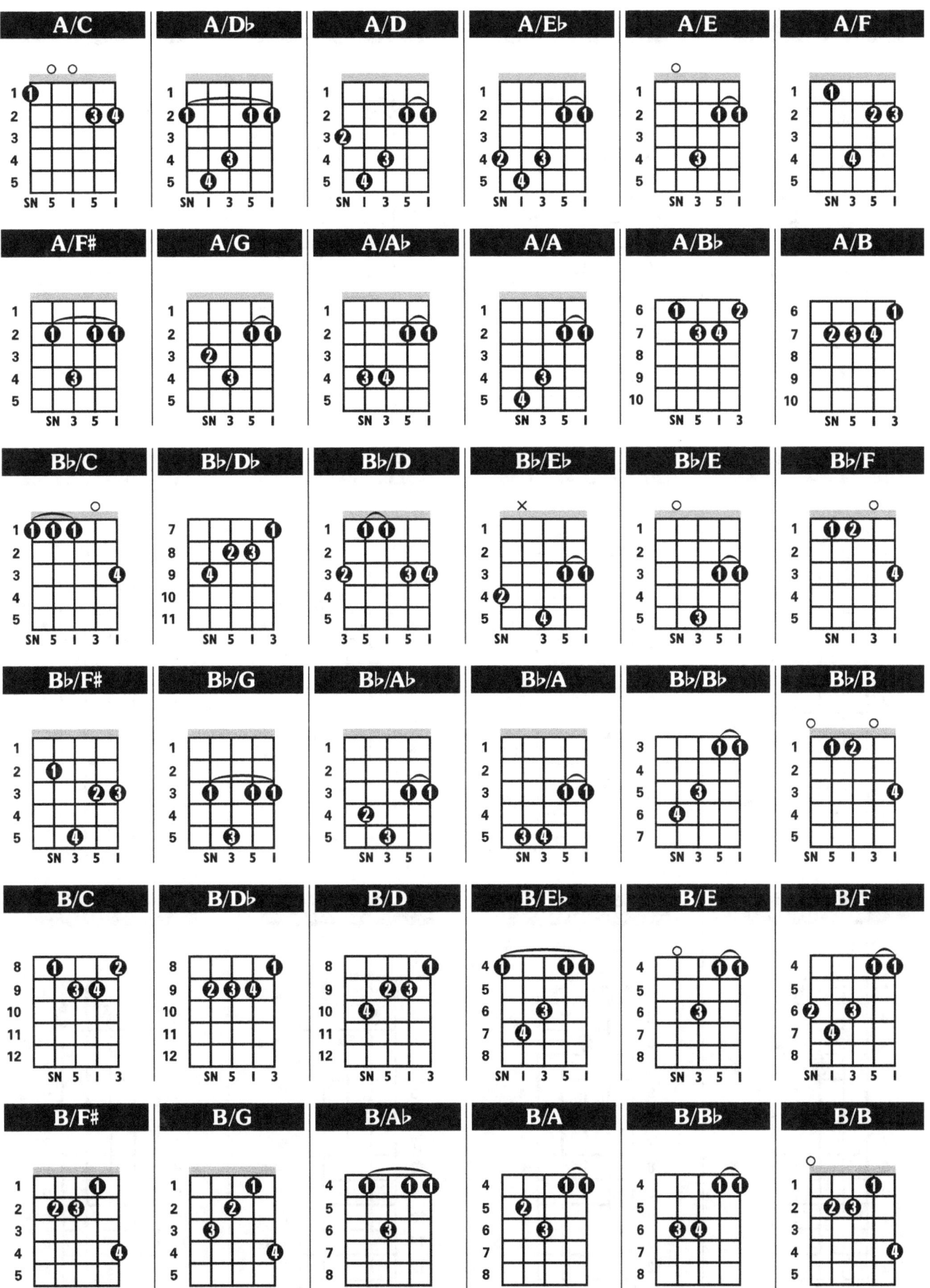

A Selection of Moveable Chord Shapes

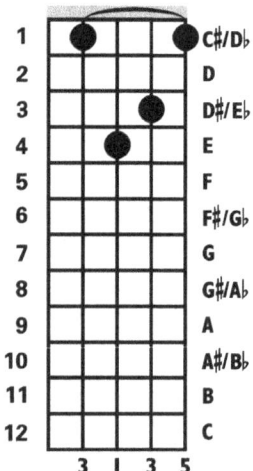
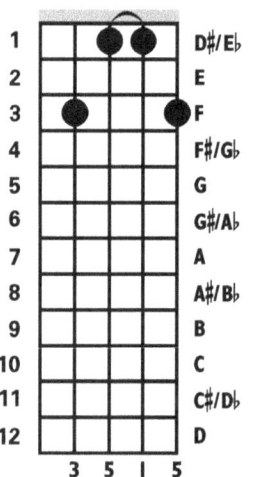
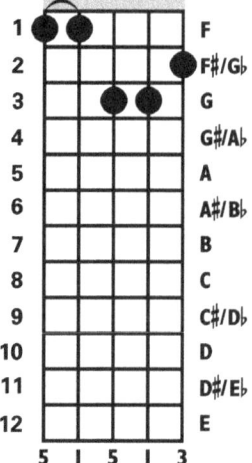
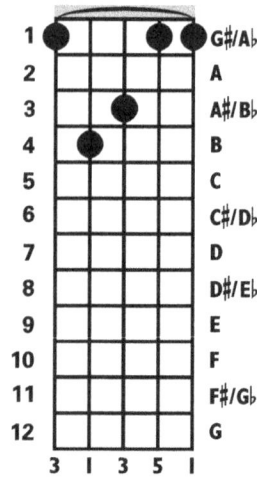

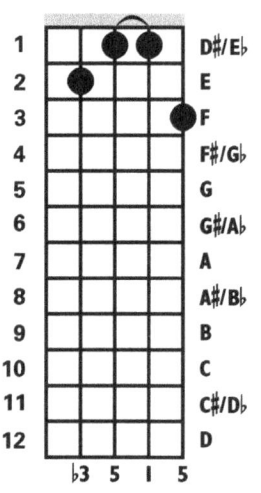
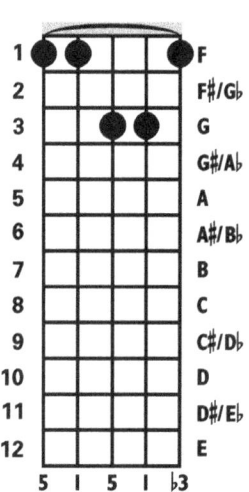
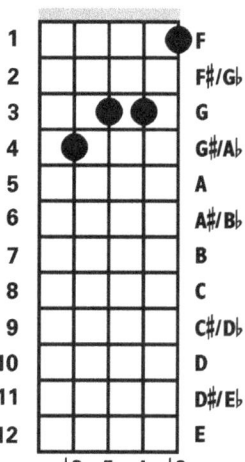
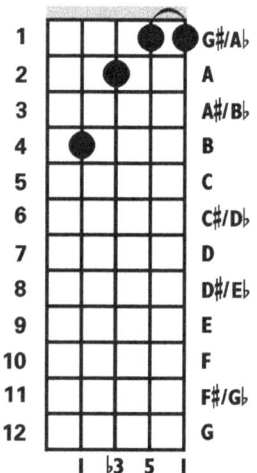

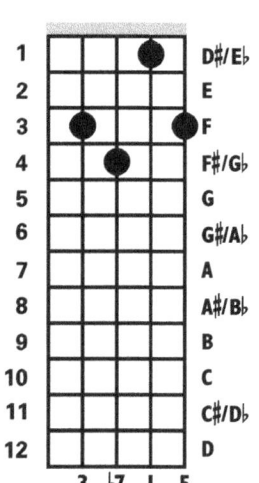
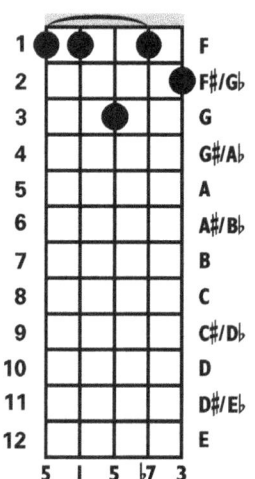
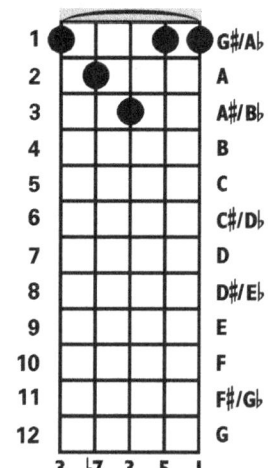
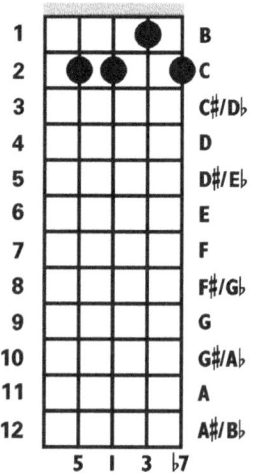

A Selection of Moveable Chord Shapes

Minor Seventh
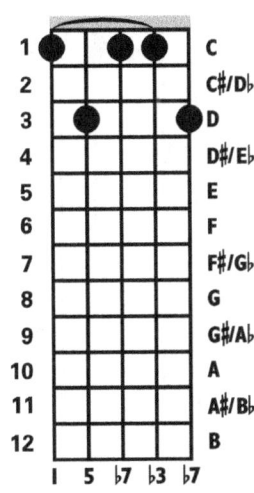

Minor Seventh
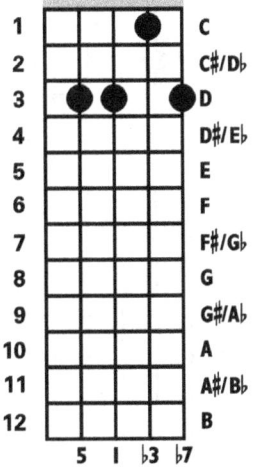

Minor Seventh
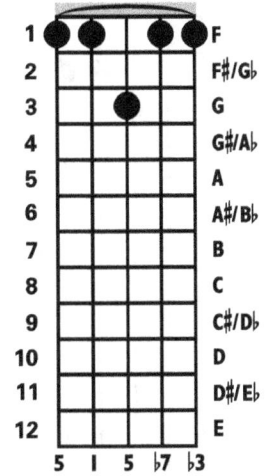

Minor Seventh
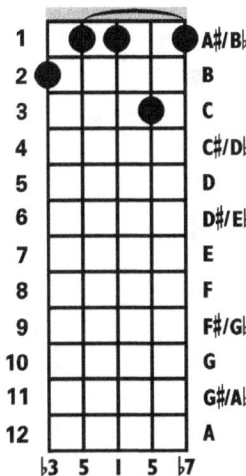

Sixth
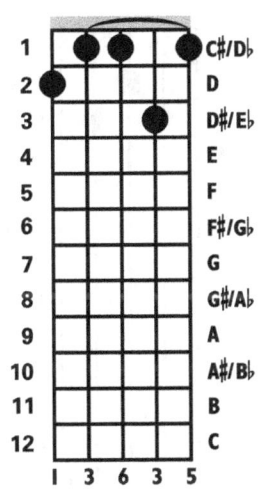

Sixth
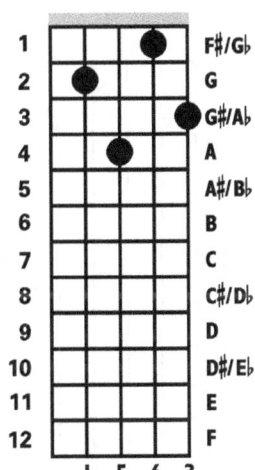

Sixth
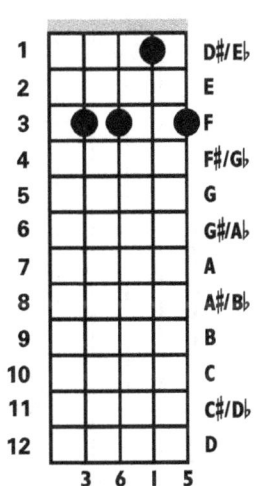

Sixth
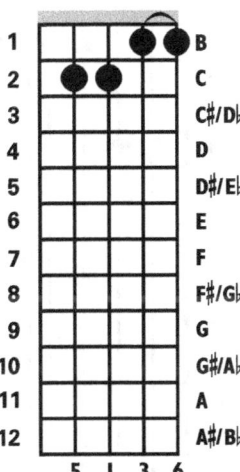

Minor Sixth
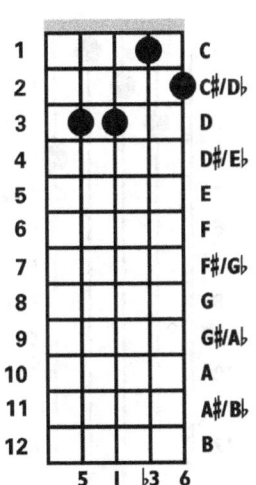

Minor Sixth
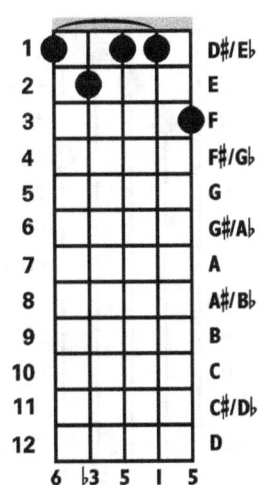

Minor Sixth
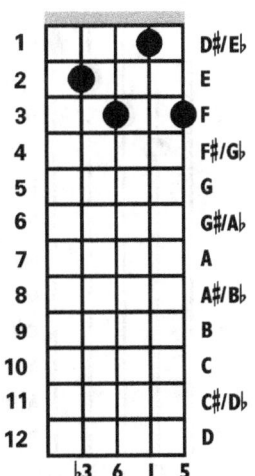

Minor Sixth
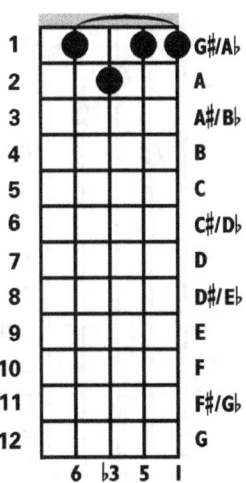

A Selection of Moveable Chord Shapes

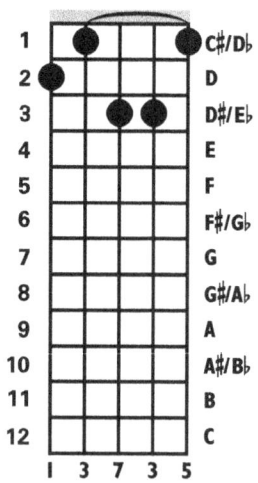
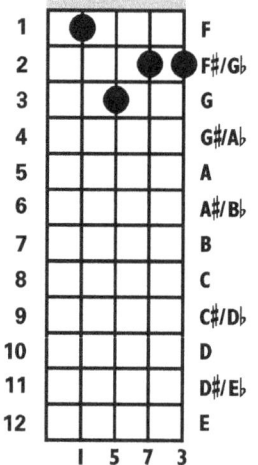
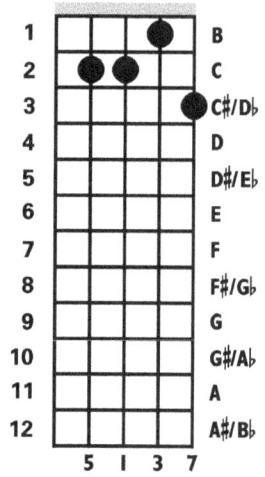
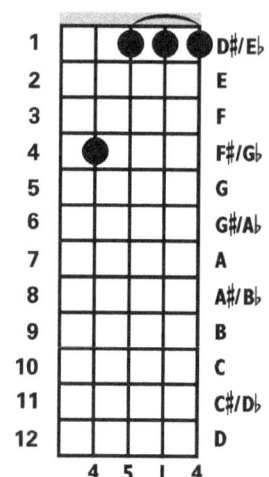
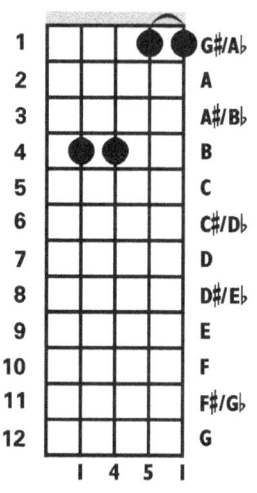
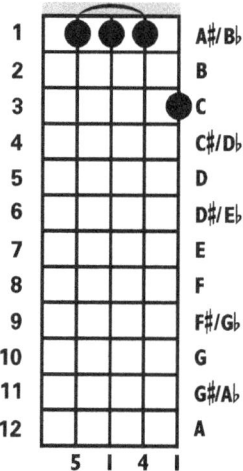
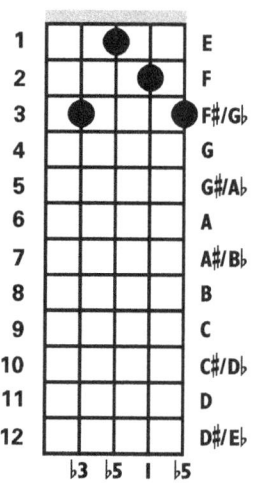
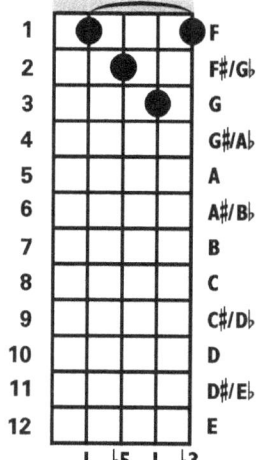
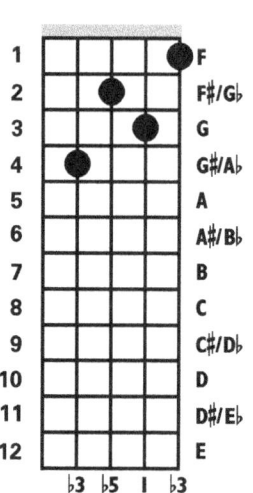
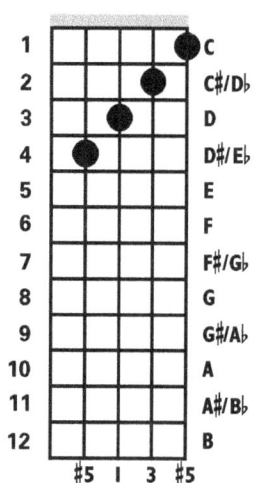
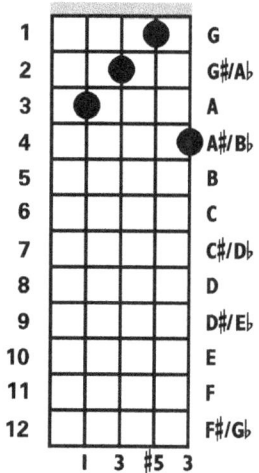
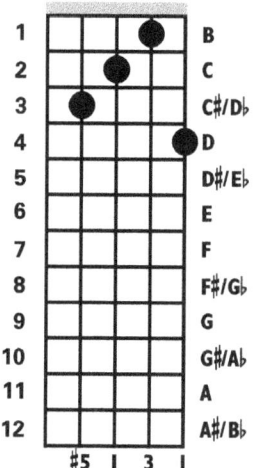

A Selection of Moveable Chord Shapes

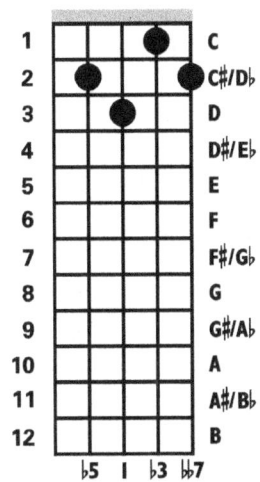
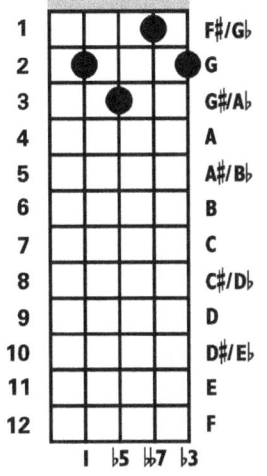
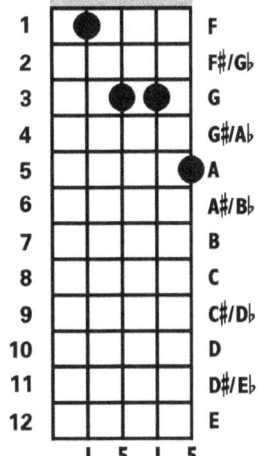
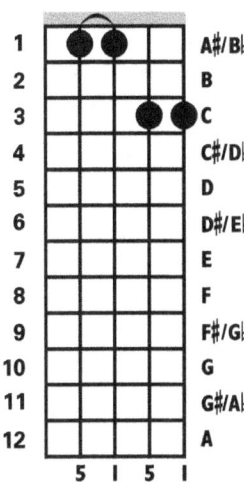

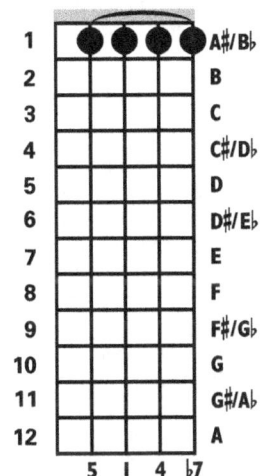
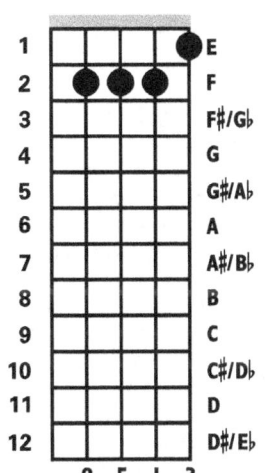
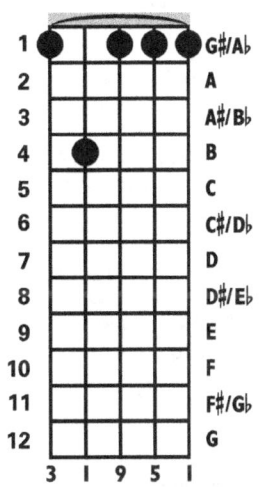
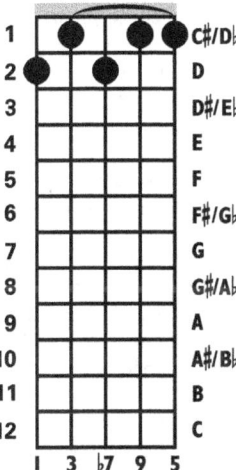

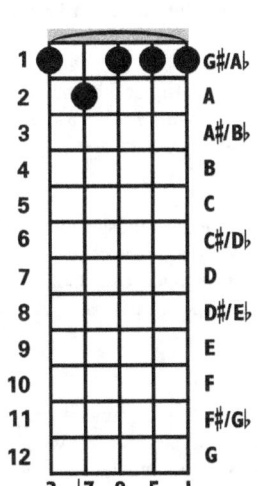
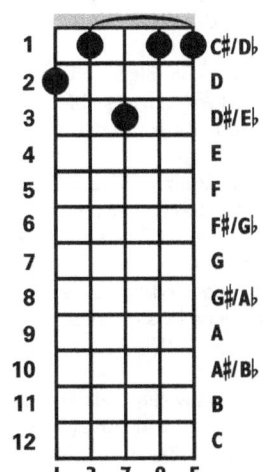
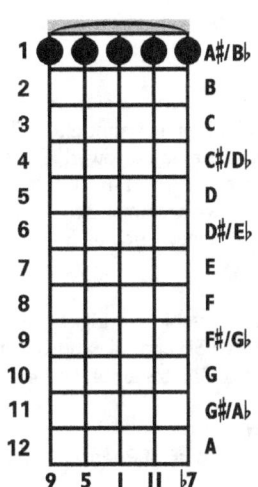
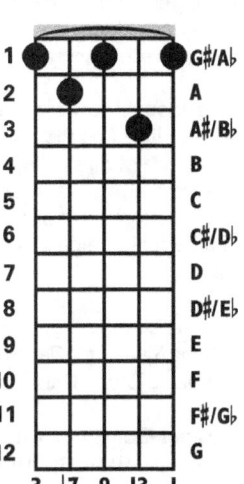

PUERTO RICAN CUATRO FAMILY FACTFILE

Bordonúa
Like the cuatro, the bordonúa is native to the island of Puerto Rico. Its history dates back to as far as the 16th century and to an antecedent, an instrument called the *bajo de la una*, a form of early Spanish bass guitar. Physically, the bordonúa has a much deeper body than the cuatro, but still retains the configuration of 10 double coursed strings. The first 2 courses (strings 1-4) are tuned in unison pairs, with the remaining 3 courses strung in octaves (strings 5-10). Standard tuning for the bordonúa is A-D-F#-B-E.

During the nineteen twenties and thirties leading players developed a distinctive tremelo technique that was achieved by wiggling and squeezing the strings over the frets. This method of playing is referred to as *gemido* (moan) or *lloriqueo* (crying). Important bordonistas include: Candelario Vásquez, "Don Candó," of Juncos and Eugenio "Yuyo" Velásquez of Aguas Buenas.

Cuatro Antiguo & 8-String *Southern* Cuatro
An early 17th century design of cuatro featuring 4 gut or stripped leather strings and shaped like an upsidedown keyhole. This instrument fell out of favour and eventually vanished during the middle of the last century. It did enjoy a revival of sorts in the form of the beautifully intricate *Southern Cuatro*, but eventually the new 8-string metal-strung variant suffered the same fate as its earlier relative. Leading exponents of the latter included Heriberto Torres and Norberto Cales.

Apart from the cuatros mentioned above, other variants have made an appearance over the years, including:

Dos Puntos Cuatro: *An 8-string model shaped like a mandolina, originating in the Puerto Rican city and municiality of Yauco.*

Tulipán Cuatro: *As the name suggests, a tulip-shaped cuatro with many of the features of the Antiguo design, from Yauco and Ponce in the South and South West of Puerto Rico.*

Higuera Cuatro: *An oval-shaped cuatro constructed from a gourd which were made and played by African slaves brought to the island. These instruments, like the Antiguo featured 4 strings. Modern day models are now made with 10 metal strings and often have designs carved into the backs.*

Cuban Tres *or* Tres Cubano
The tres is a 3-course/6-string Cuban guitar tuned to an open C or D major chord (either G-C-E or A-D-F#). Originally, the tres was mandolin shaped, probably dating back to its European origins. However, this was soon to be superceded by the guitar shape that's universally favoured today. The idea came from leading tres player and composer Arsenio Rodriguez who adapted a standard Spanish guitar to give him a bigger bodied instrument for more volume and projection. Although the majority of tres cubanos feature 6 paired strings, some instruments triple these up in much the same way as the tiple.

The tres is thought to have originated in the *Oriente* region of Cuba where it was played by the *guajiros* (or local farming community). The Cuban *Son* style of music that developed in this area borrowed its main influences from a mixture of Spanish songs and African musical styles, where it was performed as a song and salon dance accompaniment. This in turn had a major impact on future musical genres such as *Salsa* and *Latin Jazz*.

Important *tresistas* (or tres players) include: Arsenio Rodriguez, Isaac Oviedo, Nené Manfugás, Carlos Godines, Eliseo Silveira, Alejandro "Mulato" Rodríguez, Reyes 'Chito' Latamblet, Félix Ganuza among others.

Puerto Rican Cuatro *or* Cuatro Moderno
Although today's 10-string cuatro is considered to be of Puerto Rican origin, it's antecedents can be traced back to 16th and 17th century Spain and the subsequent colonization by Spanish settlers. The history of similar stringed instruments goes back even further to Persia (modern day Iran) and the Moorish population that had such an influence on Spanish culture at the time. This may also be the origin of the word *cuatro* which could have evolved from the Moorish word *al-qatr*, meaning stringed instrument. An alternative derivation of the word cuatro which appears equally plausible comes from the Spanish word for four. This seems illogical today as the instrument has 5 courses and 10 strings, but this hasn't always been the case. Early cuatros, such as the Antiguo, began their existence as simple 4-stringed instruments, with the 10-stringer we know today, only appearing relatively recently in historical terms.

How the cuatro came to be violin-shaped is something of a mystery. One theory concerns a local luthier, Miguel Hernández who lived and worked in the Arecibo area of Puerto Rico in the early 20th century. This region was known for its violin making, so it's not a giant leap of supposition to imagine Hernández being heavily influenced by what he saw around him. In pure playing terms, the cutaways are nothing more than ornamental, unlike those of the violin which are shaped in this fashion for unobstructed bowing. This style of cuatro is referred to as having an *aviolinado* design.

Traditionally, the cuatro was adopted by the *Jibaro* people of Puerto Rico where it formed an important part of cultural and religious life. It was played at many formal occasions such as rosaries, wakes, sayings of vows, Christmas and Epiphany among others. The name *Jibaro* is derived from the *Taino* language (an early sea-faring people from the Antilles region) and means forest people.

Standard tuning for the 10-string steel strung cuatro is B-E-A-D-G (from low to high), with the 4th and in 5th courses strung in octave pairs. Occasionally the 3rd course will also feature an octave configuration, but generally strings 1-6 are in unison pairings. Although in recent times instrument-specific sets of strings are readily available for the cuatro, originally local musicians had to make do with cheap imported guitar strings and settle on the gauges that were available. The main supplier was the *Chicago Musical String Company* whose strings were referred to locally as *Cuerdas Campana*, due the image of a bell on the packet as the logo design. Modern day string manufacturers include: *D'Addario*, *GHS* and *La Bella*. Musically, the cuatro creates the same kind shimmering audio effect as the 12-string guitar, albeit pitched higher up the scale. The tuning configuration is also very similar to the guitar with it's fourths arrangement, where the next string is always 5 frets higher than the last.

Seis
The seis as the name suggests features 6 courses of strings instead of the traditional five of the 10-string cuatro. This new incarnation of the Puerto Rican national instrument was the result of musicians requesting an additional course of strings to extend the range either above or below the standard B-E-A-D-G tuning to F#-B-E-A-D-G.

A seis was commissioned from luthier William Cumpiano by production staff for Paul Simon's ill-fated musical, *The Capeman*. The $11 million production ran for under three months following poor reviews.

Thinline Puerto Rican Cuatro
A narrow-bodied version of the cuatro, designed by master luthier William Cumpiano. The slimmer and lighter instrument was created mainly for the stage, where it's ideally suited for prolonged use. Cumpiano's world renowned work also includes guitars, tiples, cuatros, seises and other stringed instruments.

Tiple
Unlike its Hawaiian relative the ukulele, the tiple (pronounced *tea-play*) in its many incarnations, is generally strung with steel strings which are arranged in triple and double courses. The version familiar to American

and Western musicians was designed by *C.F. Martin & Company*, better known for their prowess in acoustic guitar design. The *Martin* tiple is usually tuned A-D-F#-B with the middle two courses tripled and the two outer courses doubled.

The Puerto Rican tiple or *Tiple Doliente* is probably best described as keyhole shaped and is tuned in a similar way to its cousin, the cuatro, with an additional course at the top instead of the lower B (E-A-D-G-C).

Other types of tiple include:

Banjo Tiple (Peru): *A little banjo with 4 double courses of strings.*

Colombian Tiple: *12-string guitar-like instrument divided up into 4 triple stringed courses.*

Marxochime Hawaiian Tiple: *A zither-lap steel guitar hybrid tiple.*

Spanish Tiple (Spain): *A little guitar style tiple from Menorca.*

Tiple Argentino (Argentina): *Little guitar-style instrument with 6 strings.*

Tiple Cubano (Cuba): *Cuban instrument with either 5 single strings or 5 double courses (like the taropatch or charango).*

Tiple Doliente (Puerto Rico): *A popular five stringed instrument probably derived from Spanish guitarrillos and Canary Island timples. These little instruments would have been brought to island by early colonizers. Along with the cuatro and bordonúa, the tiple doliente is one of Puerto Rico's most important national instruments. Like the cuatro, it's tuned in fourths (E-A-D-G-C).*

Tiple Dominicano (Dominican Republic): *5 double coursed bandurria-like instrument*

Tiple Grande de Ponce (Puerto Rico): *A narrow waisted, larger member of the tiple group.*

Tiple Peruano (Peru): *Peruvian tiple with 4 single or double strings.*

Tiple Requinto Costanero (Puerto Rico): *Small version of the tiplón.*

Tiple Requinto de la Montaña (Puerto Rico): *Small 3-stringed version of the doliente.*

Tiple Uruguayo (Uruguay): *A little guitar-style of tiple with 6 strings.*

Tiple Venezolano (Venezuela): *Smaller version of the Colombian tiple, featuring 4 triple string courses.*

Tiplón or Tiple con Macho (Puerto Rico): *The largest family member with a 5th tuning peg much like the 5-string banjo.*

Other tiples: Tres Cuerdas, Quinto, Mandurria, Mayor and others.

Venezuelan Cuatro

The South American cuatro's history can be traced back to its long defunct ancestor, the 4-string Spanish guitar. Again, like several of the instruments in the ukulele family group, the cuatro is tuned to the same fundamental intervals as the first four strings of a classical guitar - in this case A-D-F#-B, like the soprano uke's D6 tuning. Where it differs is in the positioning of the re-entrant strings. With the ukulele and rajão, the higher strings can be found on the 4th and 5th strings. With the cuatro, the 2nd and 3rd strings are re-entrant (namely the D and F#). Although most musicians use this tuning, an alternative was created by reknowned cuatro player, Fredy Reyna in 1948. Rebelling against the re-entrant standard, Reyna re-strung the cuatro to a more recognizable low to high tuning (E-A-C#-F#), but still retained the relationship, based on guitar tuning (transposed into the key of A6).

Very much akin to the English language aide-mémoire *"my dog has fleas"*, the cuatro's tuning can be remembered by singing the following two words, *"Cam-bur pin-tón"*, or ripe banana!

The 4-string or Venezuelan cuatro is not to be confused with the Puerto Rican cuatro which has 10 steel strings in 5 double courses. The design bares little or no resemblance to the more guitar-like mainland instrument (the tuning is B-E-A-D-G). The shape is very reminiscent of a member of the violin family with it's instantly recognizable sculpted waist and upper/lower bouts.

Notable Venezuelan cuatro players include: Hernán Gamboa, Fredy Reyna, Cheo Hurtado, Juan Carlos Salazar, Rafael Brito, Leonardo Lozano and Raúl Landaeta.

Puerto Rican Cuatro Family Tunings

Bordonúa 6-String - Standard Tuning	F#BEEAD
Bordonúa 10-String - Standard Tuning	ADF#BE
Cuatro Antiguo - Traditional Tuning	AEAD
Puerto Rican Cuatro - Standard Tuning	BEADG
Seis - 4ths Standard Tuning	F#BEADG
Seis - Guitar Tuning	F#BEAC#F#
Tiple Columbiano - Standard Tuning	DGBE
Tiple Doliente - Standard Tuning	EADGC
Tiple Dominicano - Standard Tuning	CFB♭DG
Tiple Peruano - Standard Tuning	AEBF#
Tiple Uruguayo - Standard Tuning	BEADF#B
Tiple Venezolano - Standard Tuning	DGBE
Tiple Venezolano - Alternative Tuning	ADF#B
Tiple Venezolano - Alternative Tuning	CFAD
Tiple Venezolano - Alternative Tuning	CDAF
Tres Cubano - Traditional Tuning	GCE
Tres Cubano - New Alternative Tuning	ADF#
Venezuelan Cuatro - Standard Tuning	ADF#B

ALTERNATIVE CHORD NAMES

C	**CM** or **Cmaj**
Cm	**Cmin** or **C-**
C-5	**C-5** or **C(♭5)**
C°	**Cdim**
C4	**Csus4(no 5th)** or **Csus(no 5th)**
C5	**C Power Chord** or **C(no 3rd)**
Csus2	**C(sus2)** or **C2**
Csus4	**Csus** or **C(sus4)**
Csus4add9	**Csus(add9)**
C+	**Caug**, **C+5** or **C(♯5)**
C6	**CM6** or **CMaj6**
Cadd9	**Cadd2**
Cm6	**C-6** or **Cmin6**
Cmadd9	**Cmadd2** or **C-(add9)**
C6add9	**C6/9**, **C$^6_9$** or **CMaj6(add9)**
Cm6add9	**Cm6/9** or **Cm$^6_9$**
C°7	**Cdim7**
C7	**Cdom**
C7sus2	**C7(sus2)**
C7sus4	**C7sus**, **C7(sus4)** or **Csus11**
C7-5	**C7♭5**
C7+5	**C7+** or **C7♯5**
C7-9	**C7♭9** or **C7(add♭9)**
C7+9	**C7♯9** or **C7(add♯9)**
C7-5-9	**C7♭5♭9**
C7+5-9	**C7♯5♭9**
C7+5+9	**C7♯5♯9**
C7add11	**C7/11** or **C$^7_{11}$**
C7+11	**C7♯11**
Cm7	**C-7**, **Cmi7** or **Cmin7**
Cm7-5	**Cm7♭5**, **C-7-5** or **C^ø**
Cm7-5-9	**Cm7♭5♭9**
Cm7-9	**Cm7♭9**
Cm7add11	**Cm**
Cm(maj7)	**Cm♯7**, **CM7-5**, **CmM7** or **C-△**
Cmaj7	**CM7** or **C△(Delta)**
Cmaj7-5	**CM7-5**, **C△♭5** or **Cmaj7♭5**
Cmaj7+5	**CM7+5**, **C△5+** or **Cmaj7♯11**
Cmaj7+11	**CM7+11**, **C△+♯11** or **Cmaj7♯11**
C9	**C7(add9)**
C9sus4	**C9sus** or **C9(sus4)**
C9-5	**C9♭5**
C9+5	**C9♯5**
C9+11	**C9♯11**
Cm9	**C-9** or **Cmin9**
Cm9-5	**Cm9♭5**
Cm(maj9)	**Cm9(maj7)**, **CmM9** or **Cm(addM9)**
Cmaj9	**CM9**, **Cmaj7(add9)**, **C△9** or **CM7(add9)**
Cmaj9-5	**CM9-5**, **Cmaj9♭5**, **C△9♭5** or **CM9♭5**
Cmaj9+5	**CM9+5**, **Cmaj9♯5**, **C△9♯5**
Cmaj9add6	**CM9add6** or **C△9add6**
Cmaj9+11	**CM9+11**, **Cmaj9♯11**, **C△9♯11** or **CM9♯11**
C11	**C7(add11)**
C11-9	**C11♭9**
Cm11	**C-11** or **Cmin11**
Cmaj11	**CM11**, **Cmaj7(add11)**, **C△11**, **CM7(add11)**
C13	**C7/6(no 9th)** or **C7(add13)**
C13sus4	**C13sus** or **C13(sus4)**
C13-5-9	**C13♭5♭9**
C13-9	**C13♭9**
C13+9	**C13♯9**
C13+11	**C13♯11** or **C13aug11**
Cm13	**C-13** or **Cmin13**
Cmaj13	**CM13**, **Cmaj7(add13)**, **C△13** or **CM7(add13)**

M	**major**
m	**minor**
-	**minor**
dim	**diminished**
°	**diminished**
ø	**half diminished**
sus	**suspended**
aug	**augmented**
+	**augmented**
add	**added**
dom	**dominant**
△	**delta / major seventh**
Q(3)	**quartal / double fourth**
♯	**sharp**
✕	**double sharp**
♭	**flat**
♭♭	**double flat**
Do	**Spanish for C**
Dó	**Portuguese for C**
Re	**Spanish for D**
Ré	**Portuguese for D**
Mi	**Spanish & Portuguese for E**
Fa	**Spanish & Portuguese for F**
So	**Spanish for G**
Sol	**Portuguese for G**
La	**Spanish for A**
Lá	**Portuguese for A**
Si	**Spanish & Portuguese for B**
H	**German for B**

English Tonic Sol-fa

Do	**C**
Re	**D**
Me	**E**
Fa	**F**
Sol	**G**
La	**A**
Ti	**B**

The majority of music books will use the chords featured in the first column (on the far left and top right), but should you come across alternatives, consult this guide for other naming conventions.

The list above includes most of the symbols and abbreviations that you're likely to encounter in the majority of music books.

NOTES

NOTES

NOTES

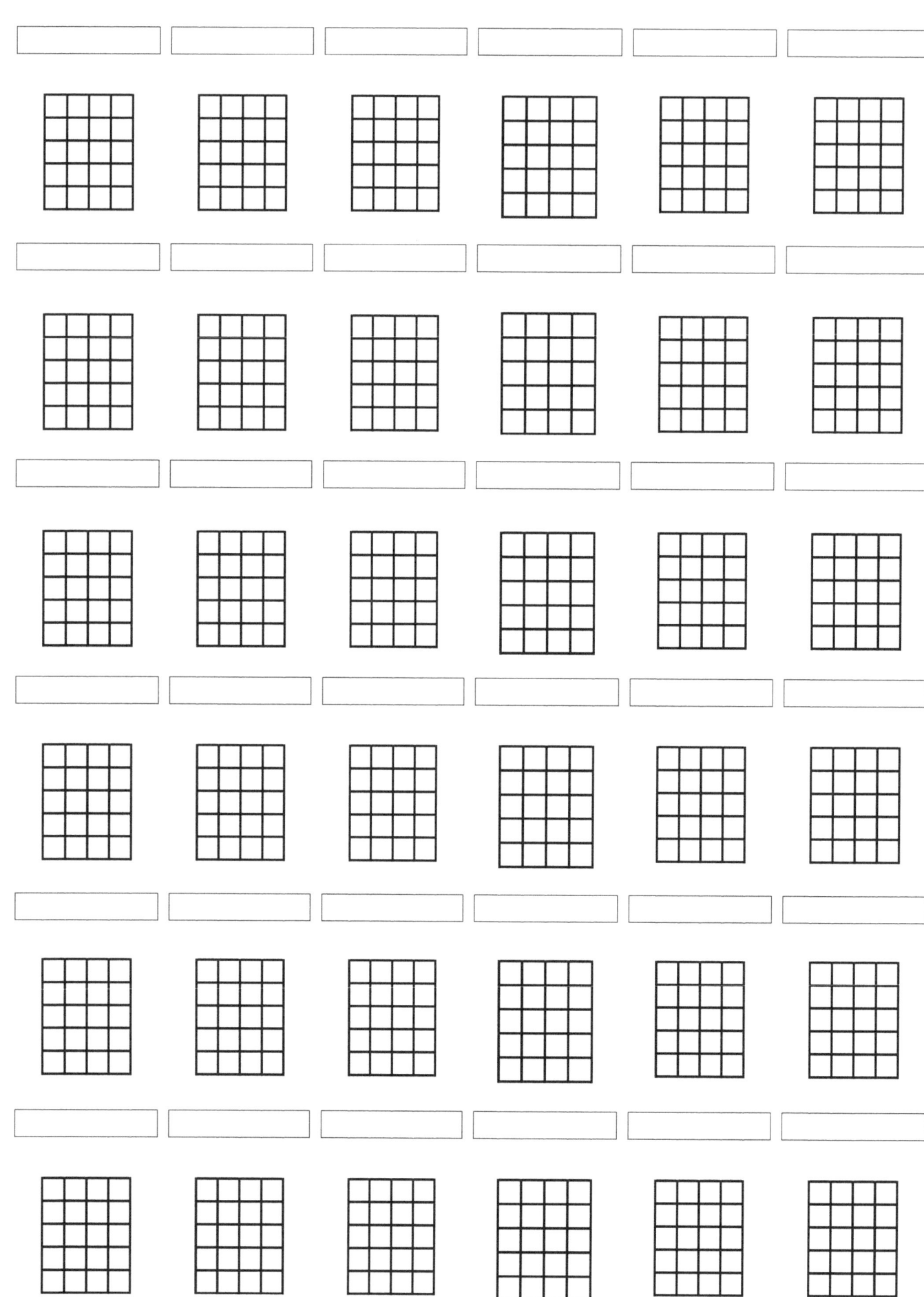

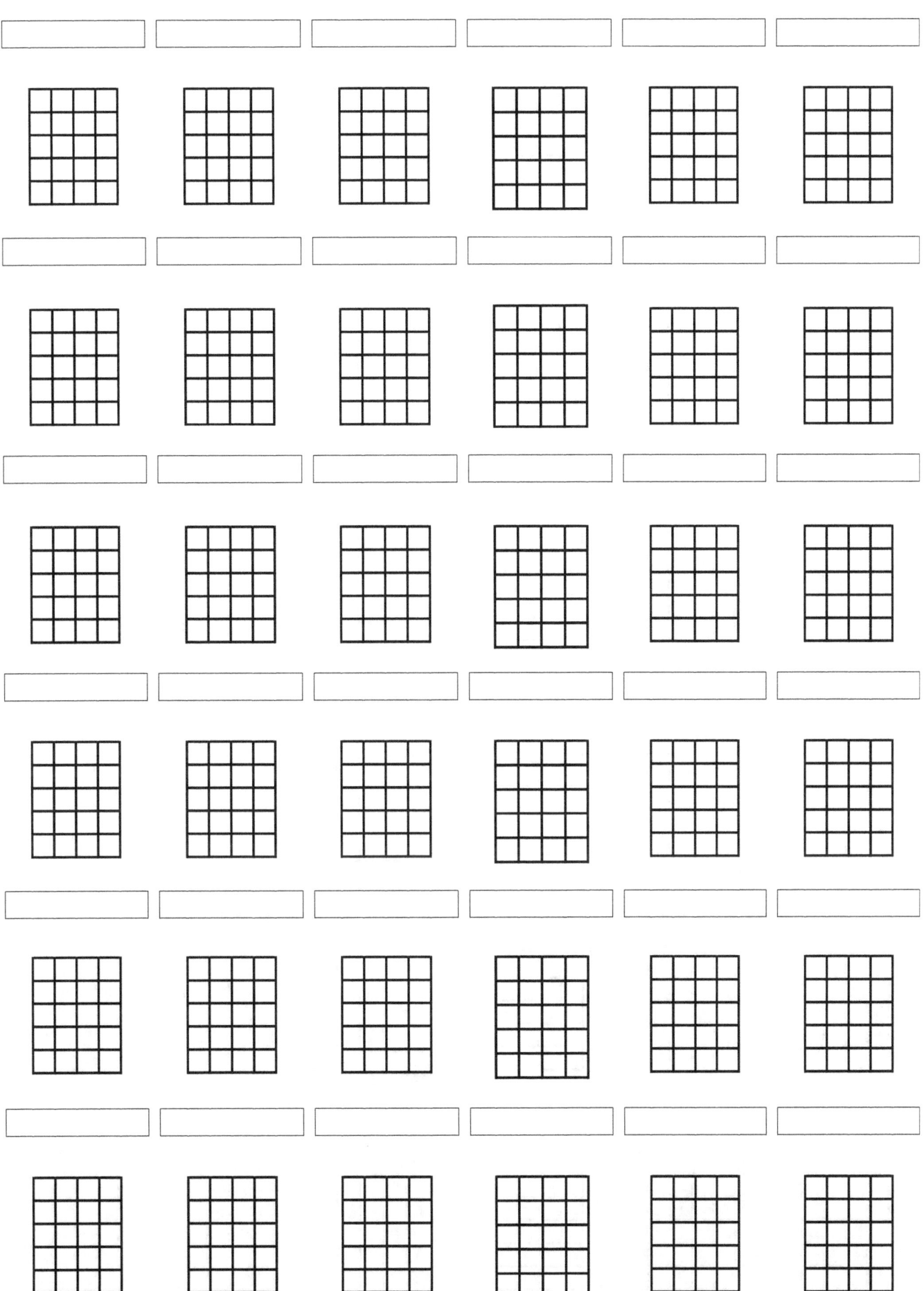

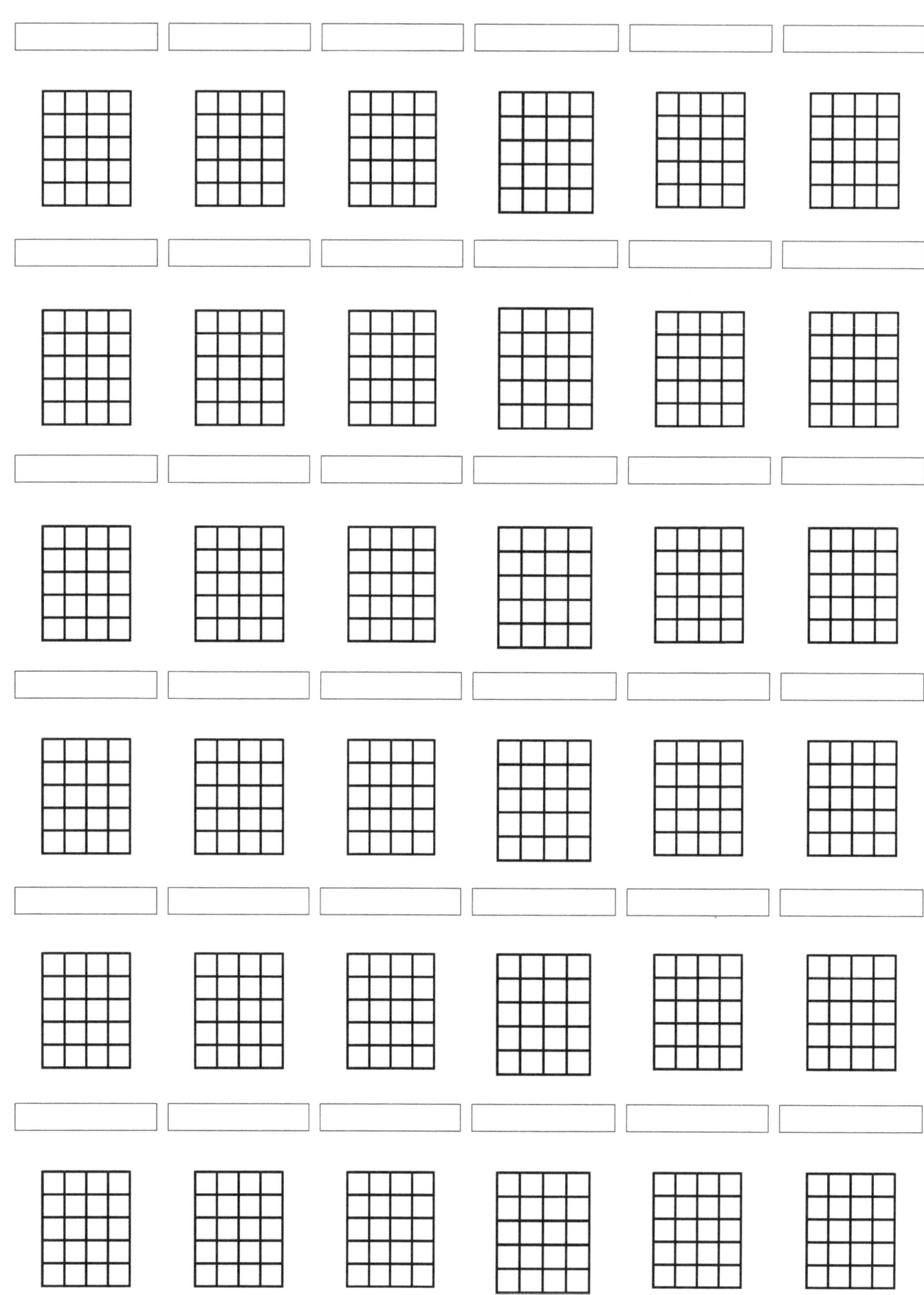

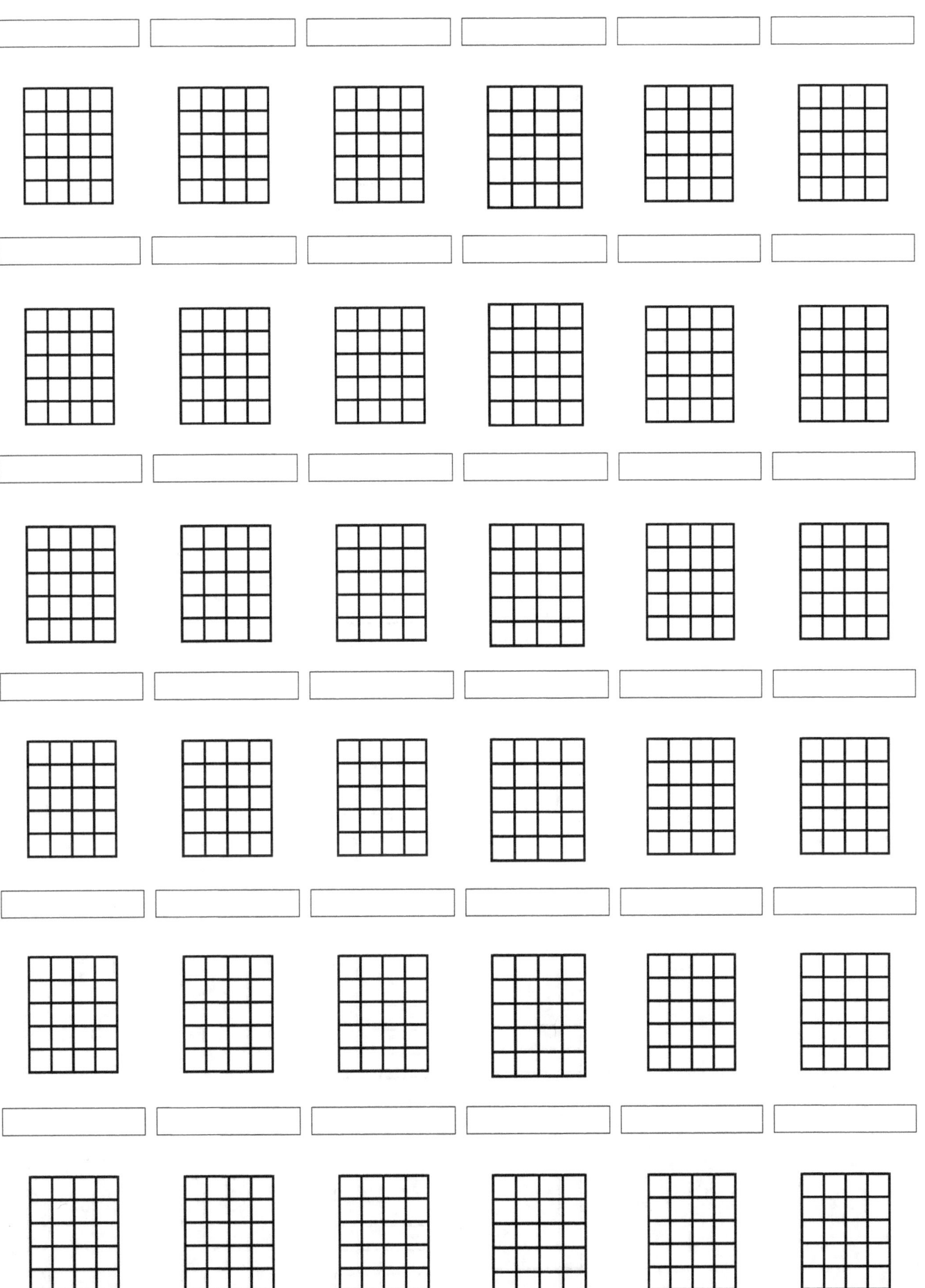

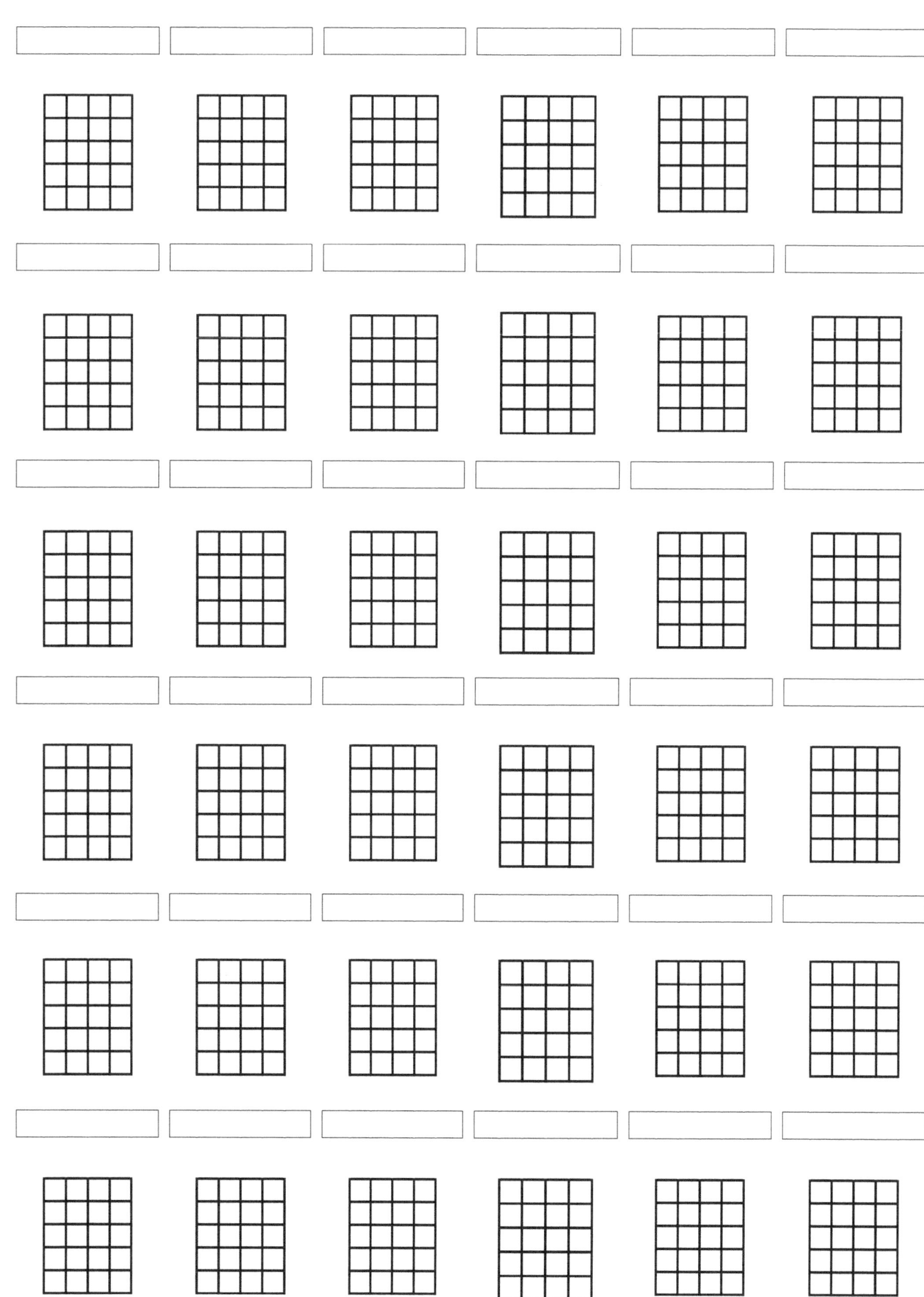

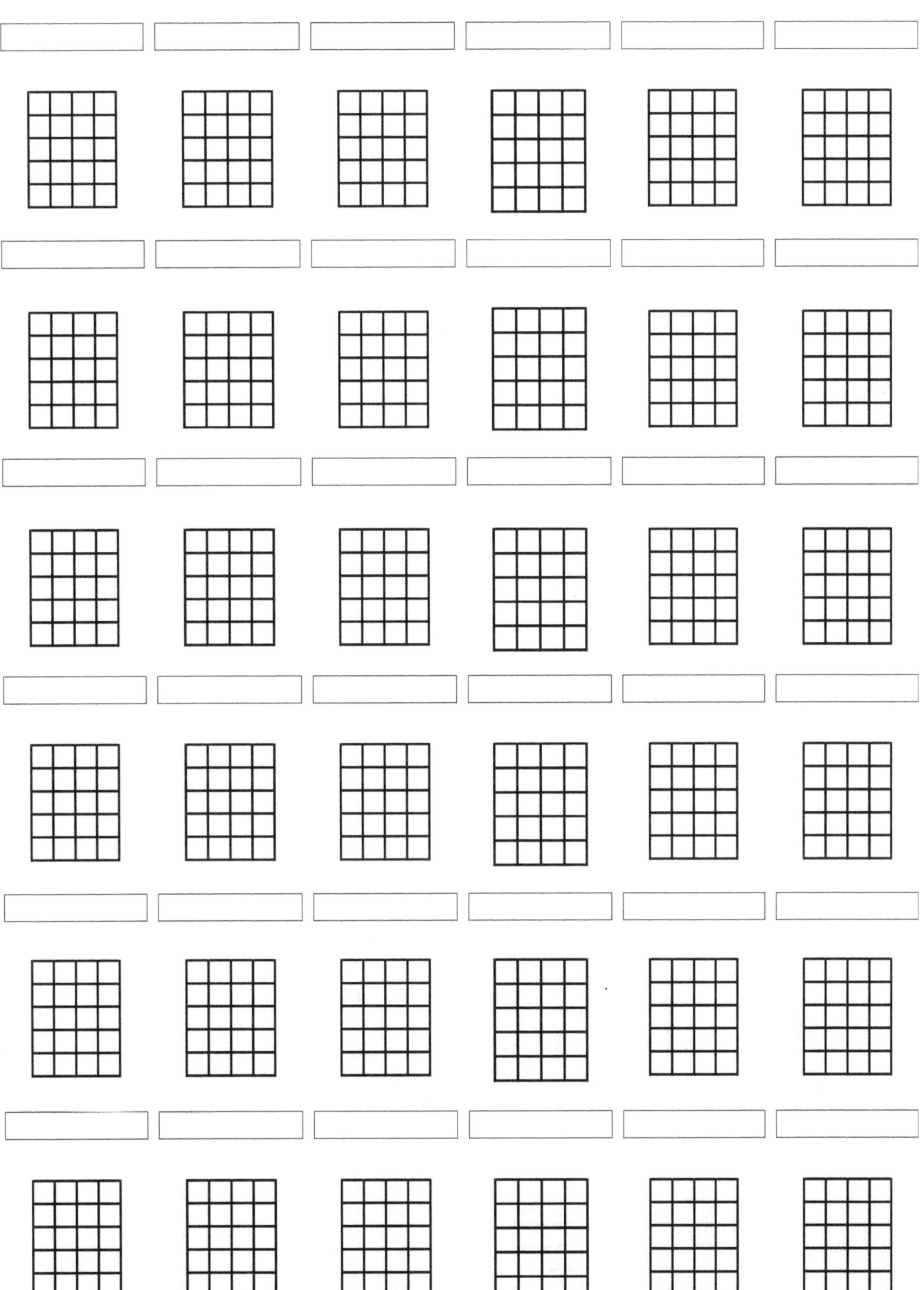

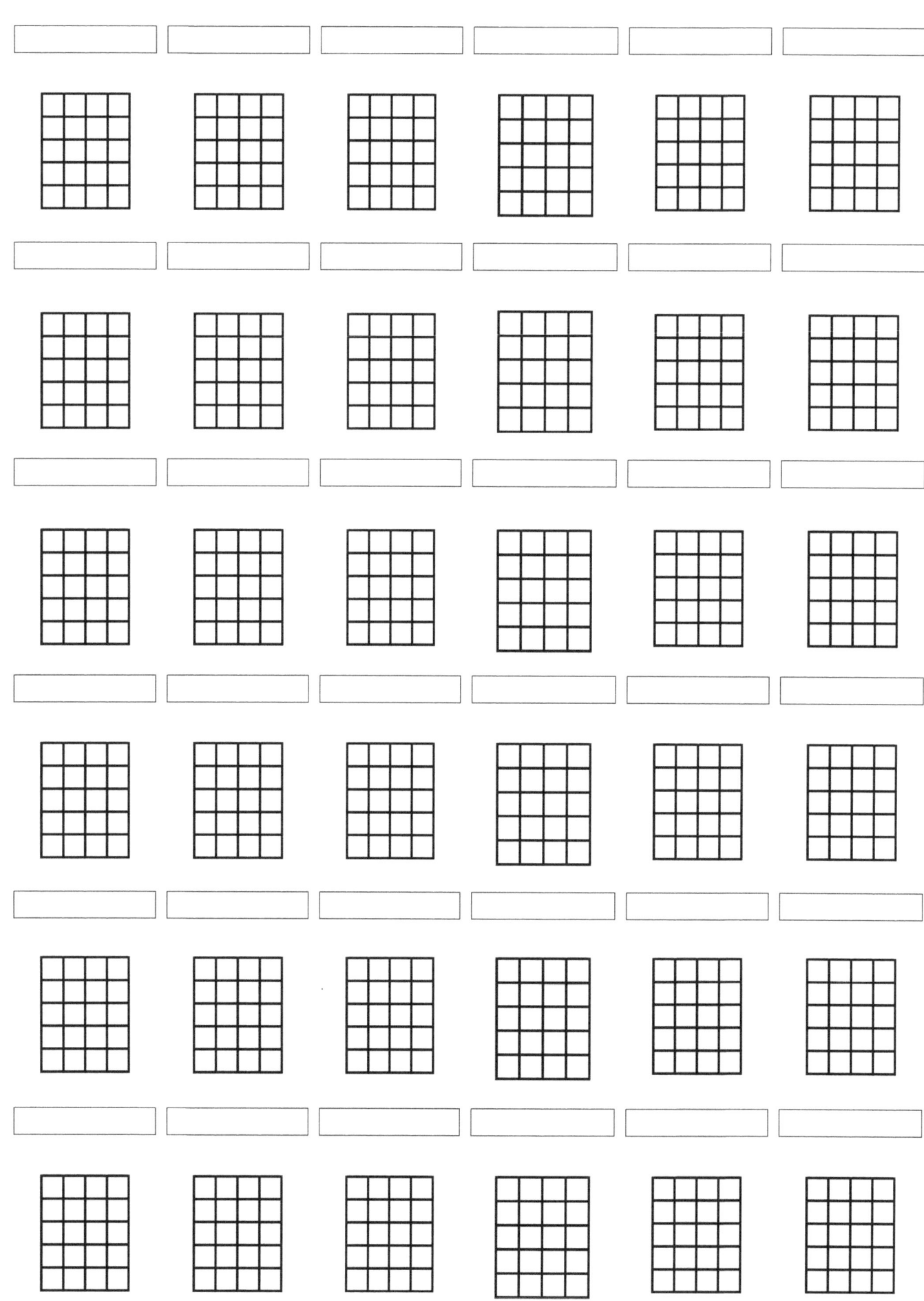

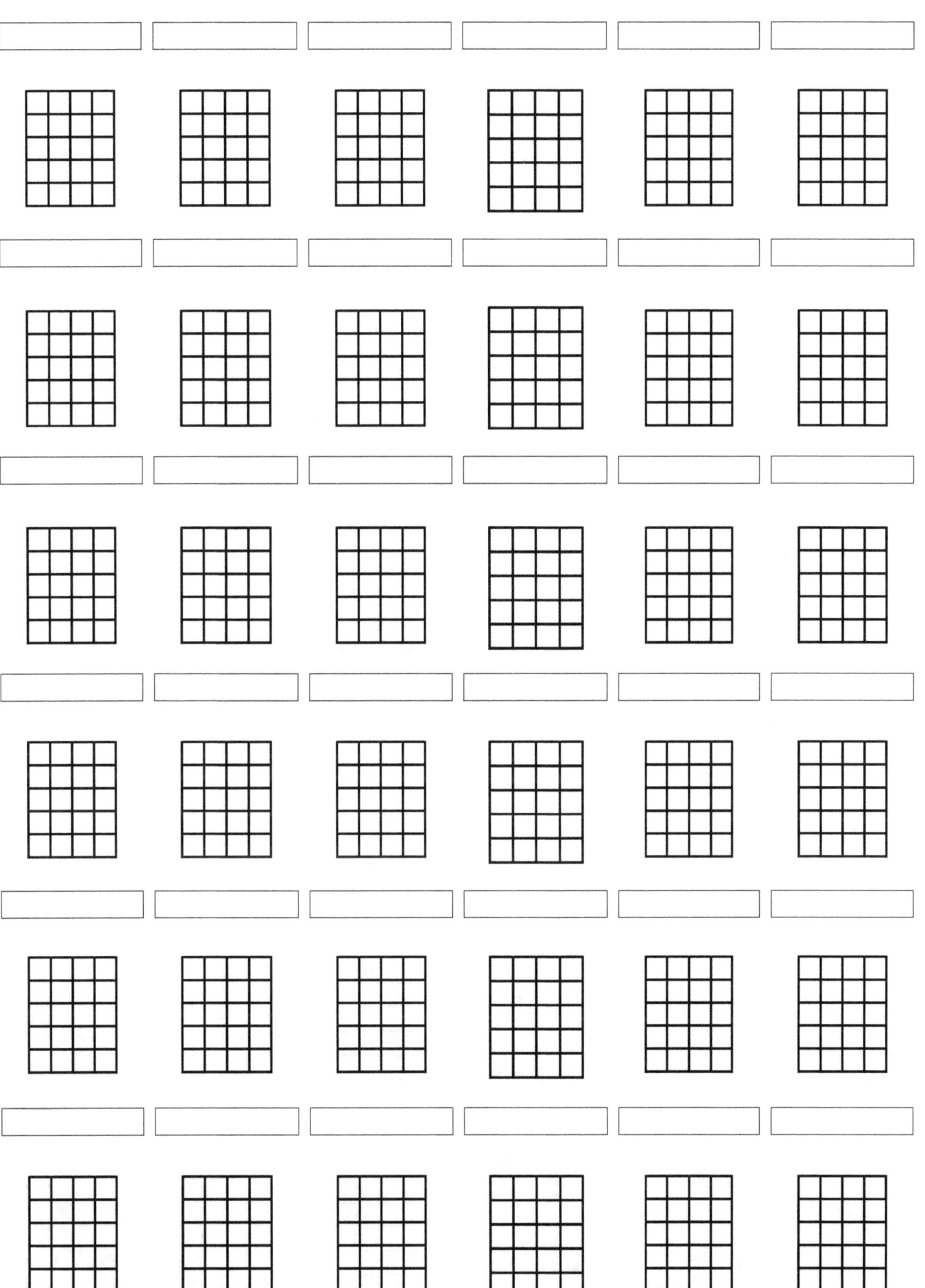

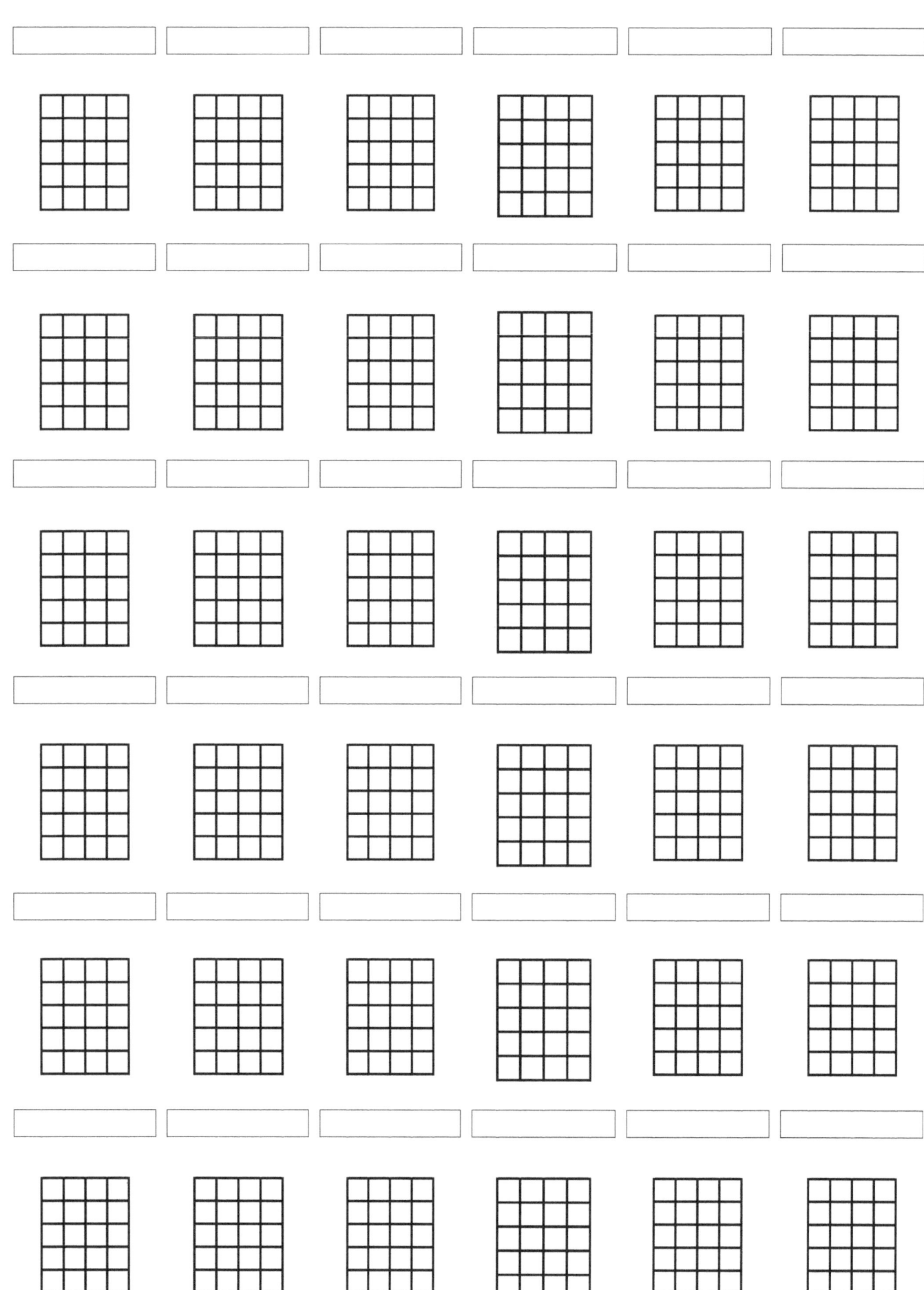

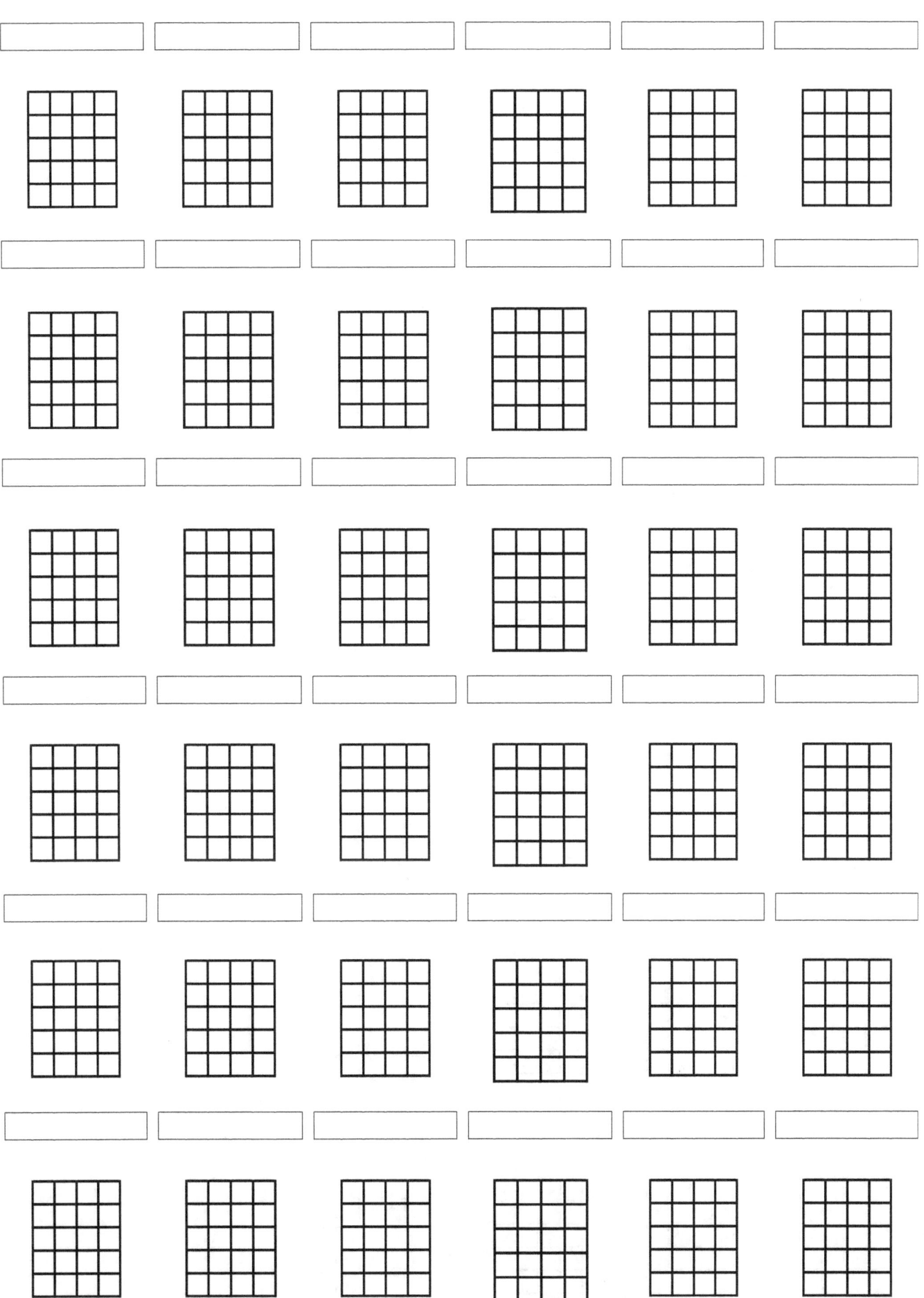

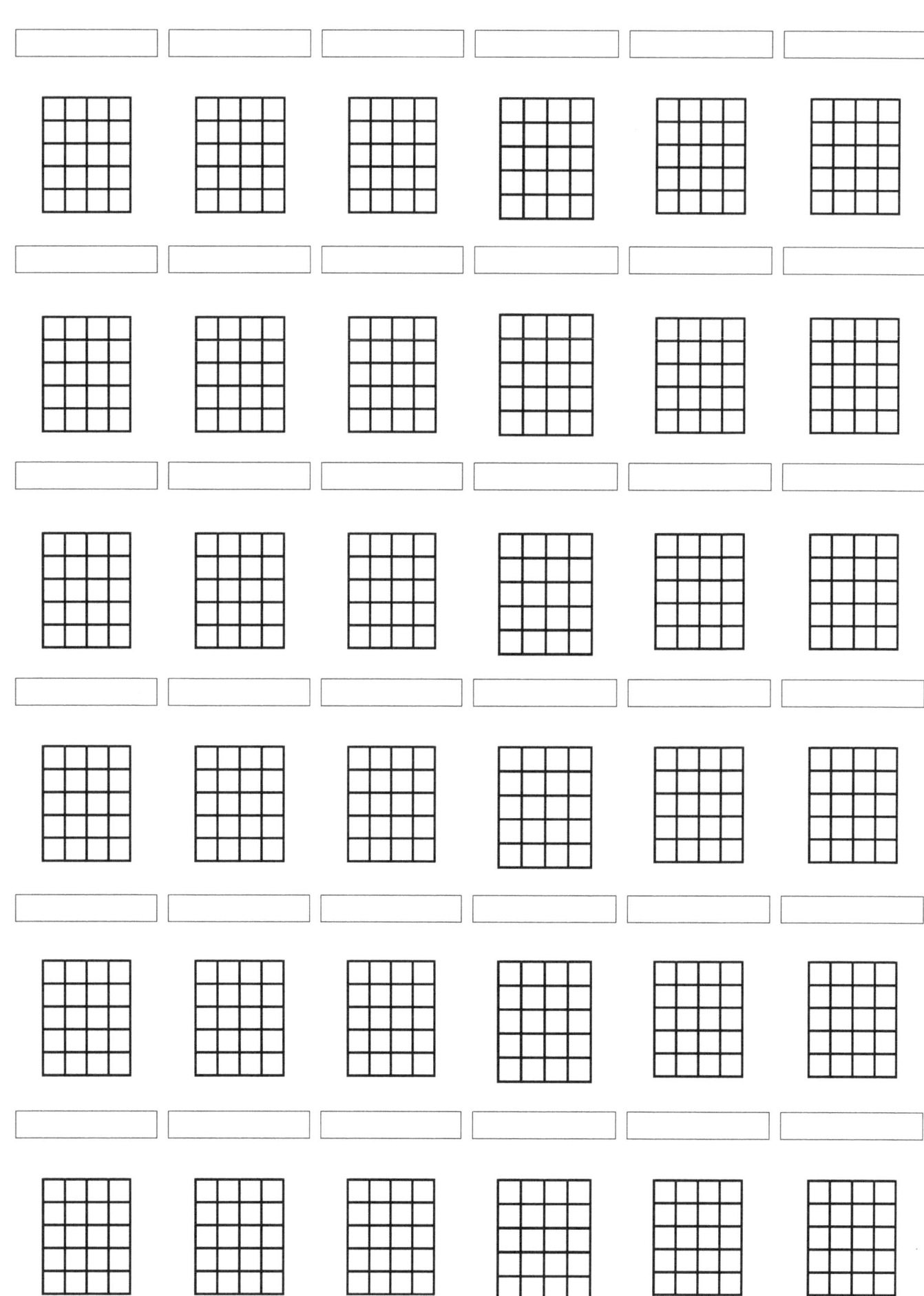

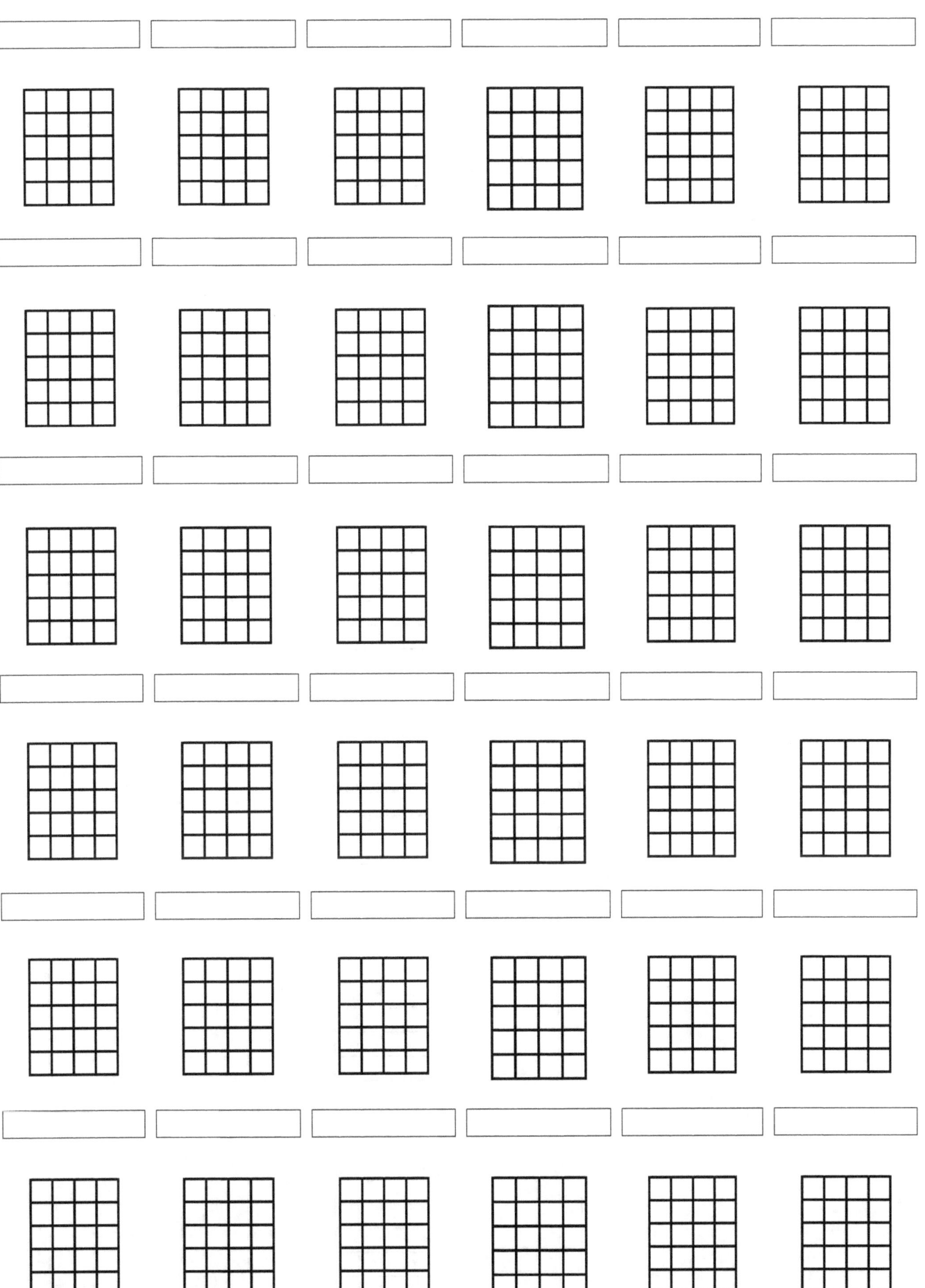

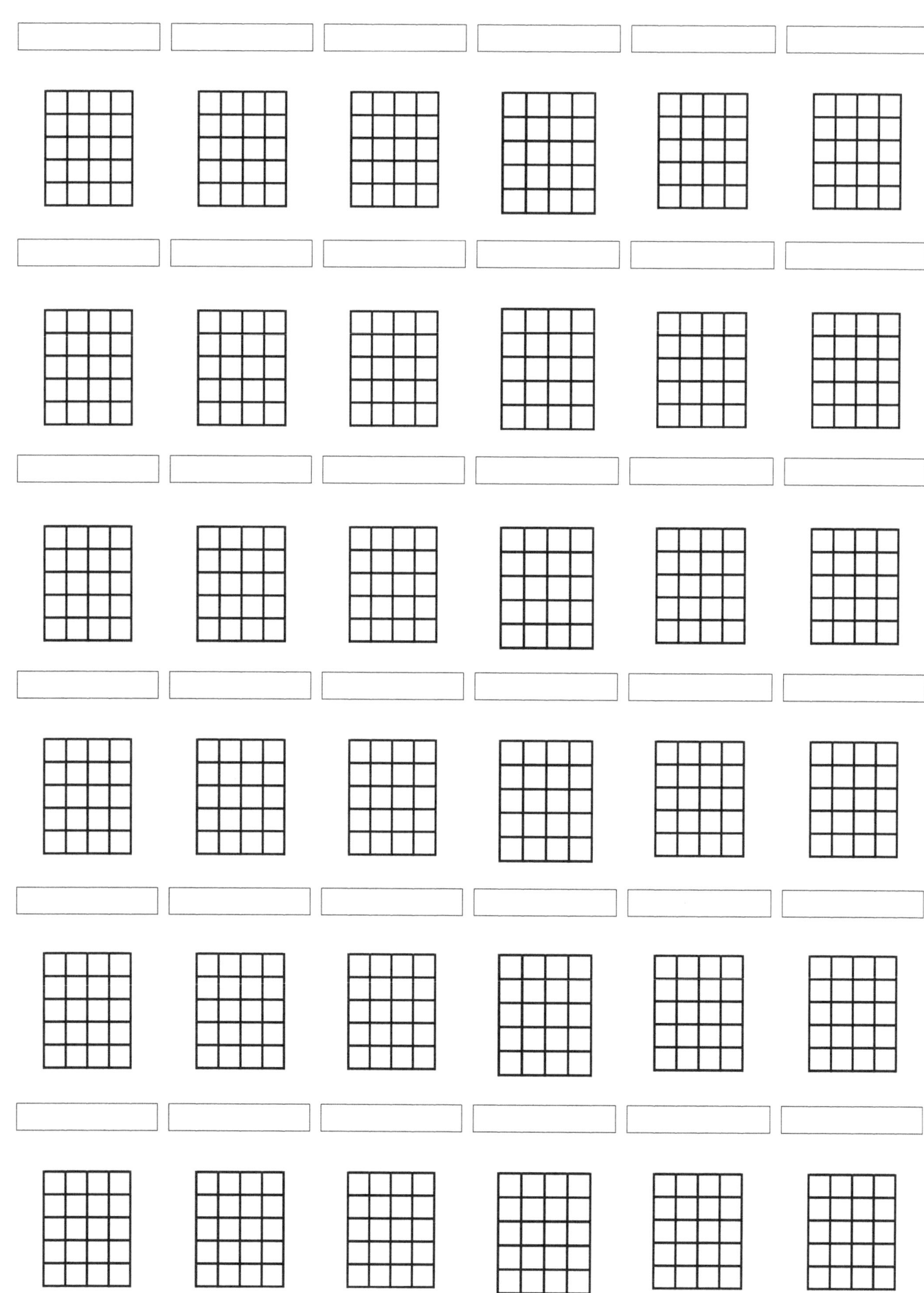

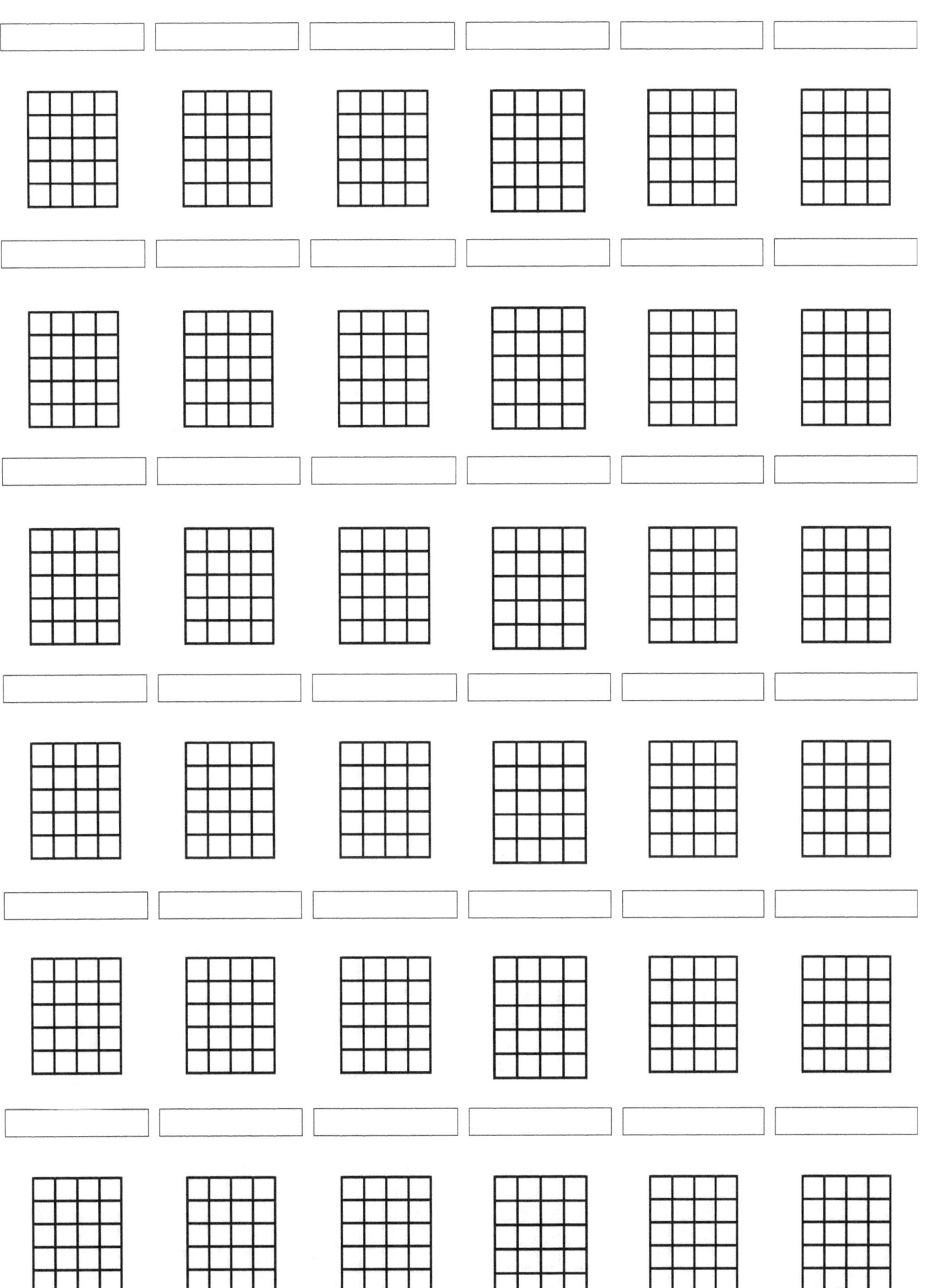

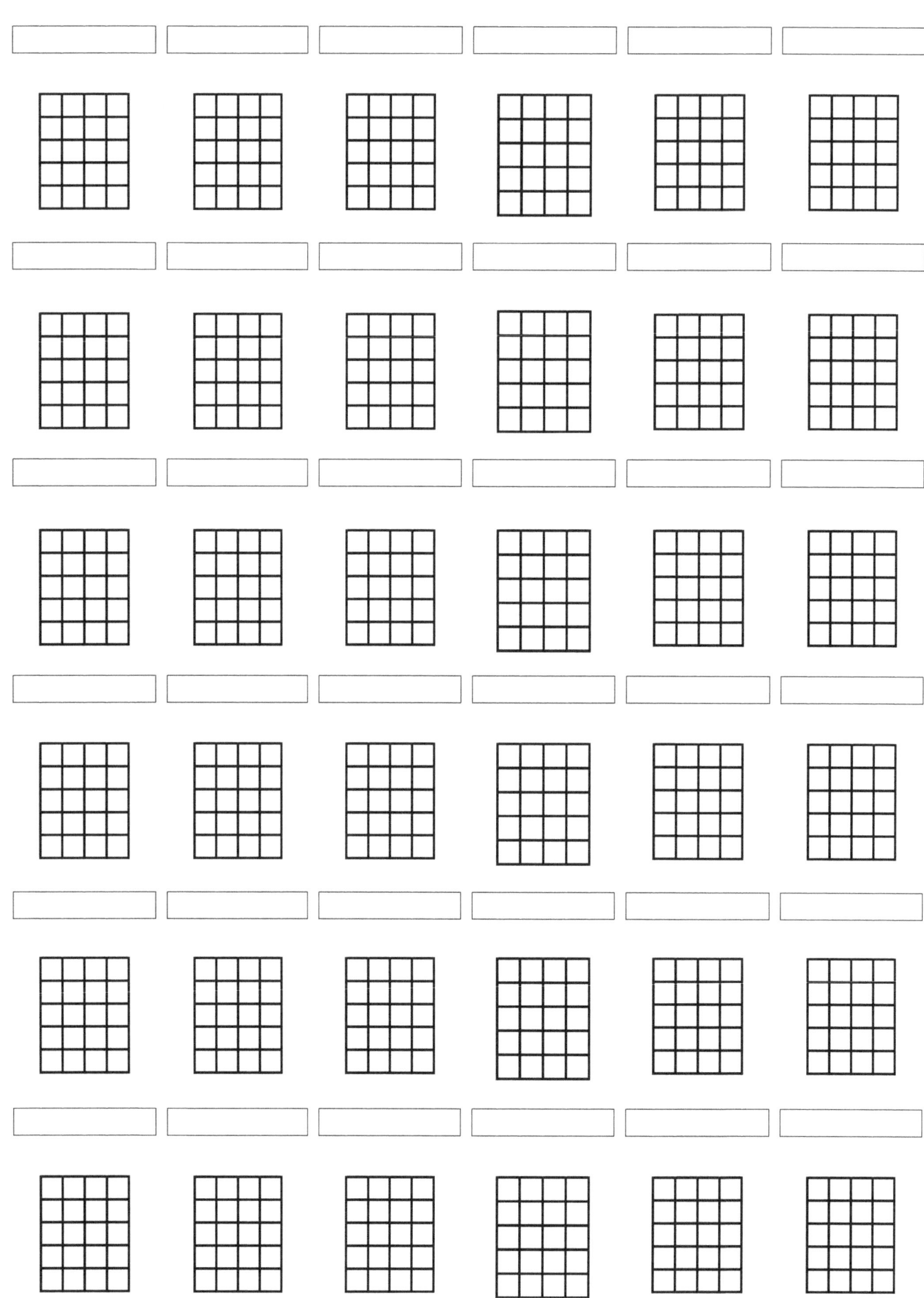

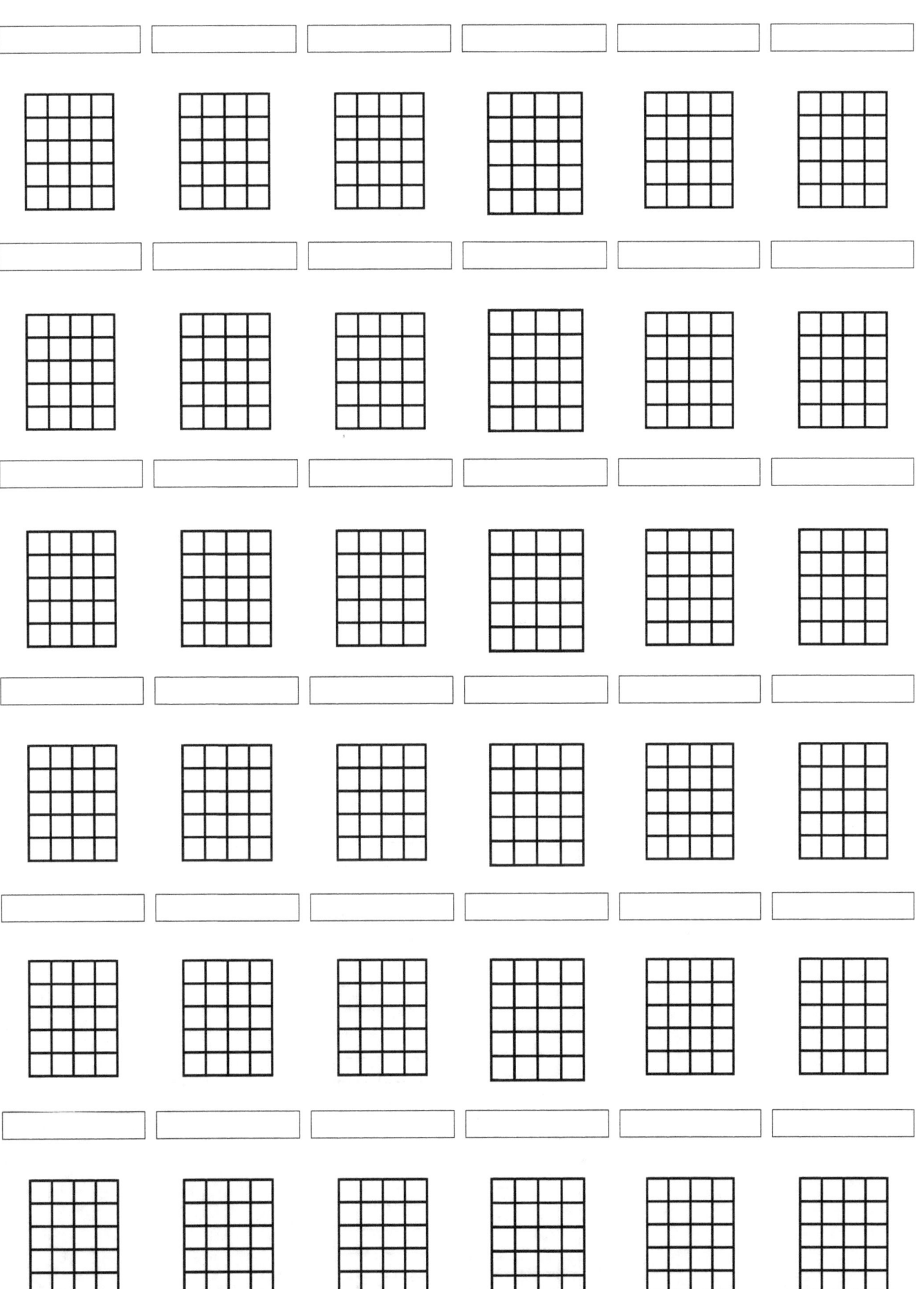

101

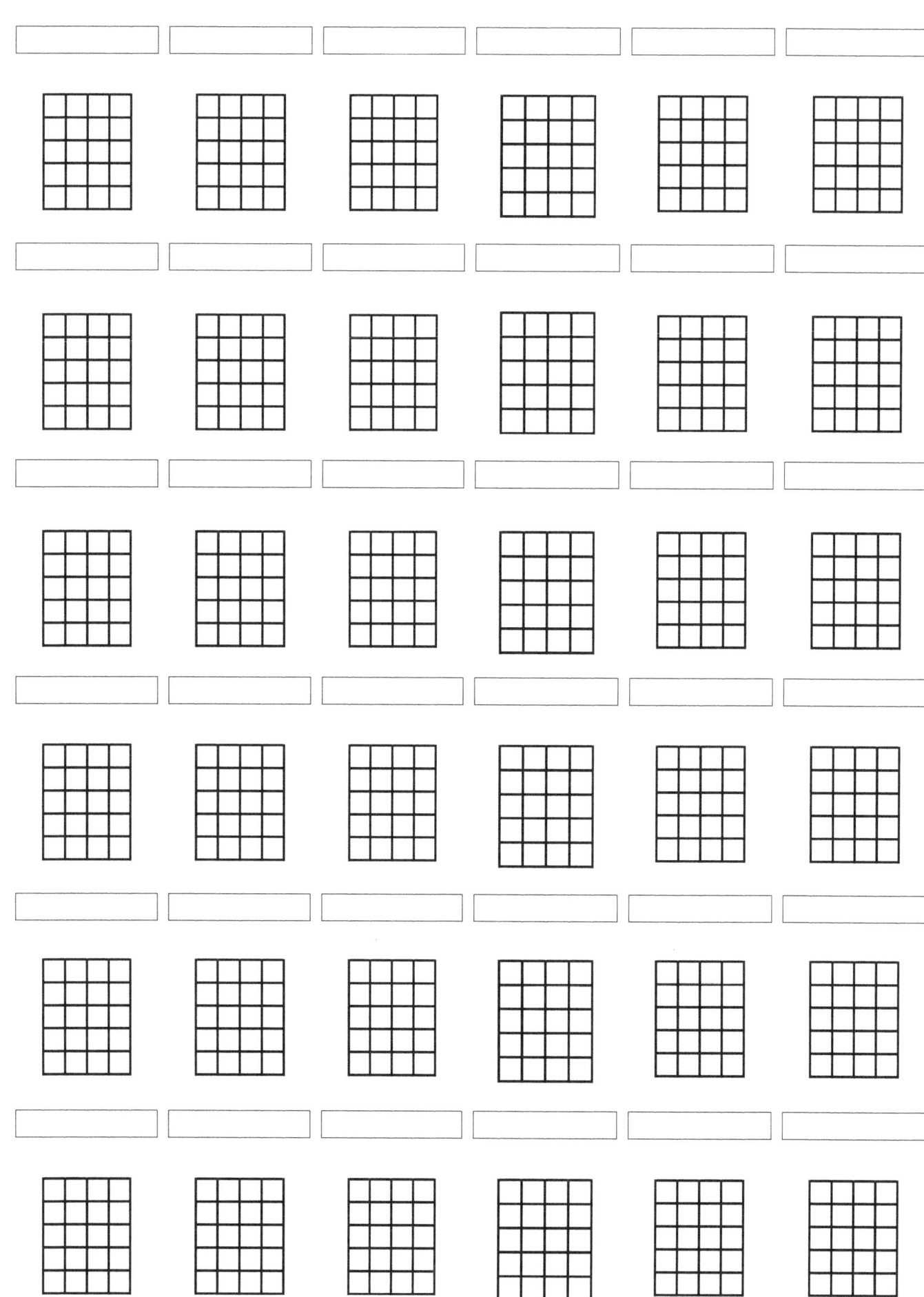

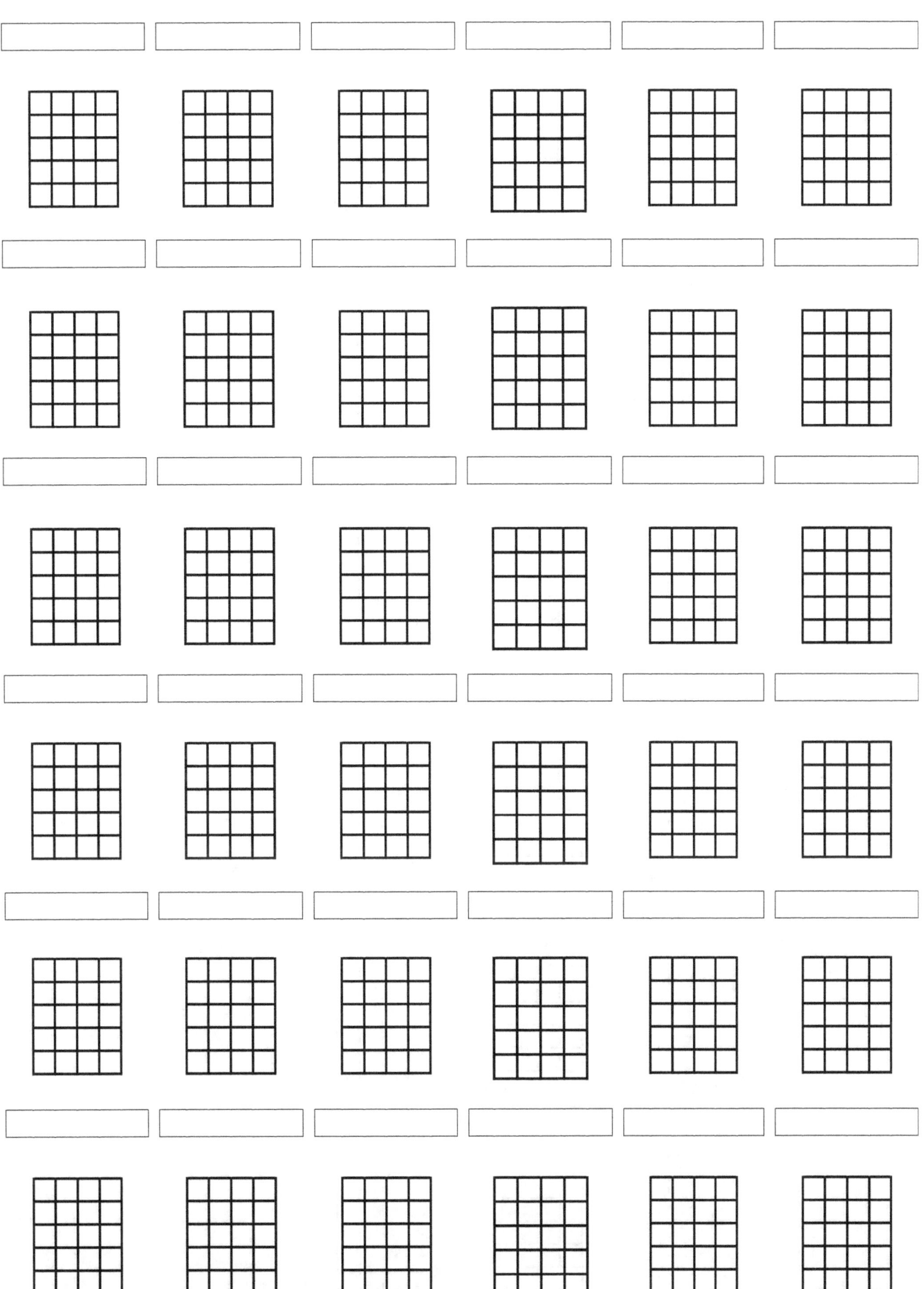

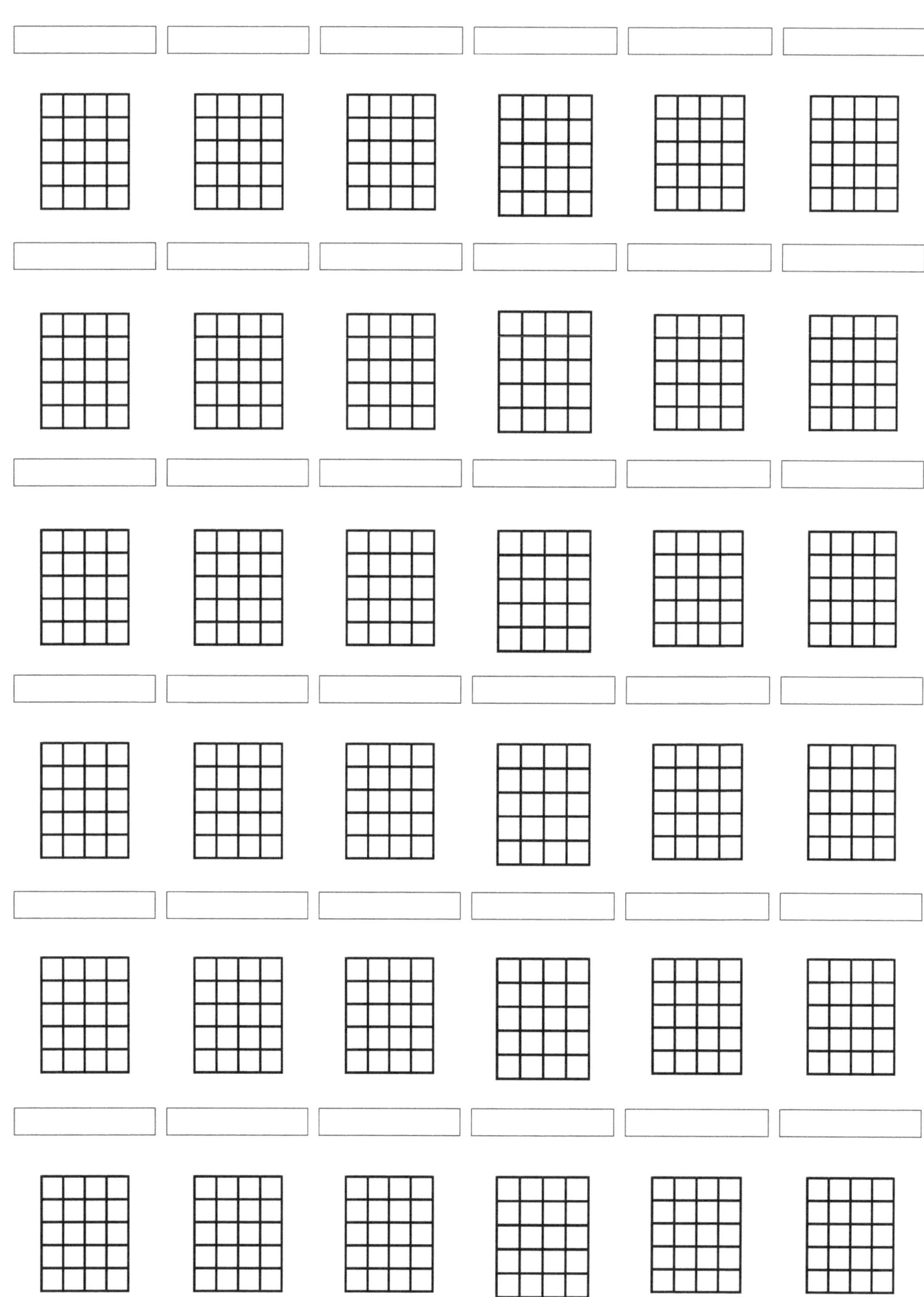

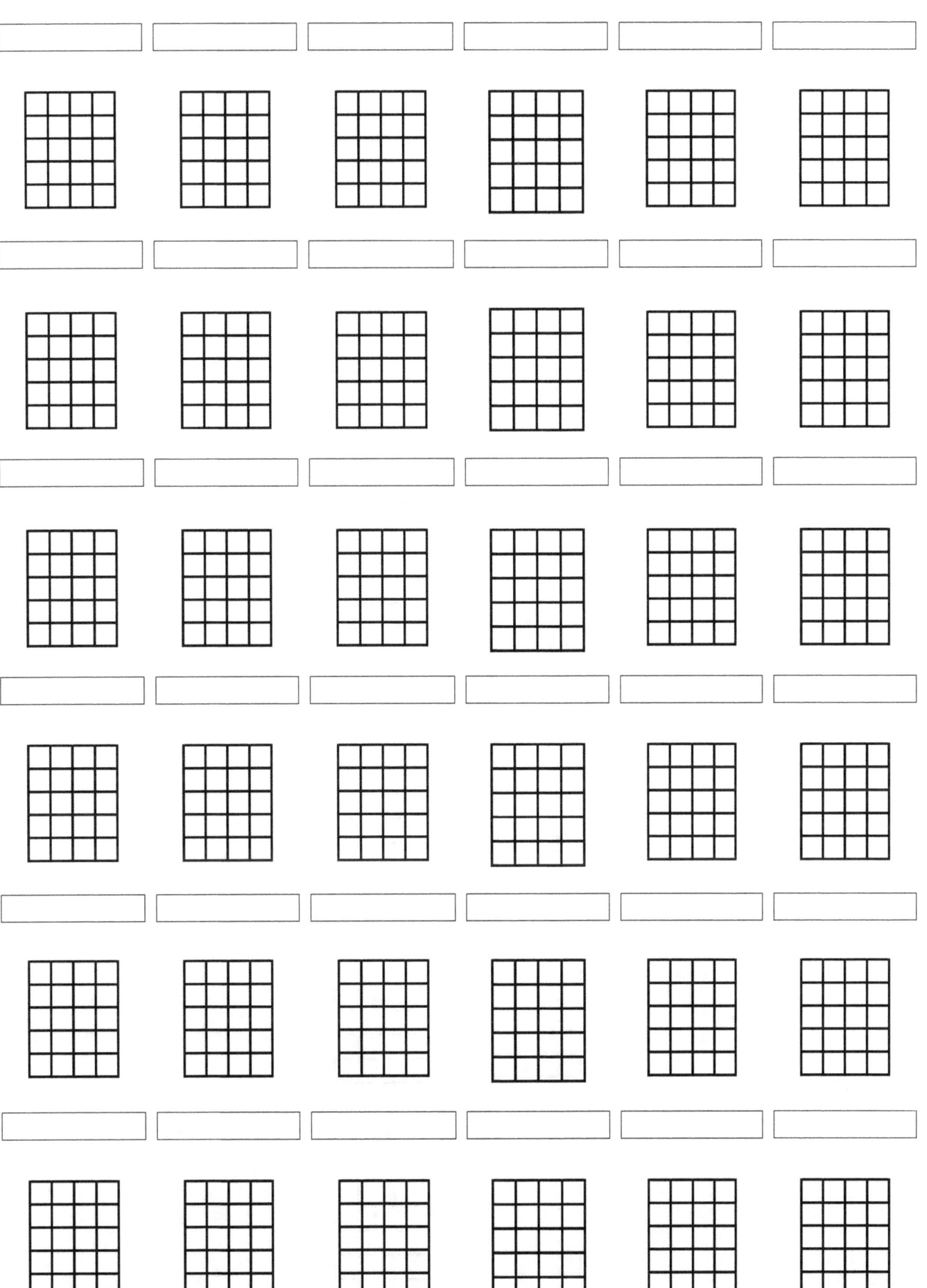

105

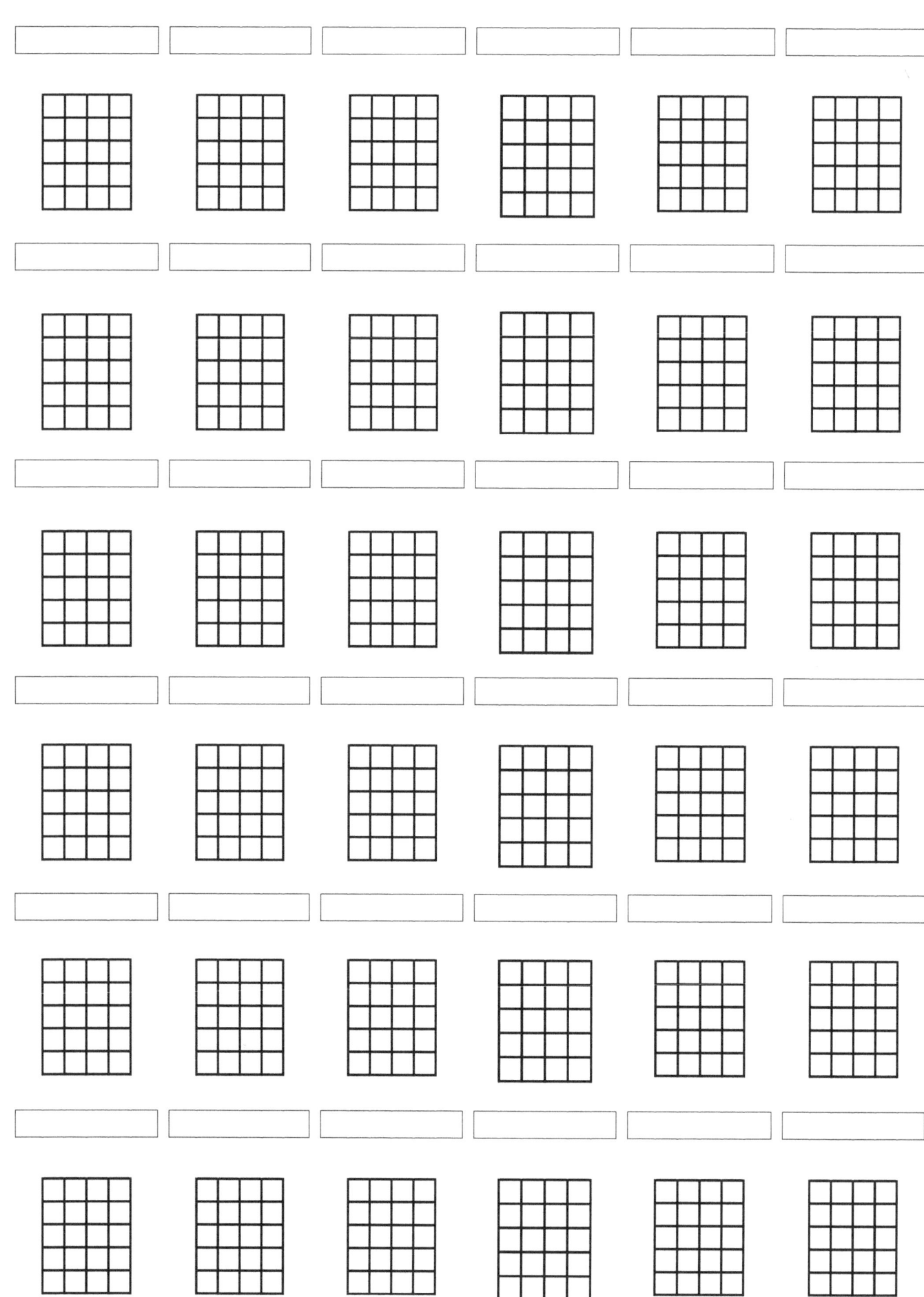

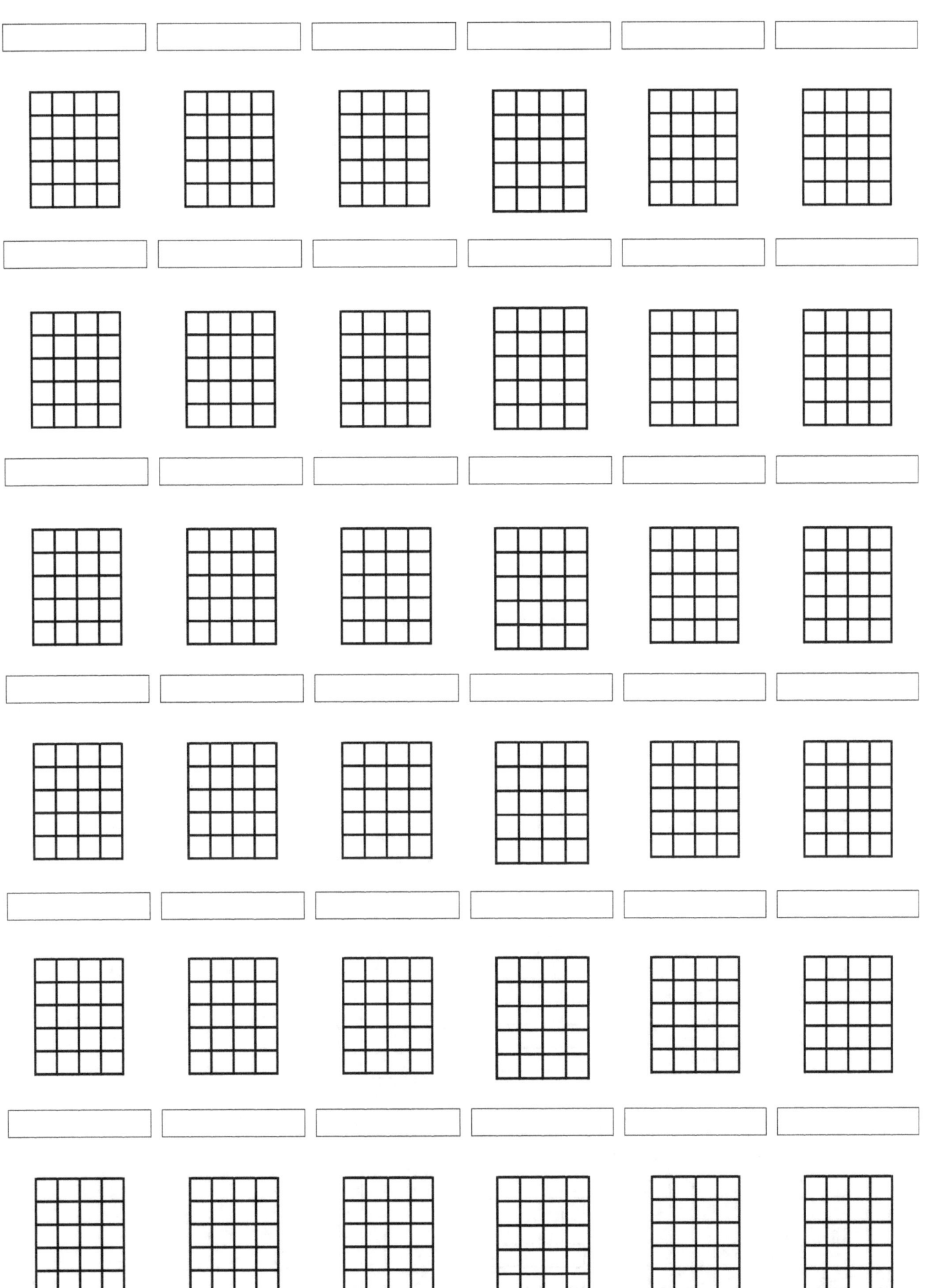

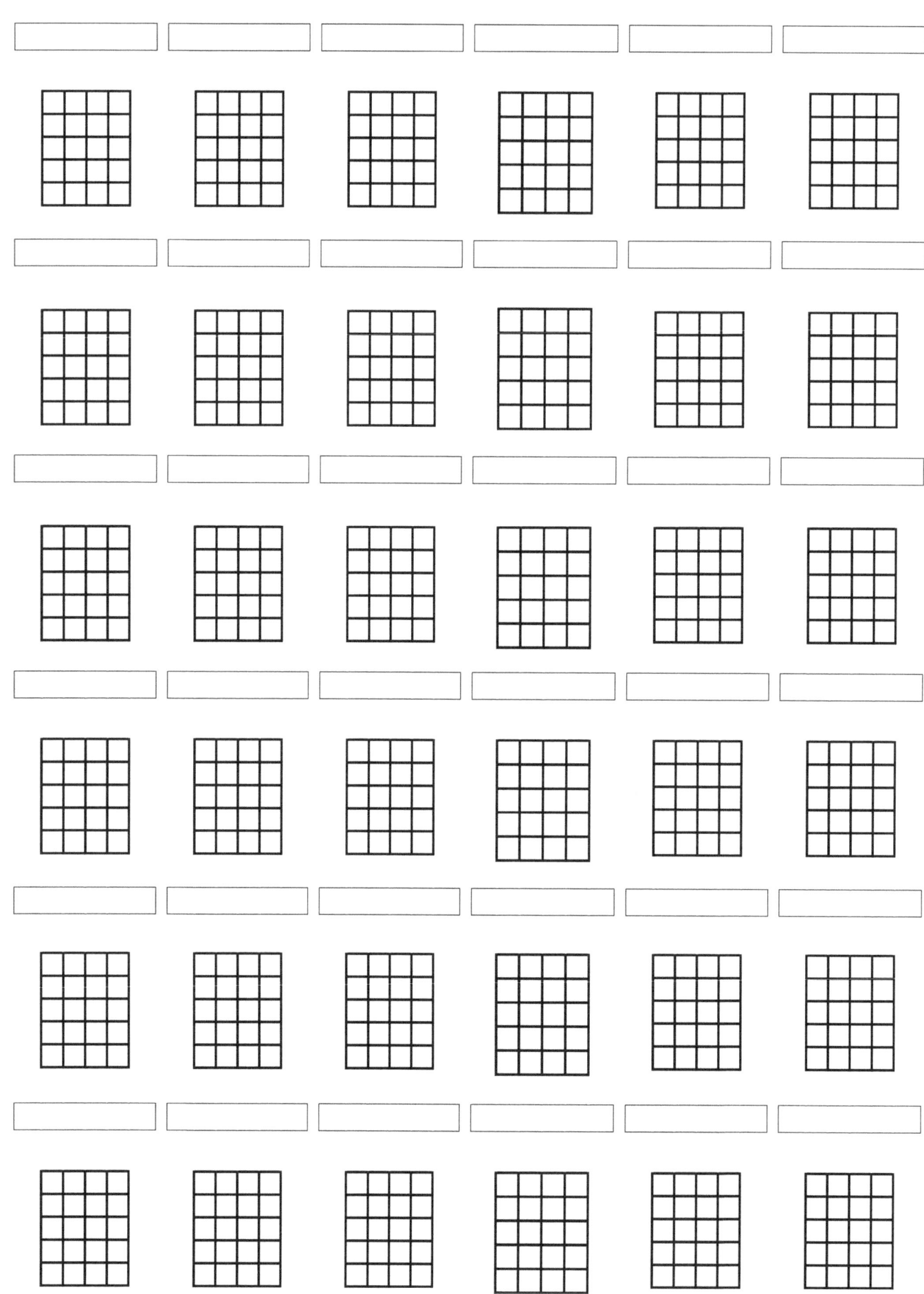

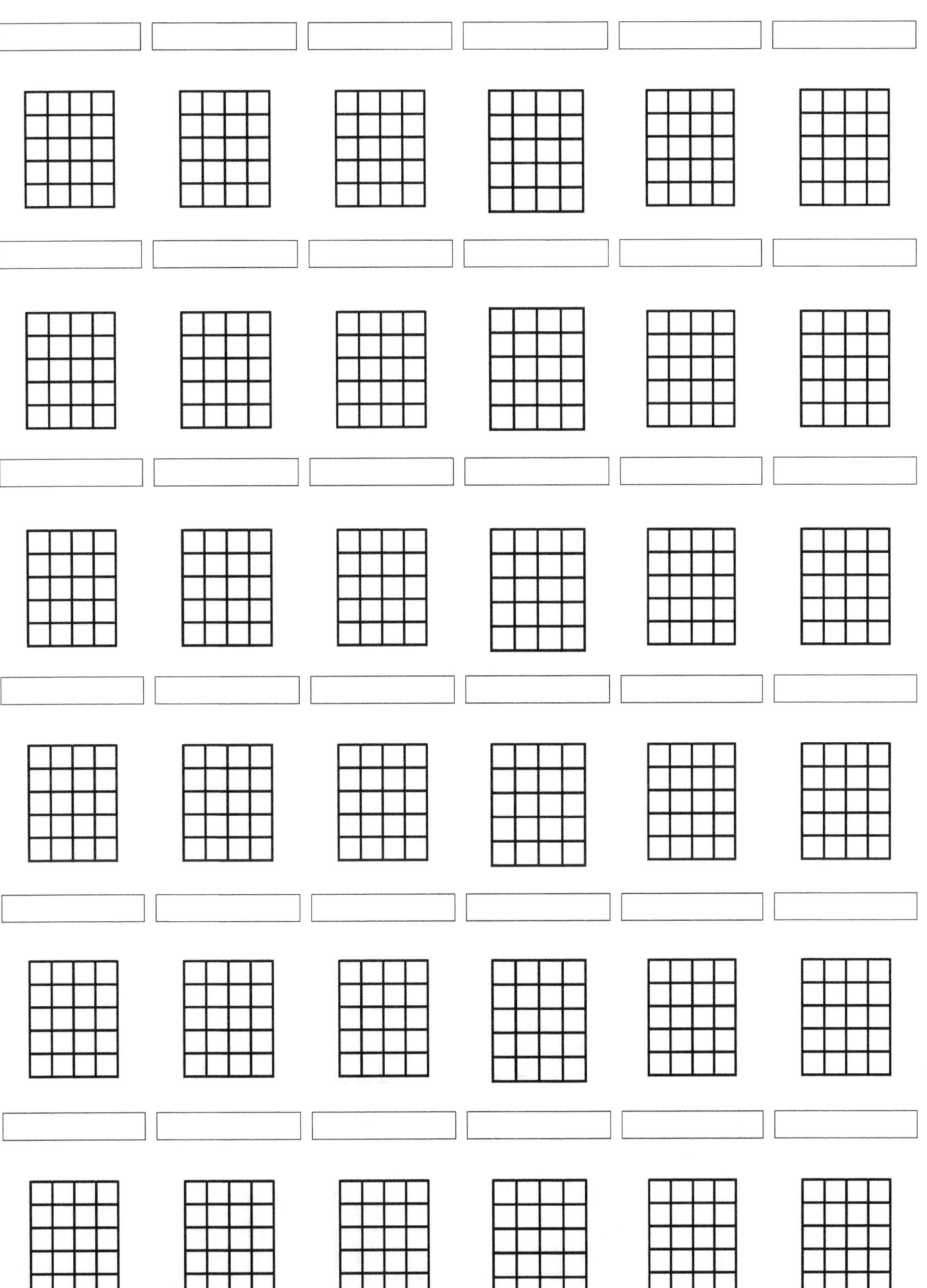

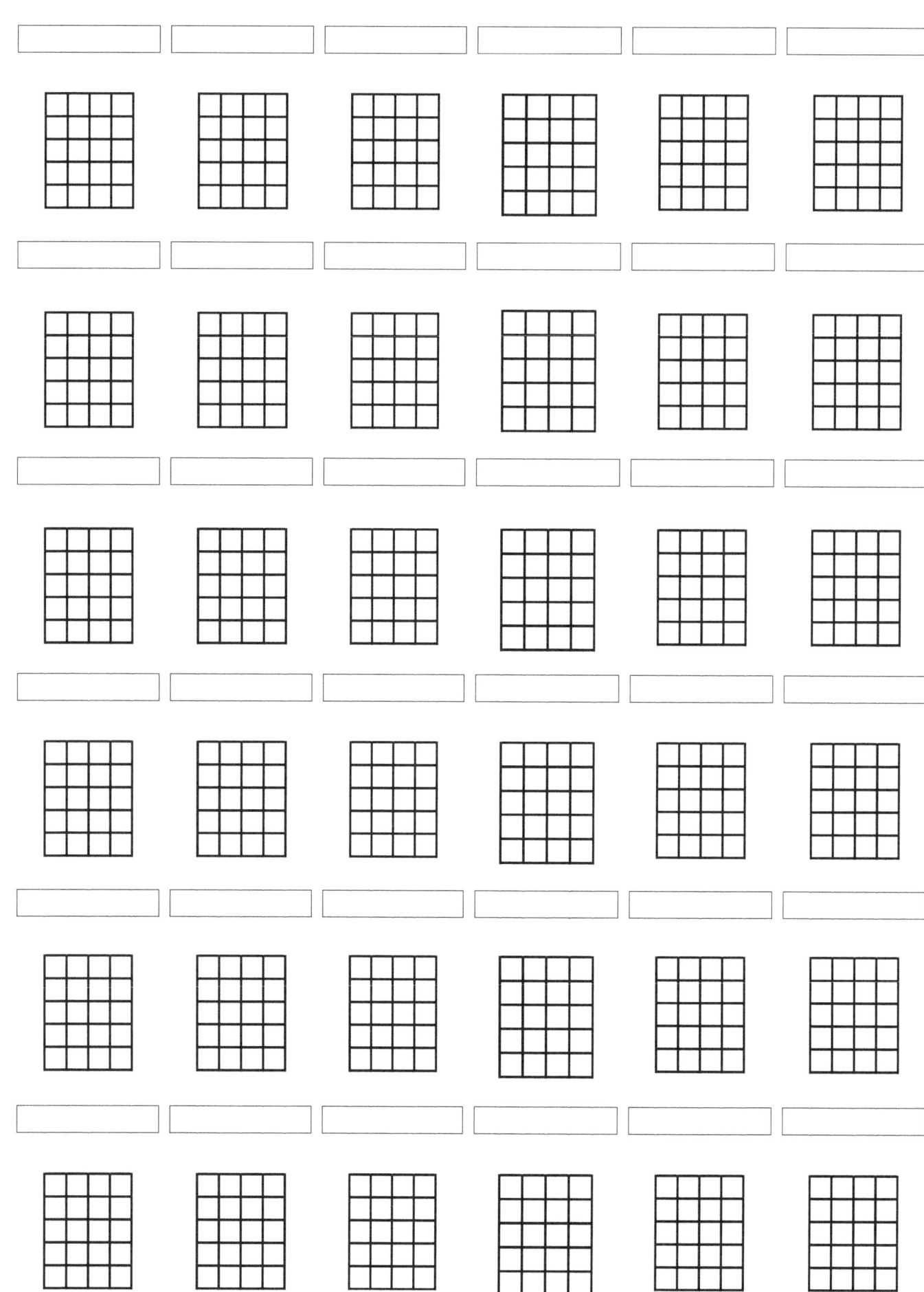

www.ingramcontent.com/pod-product-compliance
Lightning Source LLC
Chambersburg PA
CBHW081119080526
44587CB00021B/3660